Bitter Fruit

Bitter Fruit

Dysfunction and Abuse in the Local Church

KEITH GORDON FORD

WIPF & STOCK · Eugene, Oregon

BITTER FRUIT
Dysfunction and Abuse in the Local Church

Copyright © 2021 Keith Gordon Ford. All rights reserved. Except for brief quotations in critical publications or reviews, no part of this book may be reproduced in any manner without prior written permission from the publisher. Write: Permissions, Wipf and Stock Publishers, 199 W. 8th Ave., Suite 3, Eugene, OR 97401.

Wipf & Stock
An Imprint of Wipf and Stock Publishers
199 W. 8th Ave., Suite 3
Eugene, OR 97401

www.wipfandstock.com

PAPERBACK ISBN: 978-1-6667-0349-8
HARDCOVER ISBN: 978-1-6667-0350-4
EBOOK ISBN: 978-1-6667-0351-1

06/04/21

Unless otherwise stated, Scripture quotations taken from the (NASB®) New American Standard Bible®, Copyright © 1960, 1971, 1977, 1995 by The Lockman Foundation. Used by permission. All rights reserved.

To Michelle
who deserved better
and my friends (you know who you are)
who stuck with me as we passed through the fire

Contents

List of Figures | ix
Preface: Speaking Prophetically | xi

Introduction | 1

1. **The Fruit** | 9
    1.1 Dysfunction | 11
    1.2 Abuse | 34

2. **The Soil** | 53
    2.1 Anxiety | 55
    2.2 Anxiety: Do I Belong? | 68

3. **The Seed** | 81
    3.1 The Seed | 83

4. **The Trellis** | 103
    4.1 Unquestionable Power and Authority | 105
    4.2 Unwanted Conflict | 116
    4.3 Unity above All | 126

5. **Shallow Roots** | 137
    5.1 Shallow Theology of Forgiveness | 139
    5.2 Shallow Judgments of Character | 158
    5.3 Shallow Understanding of Pastoral Care | 173
    5.4 Shallow Theology of Discipline | 191

6. **The Herbicide** | 207
    6.1 The Gospel | 211

    6.2 Authenticity | 225

7. The Resistant Species | 235
    7.1 Justice | 241
    7.2 Lament | 244

Epilogue | 247
Bibliography | 251

List of Figures

Figure 1 | 17
Figure 2 | 19
Figure 3 | 86
Figure 4 | 110
Figure 5 | 147
Figure 6 | 151
Figure 7 | 153

Preface
Speaking Prophetically

THIS BOOK IS THE fruit of loss; loss of ministry and most of what was flourishing in my life by circumstances in a church that required me to leave for the sake of my own integrity and health. It was devastating and humbling. To break pride in a man takes these kinds of earth-shattering events. In the words of Job, "Shall we accept the good from God and not also the bad?" (Job 2:10). Something in me needed to die in order for something new to begin. This book is a product of that experience.

As I have come to see and understand the dysfunctions that enable abuse and abusers, I know that I must call the church to repentance and a new way of living. This book then, is also a work of the prophetic. Prophets speak words that embolden and edify and exhort. Some will listen; some won't. The voice of the prophet is a thankless task, one who declares "Keep on listening, but do not understand; And keep on looking, but do not gain knowledge" (Isa 6:9). Entrenched power ever fights to keep control.

It has been comforting in these times to learn through the study of the life of Jeremiah that the role of the pastor is in part prophetic. To understand his/her *Sitz im Leben* ("life setting") and to apply the inspired text of Scripture *is* a sacred calling. Pointing the people to a new place and a new way of understanding is a prophetic role. Pastors are called to this.

Speaking prophetically was in fact what I was doing in my last two years of ministry, without fully realizing it. It is because of this prophetic nature of my ministry and its obvious failure that I am able to see and understand much of Jeremiah's words. The first time I could relate personally with that prophet was in reading the lament of Jer 11:18–20. His experience resonated loudly with mine. Sadly, Jesus' words are true, "A prophet is not welcome in his own country" (Luke 4:24).

Now, of course, my experiences are analogous—if only in small scale—with those of Jeremiah. To put on equal footing my simple experiences with a prophet of Yahweh is to be rightly accused of having too high a view of both myself and any church. However, despite being a relatively insignificant church and an insignificant preacher, the voice of one speaking into dysfunction and abuse is a vitally important prophetic role and a sacred calling. In that sense, this book seeks to be prophetic.

With my history as a backdrop, and taking advice from my Jeremiah lecturer, I purchased a copy of Walter Brueggemann's book *The Prophetic Imagination*.[1] That text has helped shape the preface to this book. What I have come to understand in the intervening years is that dysfunctional churches in which abuse is enabled have similar characteristics and cultures that are usually, if not always, evident within them. These things can be addressed, and need to be addressed, by the prophetic. Brueggemann speaks directly into any dysfunctional church, even though this may not be his intended audience. Brueggemann's stated thesis is this:

> The task of the prophetic ministry is to nurture, nourish, and evoke a consciousness and perception alternative to the consciousness and perception of the dominant culture around us.[2]

Although Brueggemann has in mind the secular or politically religious culture in which the church and the people of God find themselves, with my church experience, I am able to narrow this focus to within the local church and recognize that what Brueggemann is exploring is pointedly relevant within that much narrower sphere.

Every church community has its own dominant culture, and in dysfunctional churches this culture can and often does enable abuse. Regardless of the form the abuse takes, what will always be true in these churches is that the dominant culture is one of coercive control by a narrow-minded, insular group of individuals. To speak prophetically into this space is to seek to provide an alternative perception to what that loud voice speaks, to give a vision for a future that is different. This, unbeknownst to me at the time, is what I was seeking to achieve, without having the language or framework to define it. It was prophetic, indeed.

---

1. Brueggemann, *Prophetic Imagination*.
2. Brueggemann, *Prophetic Imagination*, 3. (emphasis in the original).

Brueggemann speaks of the prophetic as both criticizing *and* energizing. Criticism is easy. Casting an energizing vision takes greater imagination. Attempting to help envision a community with new values requires humility and authenticity in the prophet, and these same character traits must exist in the people for there to be any change. By enunciating new values, the prophet is indirectly criticizing the existing lack of them, and when this can be seen and heard it becomes a threat to the dominant voice. That dominant voice which enunciates the dominant culture is often "uncritical" and cannot entertain "serious and fundamental criticism" and will go to "great lengths to stop it."[3] This will always be true for any dysfunctional church that is enabling abuse and abusers.

Using ancient Egypt with the pharaoh and her static gods as his example, Brueggemann employs language that can be extrapolated to any dysfunctional church. The doctrines, both theological and cultural, of the dominant voice are the "static gods."[4] They are the means of establishing order, an order that serves and benefits those in charge. As long as things are going well, these doctrines justify the order. Too often, sadly, justice is sidelined for the good of the order.

Abuse in all its forms, no matter how great or subtle, is an injustice. In the dysfunctional church that enables such behavior, criticism must be the work of the prophetic voice. It must assert that "the false claims to authority and power cannot keep their promises."[5] The promises made by the dominant voice are promises of order, control, peace, unity, and prosperity to those who toe the line, but often at great cost to those who don't. The dominant voice runs counter to the voice of a free God[6] who alone is the source of all these things. The prophet speaks to the dysfunction by helping the people to grieve for what it is they are missing and what it is they will, in the face of unrepentance, eventually lose. It is interesting to note that Paul speaks prophetically when calling his community to repent in 1 Cor 5:2, where he highlights to a dysfunctional church that they should be grieving over sin rather than rejoicing. Brueggemann, quoting Dorothy Soelle, says getting people to grieve is a way of moving them away from "cry-hearers who are inept at listening and indifferent in

3. Brueggemann, *Prophetic Imagination*, 4.
4. Brueggemann, *Prophetic Imagination*, 7.
5. Brueggemann, *Prophetic Imagination*, 11.
6. Brueggemann uses free here in the way that Barth defines free. Not only is God free to act, but the very being of God is a being in freedom. God chooses to be the God he is—a God who acts; he is not a static essence.

response."[7] The voice of the prophet in the dysfunctional community is to help them see the loss of *shalom* that the dominant voice has imposed upon them.

The community of the dominant voice—Brueggemann calls it the "royal consciousness"[8]—presents itself in *affluence*, an *oppressive social policy*, and *static religion*. The prophetic voice is the counterpoint to these cultural and social forces. In the dysfunctional church which enables abuse, the royal consciousness is always on display in one form or another.

The dysfunctional community can often perceive itself as affluent. Satiated with good things, new buildings, comfortable seats, and air-conditioned luxury, these are but a small sample of the Western vision of the good life that the dominant culture provides.[9] This, coupled with successful ministries, resulting in conversions and baptisms; what more could they want?

These things, however, come at a cost. The members are whipped into a frenzy of activity and commitment. Time, talent, and treasure are all demanded and commanded to be used for the stability and maintenance of the status quo, the vision set by the dominant voice to ensure the continuance of the dominant culture. Those close to the top bask in the glow of the favor of those in control, the rest scramble to be seen and have favor bestowed upon them. Spiritual abuse of a greater or lesser extent is common in these dysfunctional churches. The people's faith, their commitment to the cause and the kingdom, and even Christ himself, are brought into question and used as a means of control for those who fail to expend sufficient energy for the sake of unity and the cause. Like pharaoh and his bricks without straw, the people are spiritually and physically oppressed and repressed in order for the affluence of the kingdom to be maintained. Unlike Hebrew slaves, however, the people do it willingly for Jesus.

In order for affluence and oppressive control to succeed, religious sanctions are required. God must be invoked. "The sovereignty of God is fully subordinated to the purpose of the king."[10] The people know things are being done for the glory of God because the dominant voices say so, and there is a plaque on the wall to prove it. However, "the freedom of

---

7. Brueggemann, *Prophetic Imagination*, 13.
8. Brueggemann, *Prophetic Imagination*, 21.
9. See the remembrance of the good life by the exiles, Num 11:5.
10. Brueggemann, *Prophetic Imagination*, 29.

God is overcome." Brueggemann points out, "the notion of God's freedom probably is more than any religious system can sustain for very long."[11] God is now on call to do the bidding of those in charge. It is inconceivable for this God to ever speak a word that is abrasive or correcting. Like the false prophets of old, the dominant voices cry "Peace, Peace," with the affluence and order demonstrable evidence that God is on their side. "We are his chosen, we have the temple, God is pleased with us."[12]

Brueggemann declares that these three ideas (affluence, oppressive policy, and static religion) must go together, and in my research into dysfunctional churches that are enabling abuse, these three things are also common. God is domesticated and at the call of a limited number of dominant voices who act as a conduit for the blessings of God if, and only if, the people accede to their order and control. In such an environment of spiritual abuse, sexual abuse can also gain a foothold and not be dealt with because to acknowledge such abuses, whether spiritual or sexual (or any other form), would demonstrate that, like the famed emperor, this church, its leaders, its dominant voice and culture, have no clothes, that the promised blessing and order are coming at an intolerable cost. If this vision is seen by others, it will undermine their self-proclaimed godly mandate, hence it becomes something the dominant culture wishes to keep hidden.

Criticism in these environments is then silenced in one of two ways: either through crushing rebuke or "the system develops a natural immunity and remains totally impervious to criticism."[13] It is also my experience that these are examples of the kind of reaction the prophetic critic receives in dysfunctional environments. In fact, these responses to criticism are a useful diagnostic for establishing that one is dealing with a dysfunctional organization. Healthy organizations and individuals have not only a robust curiosity about how they are perceived, but a willingness to adapt and change as necessary to criticisms that reveal genuine fault.

But dysfunctional environments have the features of totalitarian regimes. Totalitarians differ from authoritarians. Authoritarians recognize their authority is a gift that comes from something that transcends them or is external to them. Totalitarians have no need for any sanction beyond themselves. They are gods unto themselves. Hannah Arendt, a political philosopher, says:

11. Brueggemann, *Prophetic Imagination*, 22.
12. See Jeremiah's temple sermon in Jer 7.
13. Brueggemann, *Prophetic Imagination*, 32.

> The source of authority in authoritarian government is always a force external to and superior to its own power; it is always this source, this external force which transcends the political realm, from which the authorities derive their 'authority', that is, their legitimacy, and against which their power can be checked.[14]

The dysfunctional organization may use the language of authority, but they are in fact totalitarians. Despite invoking the language of God and covering themselves with the religious mantle of Jesus and the gospel, the dysfunctional organization actually recognizes no authority beyond its own and operates from its own strengths and power. God has been domesticated, subject to their interpretation of his sacred writings. The system is working well, the people have comfort, there is order and control. Should that power be threatened, the dysfunctional organization can resort to scapegoating; the religiously acceptable form of violence.

There is a shrinking of imagination[15] in such organizations, and yet it is imagination that is the way out of such a morass. Dysfunctional organizations are frightened by imagination, the artist, the free thinker, the one who possesses the ability to ask the question "What if?" As Friedman says "there is an imaginative gridlock."[16] He then goes one to say:

> In any type of institution whatsoever, when a self-directed, imaginative, energetic, or creative member is being consistently frustrated and sabotaged rather than encouraged and supported, what will turn out to be true 100 percent of the time, regardless of whether the disrupters are supervisors, subordinates, or peers, is that the person at the very top of that institution is a peace monger. By that I mean a highly anxious risk-avoider, someone who is more concerned with good feelings than with progress.[17]

The prophetic voice in such organizations is the imaginative, energetic, and creative voice. Consider all the prophetic acts of Jeremiah that take on the form of performance art, designed to imaginatively and creatively paint a picture in ways words would fail, and were failing, to do. Dysfunctional organizations seek to satiate their people so that they, like a bear fattened in the zoo, are too complacent with their comfort to be able to imagine that they were never designed to be in the dominant

---

14. Arendt, "Authority in the Twentieth Century," 406.
15. Brueggemann, *Prophetic Imagination*, 40.
16. Friedman, *Failure of Nerve*, 33.
17. Friedman, *Failure of Nerve*, 14–15.

voice's cage. Numbed into being unthinking followers, too often that prophetic voice cannot and will not be heard.

There is no real place for the Spirit of God in such environments. God, particularly a God who is free like the wind (John 3), is not controllable, may upset the plans of the regime, and so must be silenced. No "Thus sayeth the Lord" is allowed, unless of course, the Lord is defined as the dominant voice and culture:

> The royal consciousness leads people to numbness, especially to numbness about death. It is the task of prophetic ministry and imagination to bring people to engage their experiences of suffering to death.[18]

In such numbing environments behavior becomes paramount. People are not allowed to feel or experience the lack of life in such controlling, stifling, self-contained environments. Behaviors are easy, they can be managed, and managed they are. Failure is never an option. The vision and dreams of the dominant voices are *the* vision and *the* dream. No voice of dissent can or will be heard. This kingdom, so it is said, will never fail. The prophetic voice must strip away these delusions and demonstrate to the people that God is not domesticated, he is free. Our puny attempts to create kingdoms in our image and call it God's will come to naught. Repent, says the prophetic, for the real kingdom of God is at hand.

The prophetic imagines the death of the established and grieves over it. Grief for what the people are losing now, and worse, what they stand to lose outside of a repentant place. Grief over the reality that in such environments the prophet is unlikely to be heard. This grief is real and must be both articulated and felt by the prophet. The prophetic voice must convey this to a numbed and satiated people, who have succumbed too willingly to the royal consciousness of their created kingdom. Jeremiah is a fitting model for the prophet who speaks grief to his people and feels deeply the rejection and abuse of these same people toward him personally. This is the grief of the prophetic.

But the prophet's work does not end there. The prophet must also energize the community with a vision of hope, a vision of what might be, a divine "What if?" if you like. The royal consciousness perpetuates the lie that this is all there is, that there is neither hope nor need for any hope of a better future, to pay no attention to the man behind the

---

18. Brueggemann, *Prophetic Imagination*, 41 (emphasis original).

curtain. The prophetic exposes the lie with hope and yearning and the language of amazement.[19]

Imagine a world in which justice and righteousness and *shalom* are the norms. Imagine the kingdom to come operating now, where the small and the weak and the oppressed are lifted up, and the powerful and mighty are laid low. Imagine the words of Mary's *Magnificat*, where the wicked imaginations of the unrighteous powerful prove to be their undoing (Luke 1:51). Imagine the promises of God becoming true in our day, and the life-affirming, human-flourishing imagination of the prophet can become the new normal. Imagine how amazing that would be.

The prophet is at a worldly disadvantage. The prophet has no power or armies or strength of numbers. The weapons are images and pictures and performance art and words, and in today's world there are no shortages of those. The prophet's voice is just another bit of flotsam in a sea of ideas. Too often, for these things to cut through, it takes intervention from God, who must bring the threatened death upon the cry-hearers who refused to hear the cry of the prophet or the oppressed in their midst. The parables of Luke 12:35–48 are a somber reminder that God may delay, but he is no ditherer. The Master will return and woe betide the unfaithful rulers.

The prophetic voice must be ever faithful, never silenced until God silences the voice, even in the face of the most ardent opposition, even unto crucifixion itself. This takes great discernment. If the royal consciousness and dominant voice would destroy the Prince of Glory, what end the simple prophet in the dysfunctional community? This is the prophet's sacred calling.

This then, is a book of prophecy, a book of grief, and a book of hope. This book seeks to speak prophetically to the church, a church that oftentimes is very unhealthy. May God give her ears to hear.

---

19. Brueggemann, *Prophetic Imagination*, 67–68.

Introduction

IN A LIFEWAY STUDY[1] report, fourteen percent of those aged 18 to 34 said that sexual advances from church people led them to attend less frequently. The same report reflects the fact that the youngest generation is two to three times more likely than the oldest generation to say they have experienced sexual harassment in the form of sexualized compliments and jokes, sexting, or prolonged glances.

This likely reflects three things. Firstly, the fact that this age group is statistically most likely to be abused in any environment. Secondly, in this #MeToo/#Churchtoo environment, they are far more attuned to what is appropriate and what is not. And thirdly, the apparent increase in this type of behavior is unlikely to represent a true increase, but rather increased reporting as a result of heightened awareness of and reduced tolerance for abuse and harassment. This means there are predators at large in our churches—the protestant, evangelical church, not just the Catholic church—and there most likely have been for a very long time.

In the same research, respondents were asked: "Do you know of someone who attends your church who has sexually assaulted someone, but it has not been found out or come to light?" Those aged 18 to 34 are most likely to select "Yes" (12 percent), while those age 65+ are least likely (<1 percent) to say "Yes."[2]

What is distressing about this research is that an increasing number of young people are starting to find that the church is not the haven it should be. For too long those in the Protestant and evangelical church felt that this form of abuse was a Catholic church problem, but it clearly is no longer the case, and perhaps never really was.

---

1. "Sexual Misconduct and Churchgoers," 83.
2. "Sexual Misconduct and Churchgoers," 118.

Recent revelations in 2018 and 2019 regarding rampant abuse in some sections of the Southern Baptist Convention in the United States is sobering reading. The *Houston Chronicle*[3]—the secular press no less—finally brought decades of cover-up to light. Say these words slowly and let the impact of them settle on you: Sex . . . predators . . . in . . . the . . . church. And not just some creepy, trench-coat-wearing cliché of yesteryear, but the lead pastors or youth pastors themselves. People who went to Bible college, got a degree, committed themselves to sacrificial pastoral service, got married, had kids, are serving Jesus, and are preying on your women and children.

Then there is the issue of narcissism and narcissistic personality disorder (NPD) in the church, and the narcissistic systems they create. A newly released book by Chuck DeGroat highlights the serious emotional and spiritual abuse that can occur when narcissism remains unchecked in the local church community.[4] People can exhibit all the characteristics of a person with an NPD, but not really be character-disordered. Under the care of a trained psychologist they would not be diagnosed as such a personality type after careful testing—fair enough. But they can still act like an NPD-disordered person. These narcissistic personality types exist on a continuum.[5] Some are, clearly, and their grandiose delusions are both obvious and indicative of this type of behavior. But it isn't always overt. There are others who exhibit behaviors and characteristics that would fall short of a diagnosable disorder, but they are still manipulative, controlling, and bullying and it isn't always obvious. It is aggressive, predatory, and designed to gain or maintain control of people or a church and her systems. George Simon calls them "covert aggressive."[6] Whether covert or overt, these people are "in it to win it" in all of their interpersonal relationships.

The church may not be filled with diagnosable NPD pastors and leaders, but there are still no shortages of people with this tendency showing up and leading our churches and ministries. If you have ever met a full-blown narcissistic type in church, you will know the damage they can cause. Just one in a church can bring it to its knees. All it takes is one narcissistic pastor and the people will be lamb dinners for a wolf. And the horrifying thing? This is the bride of Christ. Too often the

---

3. Downen et al., "Abuse of Faith."
4. DeGroat, *When Narcissism Comes to Church*.
5. DeGroat, *When Narcissism Comes to Church*. 36–37.
6. Simon, *In Sheep's Clothing*, 7.

church can seem like the bride of Frankenstein. Abuse of all kinds and in varying degrees of intensity occurring in the church is just too horrifying to consider, and yet we must.

The church, the glory of the Lord, has become a place of people abusing one another, sweeping things under the carpet, a haven for narcissists and manipulative abusers; passive-aggressive ministry leaders, and covert aggressive pastors running mini fiefdoms in the name of Jesus; individuals whose behaviors and character issues *should* disqualify them from ministry, but who instead run our churches. And of course, we should not be surprised that character-disordered individuals and other "difficult" people with narcissistic-type personalities should appear in our door and seek to rise to positions of prominence. But somehow we do seem surprised when an NPD person shows up and gets control of ministry, hurts people, and then leaves a wake of destruction in their path, only to go to another church and do it all over again. We stand, rubbing our eyes, with a dazed look, and say, "What just happened here?"

Recently, I was having a discussion with another Christian and the conversation was centered on psychopaths and narcissists. This was shocking, having this kind of discussion about Christians with another Christian in a church. Rather than talking about all the great, loving people that exist in churches, our focus was on the ones eating the church alive.

Now of course the vast majority of pastors and church leaders are non-NPD, sacrificial, kind, loving, Christlike servants of their people. And my experience in local churches is that they are in fact filled with the most amazing people that would not seek to use or abuse you in any way. They are mostly simple people genuinely seeking a closer relationship with Christ, desiring that others might know him, really wanting to sacrificially serve their communities in an infinite number of ways, and seeking to navigate their way through the labyrinth of confusion first-world living throws up at them. I would not want to give the impression that the wolves outnumber the lambs—they don't, not even close.

But the point is, Jesus promised the flock there *would be wolves*, we just don't want to believe it. I don't want to walk around with this cynical attitude all the time, wondering if the guy I am shaking hands with really wants to rape me and my children. Living with a heightened sense of alert all the time, like someone with PTSD, every time I step into church, is no way to live either. I do want to give you the benefit of the doubt; I do want to believe the best in you; I do want to trust you. In fact, society can't work if we don't at least have an initial level of trust for each other as the first port of call in our brains when we enter social situations.

And it is this trusting naiveté that so many predators count on when it comes to the church. We are nice people. We want to be nice people. We want to be kind and helpful and sharing and loving. We tell our greeters and pastoral teams to be effusive and loving and caring towards newcomers. "Make them feel welcome," we say. And boy do the wolves ever feel welcome. We want to open our homes to strangers. Jesus calls us to do it. We're lambs, and the wolves know it.

The purpose of this book is to speak prophetically and to help arm the sheep with knowledge. Knowledge not so much of how perpetrators act, groom and target, which would be extremely helpful; there are numerous books able do just that. This book is designed to arm with knowledge, not about them, but about you, the church. As Socrates said, "Know thyself."

What I will be examining here in this book are the abnormalities and dysfunctions in the culture and social structure of a church that can lead to behaviors that are abusive, that prop up abusive behavior, and that allow them to thrive, as well as dysfunctions that can blind us to the wolves or prevent us from dealing with them when we see them. I will be asking the diagnostic question, "What is it about us, as a church, that makes us attractive to individuals that will use and abuse us?"

I am not concerned about the specific form the abuse takes. I will address some of those forms, but other books exist that detail abuse far more extensively than this book aims to. Take, for example, spiritual abuse. *The Subtle Power of Spiritual Abuse*, written by Jeff Van Vonderen (with David Johnson), is an excellent primer on this insidious issue in churches.[7] It is helpful, insightful, frightening, and enlightening. And with that knowledge comes power.[8] What I am hoping to do is that once you come to recognize that *your* church *might* be dysfunctional and allowing abuse, you should come to further knowledge, by asking "What is it about us that allowed us to become that way?" I am writing this book to help answer that question.

And for those who have had to endure the hell of sexual abuse, whether in the church or elsewhere, there is an increasingly large number of books written by survivors and advocates that can help you navigate

---

7. Johnson and VanVonderen, *Subtle Power of Spiritual Abuse*.
8. See also Oakley and Humphreys, *Escaping the Maze of Spiritual Abuse*.

the nightmare of recovering from that trauma. For example, books like Mary Demuth's *#WeToo*, or Rachael Denhollander's *What Is a Girl Worth*? I highly recommend both of these books which, sadly, needed to be written. Thankfully, these brave women have done so. For those seeking to recover from sexual abuse, great organizations do exist. SNAP (https://www.snapnetwork.org/) is just one of many.

I mention all of these things briefly because, as I say, my focus is not really on abuse or its forms or how to recover; There are far better resources for this. This book is for the church, to help her understand the theologies, psychologies, and social psychologies that underly much of the dysfunction that can enable all forms of abuse.

HEALTHY CHURCHES?

Mark Dever and David Platt wrote a book entitled *Nine Marks of a Healthy Church*, which is now in its third edition.[9] Their motivation was to help churches assess the health of their organization. Now admittedly, these nine marks are not *the* nine marks, as if there is nothing to add.[10] In this #Churchtoo environment, churches can tick off nine or even more marks (even priding themselves in it) and still be an unhealthy organization. The dysfunctions that can lead to abuse may still be present enough for people to experience it. It is easy to convince yourselves that your church is really healthy because you are doing these outward things well, but inside, under the surface, running through its veins can be dysfunctions that allow for abuse.

I write this from my perspective as a member and ex-pastor of a conservative evangelical church. I write from my own experiences as a privileged white male, with thirty-five years within the evangelical conservative tradition. I write after listening to the voices of many others who have come out of similar traditions, and who have similar stories. In the research for this book, I discovered some important things about me and church, things that are in fact not unusual, and that reside at the heart of many people and many churches; things that are dysfunctional and can lead to abuse.

---

9. Dever and Platt, *Nine Marks of a Healthy Church*.

10. For instance, overseas missions and prayer are two marks which are missing from that list.

For the first time in my life, I used the word "manipulation" about someone. I always thought you had to be some kind of psychopath to engage in manipulative behavior. I found out that we all do it to some extent. I learned:

- That spiritual and other forms of abuse can and do occur in even the best of churches. It doesn't have to be an "all of church" thing, but can reside in subtle and specific places and ways.
- That narcissists live amongst us, even and especially in church!
- How important it is to deal with your own unresolved emotional stuff as a pastor or church leader, or it will negatively impact others and yourself.
- That a church full of nice people is not always a sign of an emotionally healthy place.

My goal in this book is to shine a light onto the dysfunction and abuse which can occur in churches, highlight its impact, and explore the solutions. It is not intended to be a work of pure theology, but rather of pastoral theology. I do, however, intend to be faithful in my use of Scripture.

I write this for laypeople as well as pastors, and mostly for those who have been hurt and abused by the dysfunction of churches, a dysfunction which has caused some people to become so jaded and bitter about church and church people that the mere mention of the Bible can cause unwanted angst.

I also write because there are many churches, generally good ones, where the abuse and dysfunction are not entirely obvious. You can follow blindly along with the culture for years because they may not be doing the outright, obvious things that have recently made the news in association with the #Metoo and #Churchtoo movements. You might be tempted to think, "So what is the big deal?" Abuse is abuse, no matter what form it takes or the intensity of it, and it dishonors Christ when it is allowed to reside amongst his people. It denies the gospel and is repulsive to our Lord, and people get hurt, truly hurt, by it.

The reality is that once you have experienced the taste of the bitter fruit of dysfunction and abuse, the bad taste in your mouth can linger for years, even a lifetime. This should never be. The church should be a refuge for the abused, but instead it often becomes a haven for the abuser, and the victims get spat out, thrown aside, and forgotten.

Introduction

This grieves our Savior when the bride of Christ acts in such terrible ways. She must wake up and grieve, and this begins with the voice of the prophet. The average pew-sitter, lay elders, pastors, and everyone who calls church home need to be alert to the signs of the fruit taking root in their churches and weed it out before it produces the full fruit of pain, abuse, and sin.

I write this because, although my journey has been painful and difficult, I still believe in the church. It is the bride of Christ, God's chosen vessel in which he invests the privilege of the gospel for a dying world. The gospel of Christ in the hands of a healthy church is the world's best, last, and only hope.

Also, I will remind the reader that the ultimate hope for any church is to never lose sight of the gospel. I wrote the following words to my fellow hurt and disaffected church family members when I left my church. I believe them now as much as I did then:

> The gospel begins with lament. You can't fix what you can't acknowledge and you can't acknowledge what you can't or won't see. It is God's kindness that causes us to see our failings. Only in this does his kindness lead to repentance. Seeing and owning sin is the first step to holiness, joy, and hope. This church is abundantly blessed, with faithful, dedicated, Christ-honoring saints, but with no repentance his blessing will be removed. To the repentant, God promises beauty for ashes, and oil of joy for mourning, and garments of praise for the spirit of heaviness. There is always hope in the gospel.

"Comfort, comfort My people," says your God.
"Speak kindly to Jerusalem;
And call out to her, that her warfare has ended,
That her guilt has been removed,
That she has received of the Lord's hand
Double for all her sins."

Isa 40:1–2

1

The Fruit
(What Is It?)

1.1

Dysfunction

Dysfunction–*noun*
1. Abnormality or impairment in the operation of a specified bodily organ or system.

"Dysfunction" and "dysfunctional," when applied to a church, are pretty powerful words. To call a church dysfunctional may give the impression that it is completely failing as a church, but this need not be the case at all. If your church is doing many great things for God you may conclude that it is not dysfunctional, and may actually be offended by someone describing it as such. And perhaps rightly so.

Edgar Schein[1], in his classic text on organizational culture, describes an organization's culture as consisting of three things:

1. Artifacts (things you can see, like clothing, behaviors, music etc.);
2. Beliefs and values (often printed and stated); and
3. Underlying basic assumptions (things that you can't see, but which really drive the culture). In other words, underlying assumptions are the "way we do things around here." These things aren't really discussed or written down, they are just assumed to be true and those who remain in the organization for any length of time get enculturated into this way of doing and being.

---

1. Schein, *Organizational Culture and Leadership*.

Schein observes, however, that incongruity between stated beliefs and values and underlying assumptions is a source of chronic and subconscious anxiety.[2] Highlighting the incongruity will elevate the anxiety in the system. Another researcher goes further and defines this incongruity as evidence of a dysfunctional system.[3]

What this means is that churches act in dysfunctional ways when they are in violation of their stated values and beliefs. For example, a church may declare it values women, but in practice they are marginalized to minor roles by an entrenched misogynistic and patriarchal culture. Should this be highlighted, the underlying anxiety that exists will be heightened, and in dysfunctional organizations the criticism will be minimized or outrightly dismissed, and the whistle-blower ostracized and scapegoated if they won't remain silent. This is dysfunctional activity, even if good things are being done in that church.

This dysfunction need not necessarily prevent the church from being fruitful, but she will not be living up to her full potential. Should not the church seek to be as fruitful as possible for her Savior?

DYSFUNCTION

Let me start by asking "What is church?" What metaphors does the Bible use to describe church?

These four are primarily used: body, marriage, family, and household. It could also be considered a flock, a vine, or an orchard, amongst other options.

Notice that nearly all the metaphors the Bible writers use refer to living things. The church *is* a living relational entity, and like all living entities requires certain functions to sustain life. Living organisms are capable of responding to stimuli, reproducing, growing, and developing. Failing to thrive in any one of these aspects is a dysfunction in the organism and can cause it to become diseased and eventually die. Failing in these aspects can cause the organism to become susceptible to parasites and predators.

Consider the metaphor of a grapevine, the church as a vine. It is one of the metaphors the biblical writers use (e.g., John 15). What is the purpose of a grapevine? Why plant it? What is its ultimate purpose?

---

2. Schein, *Organizational Culture and Leadership*, 309.
3. Barnard, "Examination of Dysfunctional Behaviour," 5.

The answer of course is to produce fruit that is suitable for wine or eating, or, as in some cultures, producing leaves which can be a good food source when they are young and tender. And what is the measure of the success of the vine? It produces good fruit year in and out, is resistant to disease, grows strong and consistently, and maintains the quality of the fruit through its long life. However, should you plant the vine and it produces sickly clusters, bitter fruit, inconsistent yields, and is forever struggling with disease, it would be fair to say this vine is not functioning as intended. That is, it is dysfunctional. This is the complaint God had with his nation Israel:

> I planted you in the land like a special vine of the very best stock.
> Why in the world have you turned into something like a wild vine
> that produces rotten, foul-smelling grapes? (Jer 2:21 Net Bible)

The nation of Israel, which had been planted to produce good wine, ended up producing bitter fruit. This nation had become wholly dysfunctional.

This can happen to churches as well. They are planted and started with the greatest of intentions by people with a great vision and mission for God and what they will do, but sadly dysfunctions can enter. They stop living out their professed core values, and left undealt with, this can lead to abuse.

Imagine a church with a highly controlling, spiritually abusive, narcissistic pastor. (Yep, sadly they exist.) Yet the church still proclaims Christ as Lord; still declares salvation by grace alone, by faith alone; declares that God is love, and that love is one of their values. People come to faith and baptisms occur. As Paul says, whatever the motivations, as long as Christ is preached, that is good (Phil 1:15–18). But a controlling and abusive leader is the exact antithesis of love, the very value which is being espoused. The dysfunctional church is nevertheless still producing some fruit. It is the occasional fruit that is used by those kinds of leaders to keep doing what they are doing. If there were no successes, maybe things would change. But one grape every so often is all that is needed to encourage the dysfunction to continue for generations.

This is what I mean by dysfunctional. Perhaps the church is violating its values and the values of Christ, but the vine still is producing some fruit. It is not entirely dead, it is not entirely worthless, but it fails to live up to the promise of its potential, it fails to thrive. So it is with dysfunctional churches; they are not entirely dead (at least not initially).

But abnormalities exist within the culture and organizational structure of the church, which result in a body that is not living up to its full potential, leaving it susceptible to attack.

Or imagine another church that has a cyclical process of crisis and recovery over and over for decades. In the good years it is very good, but then there are the bad years. I have a mandarin tree that produced good fruit for about seven years, then for about two years it produced nothing, then it was good for two more years, and now it has again produced nothing for two years. This is not a thriving tree, despite the good years of fruit. Something dysfunctional about that tree requires further investigation. It is meant to produce fruit every season, and abundantly, so when it produces nothing it is not living up to its potential. Some churches are like this. I would like to suggest that a church that lurches from crisis to crisis is not a healthy church. There is something dysfunctional about it that is worthy of serious investigation. A church that is splitting often or churning through pastors is a pointer to something dysfunctional.

The church is called to be far more glorious than she can often be. She is called to be a living organism, flourishing and producing fruit to the glory of God. So, let's look at how the major ideas of organism existence can be a metaphor for dysfunction in the local church.

PURPOSE

Consider a grapevine. The first thing to ask is why did God "plant" the church. What is he expecting to get from the vine? This is more a question of purpose as opposed to nature. Let's take a quick detour through the theology of the purpose of the church.

Wayne Grudem, in his *Systematic Theology*[4], highlights three important purposes:

- Ministry to God: Worship
- Ministry to believers: Nurture
- Ministry to the world: Evangelism

Erickson, in his seminal work[5], also includes social work as part of the purpose (which some might see as a subset of evangelism), and of

---

4. Grudem, *Sytematic Theology*, 867.
5. Erickson, *Christian Theology*.

course all of this to the glory of God. We can take these two theologians as effectively describing the majority opinion on the purpose of the church. I'll use that as the groundwork for the purposes of this discussion. In a nutshell the purpose of the church is to glorify God by:

Ministry to God through worship
Ministry to believers through discipleship
Ministry to the world through evangelism and social work

These are the things God values and are hence what a church should value. A church is a healthy, functioning organization when it achieves these purposes.

(*Responding*) As a healthy living organism, a healthy church worships God in spirit and in truth.

(*Reproducing*) A healthy church nurtures its people, disciples them, builds them up, and equips them to become images of Christ in the world.

(*Ripening*) A healthy church evangelizes the world by:

- Proclamation of the gospel, Jesus is Lord
- Displaying the fullness of God's
    - Justice and mercy
    - Love and wrath
    - Grace and law in balanced proportions.
- Engaging in efforts that seek to hold back the pain of the curse by contributing to social justice, and working for the poor and beleaguered.

It does this through total dependence upon God in prayer, so that he alone is glorified.

Conversely dysfunctional churches fail to:

- Respond well
- Reproduce well
- Ripen well

Responding

God is great, God is good
And we thank him for our food
By his hand we all are fed
Give us Lord our daily bread—Amen

We began every dinnertime with this prayer as a child. It has been more than fifty years, yet the words are tattooed onto my brain. This is worship in its simplest form. We as a family were responding to the fact that God in his gracious mercy had chosen to feed us that day and it was a recognition that we relied on him for our food tomorrow. God had done something for us. We were responding to that. And that, in a nutshell, is worship, responding to and focusing our attention on the nature of God and his actions in this world. Living organisms respond to stimuli, and the church as a living organism firstly responds to the stimuli of the Holy Spirit in her midst in acts of worship.

Although we tend to think of the songs we sing on Sunday morning as worship, two places in Scripture point us to the fact that what we do on Sunday morning is just a reflection or response to what we and God have been doing throughout the week. Worship is far more than just a song, but it is at least a song. Firstly, Paul, in Rom 12:1, states:

> Therefore I urge you, brothers *and sisters*, by the mercies of God, to present your bodies as a living and holy sacrifice, acceptable to God, *which is* your spiritual service of worship.

The *therefore* is there to say that in light of the mercies of God and the glorious grace in your salvation that I have explored in the first eleven chapters, your whole life should be a life of worship to God. Living sacrifices, as opposed to dead sacrifices. In the Jewish system, the sacrifices were dead sacrifices, slaughtered, never to be used again. But now, given what God has done and continues to do, our lives should be a continual response to this wonderful saving work as outlined in the rest of the book of Romans. God is transforming us by renewing our thinking first, reaching our hearts, and changing how we live. God informs our minds, transforms our hearts, empowers us to perform acts of worship, and ultimately conforms us into the image of Christ himself. In other words, sanctification.

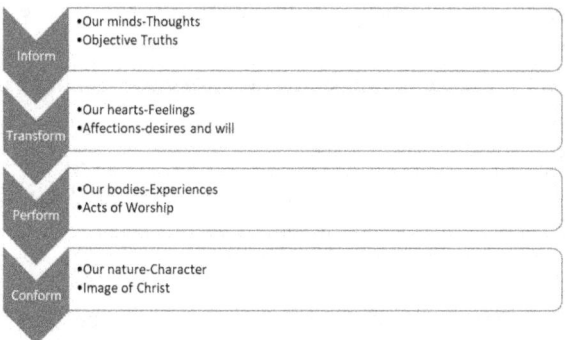

Figure 1 The inform, transform, perform, conform process.

Secondly, we see the same ideas in Jesus' words to the Samaritan woman at the well in fourth chapter of John's Gospel. She is questioning Jesus about whether it is right to worship God at the temple the Samaritans had built, or whether worship should occur at the temple in Jerusalem. Jesus' response indicates where the real heart of worship lies:

> But a time is coming, and even now has arrived, when the true worshipers will worship the Father in spirit and truth; for such people the Father seeks *to be* His worshipers. (John 4:23)

Jesus is making two points; firstly, God is not bound by buildings made with hands. This is clearly a reflection of Isa 66:1–2 and is repeated by Stephen at his trial in Acts 7. It parallels Paul's teaching in declaring that I don't have to go to some physical location and engage in certain activities for it to be considered worship. Living sacrifices don't have to go to some temple or synagogue or church. Worship is first and foremost a spiritual thing, our bodies and minds and whole persons responding in the here and now to the Spirit of God. God is a God who is everywhere if we just have the eyes to see. This kind of thinking sits at the heart of the contemplative practice of prayer. As Richard Rohr says:

> For some reason, it is easier to attend church services than quite simply to reverence the real—the "practice of the presence of God," as some have called it.[6]

---

6. Rohr, *Everything Belongs*, 18.

I think he is right. It is easier to live a life of Sunday-only "worship" that places minimal demands on me or my time the rest of the week, while failing to recognize and respond to God, to what he is saying and doing in the present in me and in those I come across. I remember having lunch with my wife once some years ago at an outdoor cafe. As we were sitting there, a homeless man, or certainly one with little to nothing, came up to our table and asked for money. We sent him away empty-handed. Later I was racked with guilt when the words of Jesus rang in my ears from Matt 25:40:

> Truly I say to you, to the extent that you did *it* for one of the least of these brothers *or sisters* of Mine, you did *it* for Me.

Jesus came to our table for lunch that day and we sent him away. This is a failure to worship.

Jesus' second point to the Samaritan woman is that not only is our spirit to be attuned to the ebbs and flows of the Spirit of God in our midst, within and without, but our minds are to be rightly informed with truth. Floating around in some spiritual ether world, ungrounded by the propositional truths of God, is a recipe for spiritual aberration, otherwise known as heresy. The gnostic and docetic controversies of the early church are evidence of what happens when we worship in Spirit devoid of truth. Legalism is the evidence of what happens when we worship in truth without Spirit. Head informed by truth, and heart attuned to the Spirit of God, both in balance, so that we may engage in acts of worship that please our God and give him glory. In the words of John Piper:

> Mind corresponds to the understanding of the truth of God's perfections. Love corresponds to the delight in the worth and beauty of those perfections. God is glorified both by being understood and being delighted in.[7]

---

7. Piper, *God's Passion for His Glory*, 82.

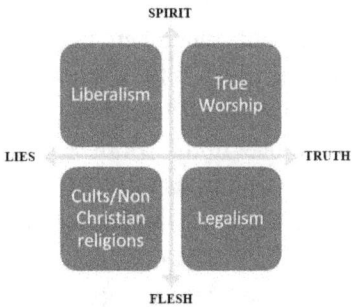

Figure 2

What the above figure is showing is that true worship exists when truth and spirit are equally balanced; this is the upper-right quadrant of this diagram.

Too much Spirit and not enough truth can lead to liberalism, which is a dysfunction of being insensitive to the stimuli of the objective truths of God's word. God has revealed things in his word which are designed to aid in human flourishing. To deny these things for the sake of subjective experiences and the freedom of the Spirit can lead to abuse. In this quadrant lie gnosticism and docetism, for instance, dangerous heresies that the first-century church battled.

This kind of imbalance can turn the process by which God works in us on its head. Looking back at Figure 1, instead of objective truths informing us, we allow subjective experience to inform us, affect our feelings, and then help us to decide what is true. So, I might have the subjective experience of suffering, which produces a great anguish in me and convinces me that God does not care. This is objectively not true as all of Scripture affirms God loves and cares for his children.

The health, wealth, and prosperity gospel can also run the risk of this dysfunctional extreme. I can turn my subjective experiences of God having met my needs, performed a miracle for me or some other great thing, into certitude that everyone's needs will be met if they just have enough faith. If God does not meet someone's needs, they may decide "I failed or God failed or the church failed." (I hate thee or I hate me.) People's lives have become shipwrecked as a result. This kind of teaching, that determines the blessings of God are predicated on the quality and strength of my faith, is abusive, unbalanced, and does not reflect the full teachings of the objective word of God.

Likewise, too much truth and not enough Spirit (lower right of diagram) can lead to legalism which is the dysfunction of being insensitive to the leadings and convictions of the Spirit of God. A strict adherence to certain interpretations of Scripture, or of certain authors, or of certain preachers, or to the truth as only espoused by the leader, can lead to a legalism which quenches the Spirit of God and can lead to abuse.

For instance, any opinion that does not fit within the strict guidelines of the truth as espoused by these organizations is viewed with suspicion, as is anyone who would put forth those ideas, especially if they differ from the established view. People are made to feel guilty for not believing the right things. I remember once being questioned because I quoted a Catholic author in a sermon. My critic viewed Catholics with suspicion because some of their theology did not fit our understanding of the gospel, and hence all of their words were deemed to be suspect. For me to quote a Catholic theologian made me suspect as well. It was an attempt to make me feel guilty.

You can see this in some churches that hold to an absolutely-no-compromise view of young earth creation. No space or grace is given to any view that falls outside this strict interpretation of Genesis. This can lead to the abuse of those who would dare suggest an alternative interpretation.

In extreme examples of organizations in this quadrant it is difficult for them to accept, in *X-Files* fashion, that there is a truth out there that is not in the Bible. But all truth is God's truth and true worshippers are sensitive to the Spirit of God as he illuminates the objective truths, whether in the Bible or elsewhere.

No truth and no sensitivity to the Spirit of God (bottom left, Figure 2) is the hallmark of all false religions, dangerous sects, and cults. Jim Jones and his cult is an extreme example of this.

One prime reason that dysfunctional churches, and in particular the leadership, are unresponsive to the stimuli of word and Spirit, is fear of losing control. In dysfunctional organizations, the more abusive they are, the more controlling they are. Control is a big deal to these leaders. They need to control the narrative, the thinking, and the behaviors of the flock. The more abusive they are, the more the leaders will declare themselves the only arbiter of truth. If people were open to what the Spirit of God was saying to the churches (Rev 2:29), then those at the top might lose their nice neat cozy arrangement of power and authority (and often the monetary perks that go with it). If people were to interpret the Scriptures for themselves, they might find out the leadership was corrupting truth for the sake of control.

As a living organism, the church is called to be responsive, to live out lives of sacrificial service and humble obedience in response to the promptings and stimuli of the Holy Spirit of God and his holy word. In dysfunctional organizations there is an imbalance in leaning towards one or the other. The more imbalanced the church becomes, the more dysfunctional it becomes. This chokes off the life force that God intends to be the means by which the community reproduces and ripens.

Reproducing

In one simple verse Jesus gave his disciples marching orders. Go and make more of you. Baptize them and teach them to obey my teachings. I am always with you . . . Now go do it (Matt 28:18–20). It is a pretty simple thing for him to have said, and the disciples did it and turned the world upside down in the process (Acts 17:6).

Healthy, living organisms reproduce more healthy, living organisms. This is the way it is meant to be. A healthy grapevine is called to produce healthy grapes. Now grapevines are a useful metaphor here, because I was thinking, "How do you get new vines?" How does a viticulturist get more grapevines? I thought you just get grape seeds and plant them, right? But no, this does not happen by planting the seeds of the grapes, but by taking cuttings from the existing good vines and grafting them onto good root stock. Something vital in the original vine, energized by the life of the root, is necessary to create another good vine. Now every metaphor has its limitations and we dare not stretch it too far, but why this is such a good metaphor of disciple-making is because it reflects the words of Jesus in John 15:4:

> Remain in Me, and I in you. Just as the branch cannot bear fruit of itself but must remain in the vine, so neither *can* you unless you remain in Me.

The genetic material, the DNA of the good grapevine, the sap in the veins, the life of Christ, runs through the plant, through the branches, not through the seeds. Plant the seeds of a grape and you can get any kind of aberration. They don't produce consistently after their kind. Sometimes the seeds are sterile and will never germinate. To get the good plant requires the good branches. New plants and new fruit are not a result of the fruit dying, but by means of the life of Christ running through the veins of each individual branch that then produces fruit. Each of us is called to abide or remain in him, because only by remaining in Christ can we produce fruit. Discipleship, therefore, can be seen as the process of abiding.

Abiding as remaining

Firstly, John 15:4 has often been translated *abide*, but the NASB gets the real sense of the word right when it translates the underlying Greek word as *remain*. Abiding means remaining in Christ.

The word also can carry the sense sense of not to become different as in John 15:16. The obvious point is that disciples of Jesus look like Jesus, become like Jesus, remain in the state of becoming more like Jesus, and don't look or act differently than Jesus. This is because they are attached to Jesus, his sap runs through their veins. Disciples of Jesus don't jump off the vine and start their own vine.

And the primary reason you would want to remain in Jesus? Because as he states in John 15:1, "I am the true vine." Now anyone could declare themselves to be a true vine. Jesus backs this claim up with his life, death, and, most importantly, his resurrection, which is the exclamation point to the statement. John continues, "These things are written that you might believe and understand that Jesus really is the *true* vine" (John 20:31).

With the life of Jesus running through them, disciples who remain in Jesus begin to produce fruit like Jesus. What Jesus is telling his disciples is that it is possible to be superficially attached to the vine, produce green leaves, and look like one who is abiding in the vine. But leaves are not evidence of abiding; the evidence of abiding is fruit.

> Every branch in Me that does not bear fruit, He takes away . . . If anyone does not remain in Me, he is thrown away like a branch and dries up; and they gather them and throw them into the fire, and they are burned. (John 15:2, 6)

This is sobering and a warning. Branches with superficial attachments to Christian religion, that have the outward appearance of Christ but through which the life of Christ is not truly flowing, will be cut off, pruned, and burned. There are, I am sure, no shortage of people who

Dysfunction

would declare themselves to be Christians because of infant baptism, or because they try to live according to the golden rule or any other such outward semblances of the Christian faith. Jesus will have none of this.

I can also run great ministries, exist in the church my whole life, see people come to saving faith through my preaching, and still not be abiding. It can all be just leaves and shoots. Jesus himself says in Matthew 7:21–23:

> "Not everyone who says to Me, 'Lord, Lord,' will enter the kingdom of heaven, but the one who does the will of My Father who is in heaven *will enter*. Many will say to Me on that day, 'Lord, Lord, did we not prophesy in Your name, and in Your name cast out demons, and in Your name perform many miracles?' And then I will declare to them, 'I never knew you; leave Me, you who practice lawlessness.'"

Disciples are not just superficially attached to Jesus; the life of Christ flows through them and they produce fruit. Abiding means fruit, not just attachment. It is worth asking: What is this fruit? J. C. Ryle, in his work on the Gospel of John, puts it this way:

> He that would know what the word "fruit" means need not wait long for an answer. Repentance toward God, faith toward our Lord Jesus Christ, holiness of life and conduct—These are what the New Testament calls "fruit."[8]

The fruit of the abiding Christian is one of constantly repenting, not just a one-off event that attaches us to the vine, but an ever-present willingness to engage in this action to help us remain. A lack of repentance in a person, even a lifelong committed churchgoing person, is evidence of lack of abiding. John says in 1 John 3:6:

> No one who remains in Him sins *continually*; no one who sins *continually* has seen Him or knows Him.

The fruit of the abiding Christian is also the fruit of the Spirit as outlined in Gal 6. This is evidence of attachment and life-flowing sap. The disciple of Jesus starts to look like Jesus, exhibiting genuine love, real joy, abiding peace, steadfast patience, overflowing kindness, genuine goodness, nonwavering faithfulness, humble gentleness, and increasing levels of self-control.

A healthy church is not one in which the members are attached to the church itself, its leaders, its books, its teachings, its constitutions, its

---

8. Ryle, *Expository Thoughts on John*, 3:107.

traditions, its popes or priests or elders or any other such person, but rather to the vine itself, to Christ and Christ alone. A healthy church is one which measures its people by the measure of Christlikeness, not churchlikeness. A healthy church is one in which the members bear the fruit of Jesus. It is healthy to ask, "What are we reproducing? Christ or us? Are we making disciples of Jesus or disciples of our church?"

Too often in dysfunctional churches, rather than reproducing disciples of Jesus we produce disciples of our church. They may call themselves model Christians, but really a model is but a cheap, plastic imitation of the real thing. In dysfunctional churches people are pressured to attach themselves to their culture, their way of doing things, to conform to their understanding of the Bible or theology and the way their culture lives. It looks like Jesus, but it isn't. Dysfunctional churches can tend to confuse their church with Christianity or Christ himself. Any criticism of the church, its teachings, its leaders, or its culture is seen as an attack on Jesus or the kingdom of God. This is what happens when churches abide in themselves and not Jesus.

Abiding as remembering

The means by which the sap of the vine flows through us, attaches to us, and keeps us is by getting the sap into us, what Jesus calls "my word":

> I am the vine, you are the branches; the one who remains in Me, and I in him bears much fruit, for apart from Me you can do nothing. If you remain in Me, and My words remain in you, ask whatever you wish, and it will be done for you. (John 15:5, 7).

I can recall a time around the communion table when the leader said that communion was to remember Jesus because we often would forget him. "Do this in remembrance of me," because we are prone to forget Jesus. While of course we don't literally forget Jesus, in a more profound sense we are indeed prone to forget Jesus. Discipleship and abiding are about learning to remember well.

Jeffery D. Arthurs, in his book *Preaching as Reminding*, helpfully explores the theological understanding of the depth of meaning behind the simple word "remember":

> In the Bible, "remembering" is more than mental recall. It involves emotion and volition as well as cognition. It not only touches the past; it articulates with the present and the futures,

helping a person connect previously acquired wisdom to current and future decisions.[9]

He describes memory as both participation and blessing:

> At times this life seems inchoate, a tale told by an idiot signifying nothing, but reminders of God's power in the past, his presence in the present and his promises for the future help God's children believe in the unseen hand that guides the affairs of their lives. Memory reunites us mentally, emotionally and volitionally to the God who watches over us.[10]

Understanding the depth of this word in biblical literature provides a basis for comprehending the depth of abiding in Christ. Abiding means remembering, remembering causes us to act, leading to acts which produce fruit. This is being a disciple of Jesus.

And how Jesus abides in us, and how we abide in Jesus is by means of his words. Here we see abiding not only as remaining, but remembering. The word of Christ abiding in us is the primary way we remember Jesus. The Christian life of discipleship is one of remembering Christ as his word reunites us mentally with his teachings, moves us emotionally, and causes us to act. Here again we see the inform-transform-perform-conform model. Paul calls it letting "the word of Christ dwell in you richly" (Col 3:16). This is a vital component of being a disciple of Jesus and reproducing the fruit of Christ in your life and in the lives of others.

Disciples abide in Christ by allowing his words, his truths, his life to flow through them, and by so doing, remembering Christ through acts of worship. So, when at communion Jesus says, "Do this in remembrance of me," it is his way of saying take and eat and consume me, let the life of me flow through you, be moved in your hearts by my life, and go and love the world as I have loved you. This is abiding, this is remembering, this is being a disciple of Jesus.

However, in dysfunctional churches there can be a failure to remember Jesus. Instead, they abide in themselves, their churches, their cultures, their leaders, and their ministries. They let their own words or the words of a celebrity pastor dwell in them richly, and then remember themselves as they reproduce copies of themselves, not Jesus, but all with the veneer of Jesus, all with Jesus' mask. They create disciples of themselves, and because of this dysfunction, abuse can thrive among them.

9. Arthurs, *Preaching as Reminding*, 13.
10. Arthurs, *Preaching as Reminding*, 14.

Ripening

Some years ago, we built a new home. At its completion the house stood on a block of land that had areas waiting for plants. So, I went to a nursery to see what I could buy. There were really cheap tube-starter plants available that were about 2–3 inches tall, in tiny tubes, ready to plant. Or you could spend ten times as much and buy bigger ones that had been grown for longer and which were ready to sell and plant. It would give a far more established look to the garden. In one corner of the nursery was the discount plant section, with lots of mature-looking plants at throw-away bargain prices. They looked just the ticket, until you looked a little closer, then you could see these plants were not that healthy: not many leaves for the size of the plant, long spindly trunks, and little leafing heads at the top. There was an orange tree that had ripe oranges on it, but they were the size of golf balls.

I knew from past experience that, although cheaper, these plants were no bargain at all. They suffered from being root-bound. They had spent far too long in the pots and were suffering for it. The roots of the plants had grown around and around in a tight knot in the plastic pot. The plant was starved for nutrients. And I knew that if I bought these plants, I couldn't just take it out of the pot and plant it. I would need to hack away at the roots, prune the top, put in huge amounts of organic material in the planting hole, tie it to a stake, and nurse it for years until it recovered. The plant would take longer to reach maturity, than if I bought a far smaller one in tube stock. Dysfunctional churches can be just like those knotted-root, pot-bound plants: stunted, not reaching their full potential, not reaching maturity, not ripening. Jesus says this in John 15:8:

> My Father is glorified by this, that you bear much fruit, and *so* prove to be My disciples.

Healthy churches mature and ripen to bear *much* fruit, not just *some* fruit. As we have seen, abiding in Christ means becoming like Christ; the fruit of Christlikeness is the evidence of abiding. But note how Jesus then goes on to say that healthy disciples not only produce fruit, but this remaining in Christ, this movement of his life through their veins, will produce much fruit.

Much fruit . . . the sign of a healthy plant, not one that is root-knotted or pot-bound; so too the sign of a healthy church. A healthy, functioning, much-fruiting church has a far greater impact on the world then the less healthy church. Both kinds of churches are producing some fruit. The healthy one produces much fruit.

Much fruit . . . the plant ripening to full maturity completes or fulfills the purpose the Father has for the vine. Teleologically, this is the end of the vine; this is its purpose, its meaning—produce much fruit so that God might be glorified. It should not surprise us to see this is the goal of the church. For years, the church has declared this to be her end. The Westminster shorter catechism declares in answer to the question, "What is the chief purpose for which man is made?" and the answer? *Now God made us to glorify him.*[11]

The church is full of people whose chief end is to glorify God. A much-fruit church is one that has ripening fruit—the glory of God. This, therefore, helps act as a diagnostic question: "Who is really glorified in our church?" In healthy churches, full of people who *Respond* and *Reproduce,* God's glory is on display. In unhealthy churches—those who don't *Respond* or *Reproduce,* or churches that do it poorly—the glory of the church ends up on display, and these are two things that can look the same, but are completely different. Too often in dysfunctional churches these two things are confused. That is to say, "If our church looks good, then God looks good." This is not necessarily the case at all. Rather, in a healthy church we should declare, "If God looks good then our church looks good," because our purpose is to make much of him and little of ourselves.

Big buildings, lots of people, big worship band, dozens of social justice ministries, missionaries overseas, kids' ministries—you name it, all of these have the appearance of fruit, much fruit. And it very well may be exactly that; hopefully so. Yet sometimes churches like this can be doing it for the glory of the brand of the church, or for the name of the preacher, and confusing this with the glory of God.

How can I tell the difference? Well, observe what happens in a crisis that runs the risk of hurting the image of the church. Trust me, these crises will come. Maybe the pastor falls into sexual sin. A major ministry leader quits under questionable circumstances. Someone stands up and speaks a prophetic word of rebuke declaring there is some form of sin in the camp. A woman comes to the leadership and declares she has been abused. You name it; the image-threatening crisis will come. The response from the leadership will soon tell you whether they are doing the ministry for the glory of God or the glory of the church.

---

11. "Shorter Catechism," Question 1.

Wade Mullen's recent book based on his PhD research describes how dysfunctional churches and organizations seek to manage their image when a crisis comes along. They will use a range of impression management techniques, including denials, excuses, justifications, and comparisons.[12] But what you won't see dysfunctional organizations doing is seeking truth as if it were something objectively outside of themselves, of which they might be blind to, and for which they may need help in seeing. If ministry is being done for the glory of God, then any dysfunction, abuse, corruption, sin, you name it, which is brought to light by means of Spirit and word, should devastate the community, producing what Paul calls a "Godly sorrow leading to repentance" (2 Cor 7:10). Watching an organization launch into those impression management techniques is a sure sign of dysfunction within.

The dysfunctional organization will, instead, let others suffer to protect itself. It's as simple and as hard as that. When maintaining the institution of the church and its image is more important than dealing honestly, openly, and sacrificially, with allegations of abuse and hurt within it, you know you are dealing with a dysfunctional organization. It is in violation of its value of love, and failing to take abuse seriously is about as unloving as you can get. The basic underlying assumption that image is more important than love comes into play. The abiding, much-fruit organization, on the other hand, will lay down its institutional life for the sake of others, the very definition of love.

That is what abiding people do who are ripening for the glory of God. Seeking to manage your image, and endeavoring to maintain control at all costs, shows the church places a far higher price on its own image than the glory of God. This reveals, therefore, in these crisis moments, that the purpose of all the God-glorifying stuff that is being done in Jesus' name is, in reality, not that at all. It is about the church and its image first, with God second. God is not embarrassed, and nor does he need to be defended when a crisis hits our churches. He is offended when we try to manage our image rather than deal with the truth. He is glorified when we deal with it honestly and transparently.

This may in fact be the primary reason God allows these crises to appear; they are his way of pruning the vine (if she is prepared to be humbled by it).

---

12. Mullen, *Something's Not Right*, 103.

God's glory not our glory

As a ripening, maturing people, a healthy church's desire is to make Christ known in the fullness of his glory and for the glorious nature of the Father to be unmistakably on display. This is seen in the evangelistic enterprise of the church in all of its manifestations, from word proclamation to social justice. The natural desire of a much-fruit church is that many more branches may be grafted onto the true vine and thus enjoy the delights of the life of Christ.

Note the progression of the words of Jesus. Abide, pray, receive, and then bear much fruit to the Father's glory. God is glorified by answering the prayers of his abiding people, so that the great things done for his glory and for his name's sake can only be attributed to him.

What I am going to say now will seem cynical and bitter, but it is simply my anecdotal observations of dysfunctional churches of all shapes and sizes from all over the globe. Too much of what we are calling "God doing great things through us" is in fact *us doing great things through us and attributing it to God*. If our plans go well, God has blessed us, if they fail, we are being persecuted. The process in a dysfunctional church can look a little like this:

- Abide in ourselves *but* say we abide in Jesus
- Reproduce ourselves *but* say we are becoming like Jesus
- Rely on ourselves *but* call it being reliant upon God
- Do great things and say God did it

Now why this is so deceptive is because great things do get done: buildings get built, missionaries get sent, and the gospel is proclaimed. They are really great things. In dysfunctional churches much of the stuff getting done, as I have said earlier, is in order to establish the brand or the image of the church, but then lay a Jesus veneer over it so it looks like that is the real driving force.

This can happen with building plans. Churches come up with the plan, come up with the borrowing strategy, they organize special giving days, they build the thing, and then slap a plaque on the wall that reads "To the glory of God." Let's be honest. They could have done this without him. How do I know? Because they just did. They used their entire God-given human wisdom and practical knowledge to build the thing. This also helps explain why, when things go awry, dysfunctional churches get so busy going into damage control and image management. They were never really relying on God in the first place, so why start now?

This is all a little too inauthentic and this is my point. Churches should be far more honest with what they are doing. If they believe that God is glorious and needs to be known (and he must!), then they should be using far more honest language like "We are using the gifts God has given us to make his name known. We ask that he bless these plans. If things fall apart, we ask that you, oh God, graciously give us the knowledge and the humility to understand our failures and to declare them honestly with our people; failures to do your will or failures to understand it. And if these plans should fail, help us to understand the lessons you are teaching through this failure. And if they succeed it is only by your good grace."

Of course, what kind of powerful visionary leadership is ever going to start a project of any sort with the idea that it could fail? It seems too weak, too uncertain. Leaders have the mind of God, don't they? If they say we are going to do something it is because God told them, didn't he? How could it fail?

Along with this kind of honest declaration of God honoring the use of their natural talents, ripening churches are also discovering the miraculous as God works in ways that only his intervention could explain.

If you read about the life of George Muller, you'll see what I mean. His life and mission are one of abiding-praying-receiving-BOOM—God gets the glory.[13] His mission to orphans has the glory of God written all over it, and the glory of man nowhere to be seen. Only the miraculous intervention of the God of heaven and earth can explain it. Our churches should be striving for this; the unexplainable happening by the unequaled God, to him be the glory. Sadly, in dysfunctional churches they bear much of their own fruit and very little for the glory of God. Just saying God gets the glory doesn't make it so. Paul calls it "having the appearance of godliness, but denying its power" (2 Tim 3:5).

Joy

A healthy, ripening church is a place that is full of love and joy, even if the big ministry things never happen. And why do I say that? Because Jesus does in John 15:9–11:

---

13. Bergin, *Autobiography of George Muller*.

> Just as the Father has loved Me, I also have loved you; remain in My love. If you keep My commandments, you will remain in My love; just as I have kept My Father's commandments and remain in His love. These things I have spoken to you so that My joy may be in you, and *that* your joy may be made full.

God is glorified when the church produces much fruit. His majesty, worth, value, grandeur, and beauty are on display for all to see. People are genuinely loved, and even in the midst of the worst trials, joy is the primary song. Because, in the end, much fruit is not so much about what we do and how much we do, but who we are and how we do it. Far better to be a healthy church of fifty people full of love and joy and doing little things for God, than to be a dysfunctional church of 5,000 doing lots of great things,"but secretly like Achen, sweeping up and hiding sin under the tent" (Josh 7:21).

The healthy church bears much fruit by *Responding* and *Reproducing*, and when she is persecuted for this, she responds with love and joy. This is the natural result of healthy *Responding* and *Reproducing*. A healthy church is one where we stand up for justice and mercy, we stand with the abused and drive away the abuser. A healthy church evangelizes the world by displaying the fullness of God's justice and mercy, his love and his wrath, his grace, and his law in balanced proportions. A healthy church engages in seeking to hold back the pain of the curse by engaging in social justice work for the poor and beleaguered. And if she is persecuted for this she responds with joy.

Fresh fruit

Ripening fruit is related to *Responding* and *Reproducing* in that every year the plant produces new crops. Having a great crop one year, a poor crop the next, fluctuating from good to bad, and from time to time going years with no new fruit, is clearly the sign of an unhealthy vine.

Healthy churches do not rest on their laurels. They are sensitive to what the Spirit of God is doing in them and amongst them. The idea here is that just as a healthy plant responds to changing seasons and conditions and continues to produce much fruit year in and year out, so, too, the healthy church responds well to changing conditions through many seasons. Our church should neither be a carbon copy of one down the street, nor a carbon copy of itself from fifty years ago.

> Churches are not franchises to be reproduced as exactly as possible wherever and whenever—in Rome and Moscow and London and Baltimore—the only thing changed being the translation of the menu.[14]

The world in which the Western church finds herself is an ever-changing place. The culture in which she finds herself is always moving, ever further away from God it would seem. The church needs to respond to this. Old ways of doing things which produced abundant fruit to the glory of God are not going to continue to do so forever. If there is one constant in church it is the need for change, not so much of substance but of form.

There are some everlasting and glorious truths in the gospel which will ever remain the same. They are the root structure which holds the vine in place. But the leaves, branches, and fruit must develop and grow and shift in the breeze, and be resilient to storms, wind, heat, and snow.

Often the means by which this happens is through new revelations of the understanding of Scripture, as the Spirit of God awakens the church to the fullness of God's revelation. One of the classic ways this occurred in the past is the way the church held so dogmatically to an earth-centric solar system universe model. The Copernican revolution changed all this. The church needed to, with humility, recognize its certitude about its understanding of the world was wrong, needed to change to reflect what was really true, and God used both science and his Spirit to move the church in this way. Imagine a church today that refused to accept the sun as the center of the solar system. She would be a laughingstock. This would be evidence of a dysfunctional church, hanging on to dry fruit.

An ever-ripening, maturing church is responsive to the changing seasons in which she finds herself.

SUMMARY

In this chapter I discussed dysfunction in two ways: first, as a failure to live out the values and beliefs that a church declares are vital, and second, by exploring the church as a vine. A healthy vine, or any organism for that matter, will respond well to stimuli, reproduce after its kind, and reach maturity.

---

14. Peterson, *Pastor*, 119.

With that said, there is no perfect church, and all churches have some dysfunctions in them. And not every dysfunctional church will exhibit all these dysfunctions to their full extent, but they will be there. What separates the dysfunctional church that allows and enables abuse and one that does not is that a dysfunctional church:

- *Fails to* respond *well to the stimuli: the word of God or his Spirit.* This means that when its dysfunctions are made evident, they are not dealt with or more likely they never are able to hear or see the dysfunctions in the first place, as they are not reacting to the stimuli of the word and Spirit. Healthy churches will be sensitive to the rebuke of the word and Spirit and make adjustments accordingly with repentance. If abuse is found to exist in the church, the healthy church will be sensitive to the rebuke of the Spirit and the word. The dysfunctional church will not be able to hear the cry of the abused because their ears are dull to what the Spirit is saying to their churches. He who has ears to hear let him hear!

- *Fails to* reproduce *Christlike individuals.* Instead, it produces copies of themselves—people who are committed to our mission, vision, denomination, and theology, and confuse the church for Christianity and Christ, although they would never consciously say this or even recognize it. This can be evident in that they cannot abide criticism of themselves or the work they engage in. A criticism of them is seen as a criticism of Christ himself. These churches can harbor abuse because the criticism or exposure of their members is unacceptable. Healthy churches are full of Christians who exhibit the fruit of the Spirit and more importantly are led by people who bear this same fruit.

- *Fails to* ripen *well.* They do great things and give God the glory for things that have the appearance of godliness, but deny his power. These churches do many great things in the name of Christ and in declaration of his glory, but a more honest assessment is that these things are done in their own strength and with human wisdom. Healthy churches mature into doing great kingdom work that can only be explained by the intervention of the great I AM.

1.2

Abuse

For this is the message which you have heard from the beginning, that we are to love one another; not as Cain, who was of the evil one and murdered his brother. And for what reason did he murder him? Because his own deeds were evil, but his brother's were righteous.

—1 John 2:11-12

THE LOVE OF CAIN

I ALWAYS THOUGHT IT strange the way John worded this section of his letter: "Don't love like Cain the murderer." Since when is murder love? But I think John writes like this for rhetorical effect, designed to contrast genuine Christian love from another form of love, what he calls "the love of Cain." And boy is it a contrast. But what kind of love is the love of Cain?

The story of Cain and Abel is the second tragedy of the story of the Bible, the first being the fall, with this being a concrete example of the first tragedy's impact. John's exegesis of the story, that Cain's deeds were evil, and Abel's where righteous, does appear on the surface to be somewhat confusing. Nowhere in the Genesis story (4:1–6) does God indicate he wants a sacrifice, nor does he describe the type he is desiring.[1] Why would animal sacrifices be considered righteous and crop sacrifices evil?

---

1. Although a mention of the time for sacrifices in verse 3 does indicate that there was already some established system in place, who decided it and how it would happen, and the timing, are all open to conjecture.

In a postcalvary world, the reader might be able to see Christ foreshadowed, but at this point in the Genesis story, it is not apparent why animal sacrifices are preferred. For Cain, God seems to randomly accept the gift of the younger brother and informs the older brother what is acceptable. Verse 6 gives the clue as to what was righteous and what was evil: it wasn't the gift, per se.

Put yourself in Cain's position for a moment. You are the first born. You are young, strong, and from the sweat of your brow you have weeded, ploughed, planted, watered, and harvested a crop. The ground is meant to bear weeds and from the sweat of your brow you must work it (Gen 3:17–19), and work it you do, and you are successful. You would be rightly proud of your efforts. You intend to show God your devotion by offering some of this labor to him as a sacrifice. Your younger brother, who has tended flocks, has done far less work. Sure, tending flocks is not simple, but a far easier task than the farming of crops. He sits around all day, watching them eat grass, and protecting them from the occasional predator. Here is Abel: younger, doing less work, and yet God favors the younger over the older. Being overlooked like this can be a shaming experience and it is not hard to imagine it being so for Cain. It may help to explain his anger at being overlooked when surely as the older, harder-working brother God should have favored him. Abel has been honored and Cain (at least in his own eyes) has been dishonored.

The unrighteous deeds of which John speaks is the refusal by Cain to accept that God alone chooses the evil from the good. God alone decides what form of worship is acceptable and what is not. It harkens back to the fruit eaten by their parents. The unrighteous deeds of Cain were his unwillingness to accept this.

The sin in Cain's heart is revealed. The desire for him alone to determine the good and the evil, apart from God, does its work. This is the love of Cain, the love of self-determination, of self-approval. This self-love is an unwillingness to allow God to be God, but rather, to seek to take that place for one's self. Cain, in anger, makes a determination of life and death, a role reserved for God himself. Deciding to remove the challenge to the focus he feels is rightly his, he removes his rival and expects God will shine his countenance solely on him with his rival now gone. Cain's exile into the wilderness (Gen 4:12) demonstrates how wrong he got this.[2]

---

2. Although in exile, God places a mark of both shame and protection on Cain. Even at his worst, God still loves and protects him. In the same way in which he provided skins for his parents, God once again reveals himself to be both justice and

This is narcissistic behavior, an all-consuming self-interest to the detriment of others, a love of self that elevates one's wants and desires above all else, including God. It is a self-love that relegates others to the status of objects to be used or obstacles to be overcome. This is the love of Cain and is ultimately at the heart of all abuse, and by definition, therefore, is as un-Christian a behavior as you can get. No, says John, don't love like that, do better.

ABUSE DEFINED

> Abuse must first be named as such and recognized for what it is, as this is how the abused individual distinguishes right from wrong in what was, or is currently, occurring and recognizes that he or she is not to blame for it.[3]

Donald Capps, in *The Depleted Self*, writes: "We deny our experience to the extent that we fail accurately to name it."[4] When it comes to abuse then it is important that we accurately see it, understand it, and name it. If we don't comprehend abuse in all its forms or have no name for it, then we will fail to recognize it when we are its agents or victims.

I think too often those of us in churches avoid the term "abuse" for several reasons. Firstly, because we think abuse is the overt crossing of personal physical boundaries, like sexual assault or physical attacks. And since, thankfully, these things aren't happening often in churches[5], it is easy to assume there isn't an abuse issue. Secondly, we avoid this language because we feel it is best left to the professionals amongst us, psychologists and counselors and the like. We feel the layperson hasn't got the right or qualifications to be making those kinds of allegations. I can remember using this language for the first time and how guilty I felt and the shame I felt for even describing someone who was a Christian as being abusive. Surely not! What did I know? And thirdly, and perhaps more insidiously, people don't like the language of abuse because they may have unresolved abuse and abusive patterns in their own past and are simply unable to detect it or call it out when it is happening right

---

mercy to Cain. Even at our worst, there is hope.

3. Novšak et al, "Therapeutic Implications of Religious-Related Emotional Abuse," 31–44.

4. Capps, *Depelted Self*, loc. 934 of 2008.

5. Although once is too often, and sadly it happens more than that.

in front of them, particularly if it is of the more passive-aggressive and covert-aggressive type. Using language of abuse with people who have unresolved emotional pain can lead to a backlash or simply a dead stare, as if you are speaking a foreign language. People need to be ready to hear the awful truth and often they simply are in no state to do so.

What I hope to do is disabuse us of this reticence and start seeing and naming abuse for what it is, in all of its forms, be they subtle or obvious, overt or covert. Recently I was at the dentist, and as he was happily drilling into my teeth, the dental technician brought in the X-rays of my mouth that they had taken earlier. As I was lying there, he said "Ah, another cavity. This tooth is numb we'll deal with this as well." After he had finished, I asked him to show me on the X-ray what he had seen. I expected a big black dot or something, but instead he showed me the faintest hint of a shadow, the barest change from the rest of the surrounding image. I said, "I never would have noticed that," and he said something quite profound.

"The eye cannot see what the brain doesn't know."

In my experience, as I began to explore manipulative behavior and abuse, lights came on for me everywhere. I now had a language and an understanding for what was going on, and continues to go on in many churches. Finally, I could see the things to which I had heretofore been blind. So, this book is written in part to help your brain understand so your eyes might see, because once you see it you won't be able to un-see it, and once you see it you will want to ask the kinds of questions this book is aiming to address, like "Why is this person allowed to get away with this behavior in our church?" and "Why do we want them to?"

So, let's begin with understanding what I mean by abuse:

> Abuse: A pattern of coercive control (ongoing actions or inactions) that proceeds from a mentality of entitlement to power, whereby, through intimidation, manipulation and isolation, the abuser keeps his/her target subordinated and under their control. This pattern can be emotional, verbal, psychological, spiritual, sexual, financial, social and physical.[6]

Webster's dictionary gives this broader definition:

---

6. Roberts, "Crying Out for Justice."

Abuse is the improper usage or treatment of a thing, often to unfairly or improperly gain benefit.[7]

Now why both of these definitions are helpful is because, as Webster's indicates, unlike the first definition, I can abuse you even if no pattern of behavior is evident. For instance, imagine I am having a particularly bad day and you cut me off in traffic on the way home. In a fit of road rage, I chase you, stop you at the next set of lights, jump out of the car, and verbally abuse you and . . . well you get the picture. Now for me this is entirely out of character, but I have used you improperly, even if only once. You were, in that instance, an obstacle to be overcome for my own benefit.

I am, however, primarily concerned with the first definition where individuals are engaged in a pattern of coercive control as their *primary or predominant* means of interacting with others. We can all have the odd bad day and can do things that are abusive in themselves, but one would hope that in a moment of clarity, apologies would be given and forgiveness offered. But the abuse I am considering is the kinds of dysfunctions in a church which can enable individuals to exert coercive control over another in a long-term repeated pattern of behavior designed to control others and maintain authority. But you needn't already have any formal authority and a position of power in a church to engage in abusive behaviors. In some instances, when the abuser has no authority and control, abuse is used in an attempt to obtain it. Coercive attempts to gain or maintain authority and control will always come as result of a sense of entitlement to and misuse of power.

Coercive control is also an important point to note here. Abusive individuals are engaging in actions that are forcing people in overt or covert ways to accept violations of their own personhood and consciences, until their consciences are calloused or they no longer have the will to resist or complain. Abuse inherently seeks to silence, to shut down the voice of the one being abused. Following Webster's definition, this is the improper "use" of a human being, the exploitation of another for the benefit of the one engaged in the abusive behavior to the detriment of the one being abused. As I have shown, this is very much the love of Cain.

---

7. *Merriam-Webster Dictionary, s.v.,* "Abuse."

Abuse as a Dehumanizing Misuse of Power

Philosophers, sociologists, and theologians, amongst others, have spent countless oceans of ink attempting to get an understanding of the concept of power. Power comes from the Latin word *posse*, which means to be able, and as such, all human beings have power. In and of itself it is both a neutral and necessary thing.

One helpful view is the work of Rollo May, who describes power as "the ability to cause or prevent change,"[8] and in human beings it exists on a continuum from the *power to be*, described as a neutral thing, inherent in the one who lives, all the way through the concepts of self-affirmation, self-assertion, aggression, and ultimately violence.[9] For May, only some forms of aggression, what he calls "destructive aggression,"[10] are inappropriate. "Aggression is a moving into the positions of power or prestige or the territory of another and taking possession of it for one's self."[11] Violence is what happens when aggression fails.[12]

Power, when used appropriately, can elevate the individual's self-worth, protect against aggression, and enable one to be a productive and socially valuable entity within community. However, when used inappropriately, power is destructive, and we all have the potential to do this.

Power can be seen as good, what May describes as *power with* (where my power aids and abets my neighbor), *power for* or *nutrient power* (where my power cares for my neighbor), and even *power against*, (as in competitive situations, where healthy debates over competing spaces can create compromise, which is in the best interests of all).[13] These good uses of power are very much within the sphere of the Christian ethic of preferring one's neighbor over self, and all of the "one another" passages of the New Testament reference this kind of good power usage.

But there are also bad usages of power, described as *power over*, which take the form of exploitation or manipulation. Exploitation subjects others to whatever means are available to control, including violence and death, the actions of Cain if you will. Manipulative power is

---

8. May, *Power and Innocence*, 99.
9. May, *Power and Innocence*, 40–45.
10. May, *Power and Innocence*, 156.
11. May, *Power and Innocence*, 42.
12. May, *Power and Innocence*, 43.
13. May, *Power and Innocence*, 105–10.

just exploitative power done in more covert ways to hopefully achieve the resultant control.

Power with, power for, and *power against* (in the right circumstances) are all valid uses of inherent power. What makes them valid uses is the aim or purpose of the use. Healthy uses of power work for the good of the other, because they see in the other a good for which they desire to work.

The aim or goal of our relationships should be a healthy means of interrelating, described by one researcher as a "mutual intersubjectivity."[14] A healthy and mature mutual relationship is one in which there "is an appreciation of the wholeness of the other person with a special awareness of the other's subjective experience."[15] This is a way of saying each person in a relationship is empathetic to the humanity of the other. Each person seeks to understand the other as a glorious, albeit fallen, image-bearer of our God. In a mutually intersubjective relationship, each person can know and be known, value the other as other, refuse to exploit or manipulate the other, and demonstrate a willingness to be open to change in the relationship.[16] At the heart of all Christian interpersonal ethic is God's declaration that all people are created in his image (Gen 1:26–27). Here is the key to understanding when power usage becomes abusive.

Behavior is abusive when it fails to operate with this form of mutuality. When one fails to recognize the other as valuable, as an image-bearer, refuses to be vulnerable with the other and instead sees the other as an object to use or obstacle to overcome, then this failure can lead to abuse in the relationship. This objectification, this willingness to exploit and manipulate, to destructively aggress, to cross over the border into the personhood of another, whether physically or otherwise, is what it means to abuse another.

For Christians the right use of power is for the elevation and good of the other for mutual benefit, because as image-bearers they have a dignity that makes them worthy of this treatment. Abusers misuse power by seeking to dominate and control what they see as objects for the own nonmutual benefit.

When an individual uses their power to aggress destructively, engage in violence, and stand over another, they are engaging in abusive

---

14. Jordan, "Meaning of Mutuality," 2.
15. Jordan, "Meaning of Mutuality," 2.
16. Jordan, "Meaning of Mutuality," 2.

behaviors, whether it is a one-off thing (the road rage incident) or a pattern of relating.

To put this together we can understand abuse as:

> *One person objectifying another by failing to honor the mutual dignity and humanity in the other, and misusing power, using exploitation and/or manipulation to coercively gain or maintain control over another.*

Abuse as Manipulation

I was fifty-six years old the first time I ever used the word manipulation about someone. That it took me so long is clearly an indication of the fact that I was completely blind to the dysfunction in my environment that included manipulative people and behaviors. Starting to see and describe behavior as manipulative, before I had a real language around it, is evidence of the fact that I was having my own personal crisis, my own "woke" moment.

I didn't ever really think about manipulation because it is such a powerful accusation to use against someone, and to use it about Christians in a church context was, for me at least, simply off the radar. If I gave it any thought at all I would associate the behavior with Goebbels, Hitler's propaganda chief, or other kinds of psychopaths. For me manipulation was the playground for only the worst of the worst of us, and never nice, normal people.

Manipulation is something we all can engage in from time to time when we want something from someone else and don't know how to ask for it, or out of fear of the reaction of the other if we are to ask for it directly. A husband might make a dinner for his wife, clean the house, buy a gift, whatever, with the intention of hopefully getting her in the mood. This is easier than outright asking his wife for sex as she might just reject him, and this would be too painful. Instead, he engages in behaviors to manipulate his wife into getting what he wants. This is an unhealthy and dishonest way of relating, yet it happens all the time.

For some people manipulation is all they know. They learned that to ask for what they need was risky or dangerous. Or maybe they were ignored as children. Neglect and abuse as children taught them that you cannot ask for what you want. Maybe as children they were raised in an abusive environment, in which showing weakness and need was a dangerous exercise. They became dehumanized and, in some sense, lost a sense of their own inherent dignity. So how do you get what you need in an unsafe environment? You act in subtle, manipulative ways to get what you need without actually having to ask for it. Now as adults, they bring this behavior into their relationships even when being direct would be easier and work better for them. This coping mechanism can be brought into adulthood even when it is now safe to ask for your needs to be met, because they have never learned to ask.

In this chapter I am using the concept of manipulation as a pejorative term designed to indicate that the perpetrator of these actions is misusing power and seeking devious/covert means:

- to manage you and keep you under control,
- to get what they want without expressly asking for it, or
- to prevent some sin or ethical misbehavior from being appropriately exposed.

George K. Simon highlights the features of covert abusive forms of manipulation in this way:

> When you're determined to have your way or gain advantage and you're open, direct, and obvious in your manner of fighting, your behavior is best labelled overtly aggressive. *When you're out to "win," get your way, dominate, or control, but are subtle, underhanded, or deceptive enough to hide your true intentions, your behavior is most appropriately labelled covertly aggressive.* Concealing overt displays of aggression while simultaneously intimidating others into backing-off, backing-down, or giving-in is a very powerful manipulative maneuver. That's why covert-aggression is most often the vehicle for interpersonal manipulation.[17]

Much manipulation in the abusive church context is covertly aggressive, but *it is* aggressive. The manipulator is seeking to gain or keep an advantage over you, but in such a way as for you to often fail to see it for what it is. Since to aggress in an overt way often will not be acceptable, underhanded methods are used, and because it is a misuse of power, as I have shown, it is, by definition, abuse.

---

17. Simon, *In Sheep's Clothing*, 21 (emphasis mine).

Manipulation revealed

In the definition of abuse quoted earlier by Barbara Roberts, she describes many forms of abuse, including:

- Spiritual abuse
- Physical abuse
- Emotional abuse
- Psychological abuse
- Sexual abuse
- Social abuse
- Financial abuse

A perpetrator can engage in one or many of these at the same time. However, associated with these forms of abuse are a range of manipulative behaviors that go along with the primary form of abuse in order to keep the victim quiet, maintain control over the victim, or to coerce the victim into behavior against their will.

For instance, rarely will there be sexual abuse without some form of emotional or psychological abuse. An adult who sexually abuses a child will use a range of manipulative techniques to keep "our little secret." These techniques are used by perpetrators of abuse because they are so effective. The fact is they flat-out work. The manipulative behaviors are abusive in themselves, because they operate in the spirit of the love of Cain, seeing others as obstacles to overcome or objects to use for the benefit of the manipulative abuser. In this chapter I will not be looking at the forms of abuse as listed above, but rather briefly revealing the forms of covert aggressive manipulative behavior.

It is my conjecture that people who engage in these forms of covert aggressive manipulative behaviors as *primary or prominent* means of relating to others are well along the spectrum of a person with a Narcissistic Personality Disorder (NPD). Chuck Degroat writes "narcissism exists along a spectrum form healthy to toxic."[18] All of us are self-centered and narcissistic to a point. From time to time our selfishness can impact others negatively (i.e., the road rage example above). But some of us have a more entitled approach to life that is more and more along the lines of one with NPD. Further along the spectrum, these manipulative

---

18. DeGroat, *When Narcissism Comes to Church*, 36.

behaviors become the behavior of choice in their interpersonal relationships. It becomes their nature, their character, and is toxic. They seek to aggressively control in these covert ways. They demonstrate many of the behavioral characteristics of someone with this personality disorder without necessarily being a person with a diagnosable personality disorder. They would be "narcissists" in the popular and perhaps overused meaning of the word, even if a thorough analysis by a qualified professional would not diagnose them with the disorder. Their interactions with others would tick all the boxes of someone with this disorder, and therefore for all intents and purposes the average person would need to view and at least deal with them as if they had this personality disorder. We don't have to diagnose or accuse, but we do need to react to individuals like this. As is often declared, "If it walks like a duck and quacks like a duck, it's probably a duck."

So, let's briefly look at the most popular forms of covert aggressive manipulation which you are likely to encounter from an abusive individual.[19]

False guilt

One of the great tactics used by abusive individuals is the tactic of false guilt.

Guilt is a state of being as a result of actions undertaken that violate an *objective* law. If I do 50 mph in a 35-mph zone, I am guilty of violating the road rules. This law is objective. It exists outside of me and is universally understood and enforceable. To violate that law is true guilt.

One definition of *false guilt* is a *perceived* state of being, as a result of actions undertaken that violate a *subjective* law. Notice I say *perceived*. You might *feel* guilty, but you are not. Imagine a church scenario. Most people who attend church regularly sit in the same spot. We are kind of creatures of habit like this. One day you sit in the seat that Mary always sits in. When she arrives, she puts enormous pressure on you about how you have no right to sit there and it is her seat. Now think about this for a minute. It isn't actually her seat, and there are no rules requiring you to sit in one place or another. These are her subjective rules and she is laying down the law to control you, in an aggressive way to ensure that you don't sit in the chair again. Jesus calls us to a law of love, a devotion of grace and

---

19. See Birch, *30 Covert Emotional Manipulation Tactics*. For a comprehensive understanding of these and many more behaviors.

kindness that gives preference to her, but this is another thing altogether (Rom 12:10). Mary is not calling you to the law of love, but to her subjective rule. This is my chair—stay away. Now, unbeknownst to you, Mary sits there because her hearing isn't what it was and she can hear best in this location rather than in others. But Mary has never learned to ask for what she needs in a healthy way, so she uses the manipulative tactic of false guilt and an aggressive manner to get her way.

Now imagine you come back the next week and the only seat available is Mary's. Several people are standing at the back because they have also faced Mary's wrath. There is an anxiety in them as to what she would do if they sat there. But you are stronger than this you think, and sit there. But then for the rest of the service you are filled with anxiety and fear because you are sitting in "her" chair. The whole worship time is tainted by this rumbling in the pit of your stomach. "Phew" you think to yourself at the end of the service when you realize, she wasn't there that week. Even though she wasn't even in the building, Mary was controlling you and others.

One of the ways you can tell you are being manipulated by false guilt is the anxiety you will feel after confrontations with someone using this tactic. You'll be anxious but not know why. So, ask yourself, "Was I being judged and measured? What standard am I being measured against?" In false-guilt scenarios you are being measured and found wanting against someone else's standard. This is false guilt.

FALSE SHAME

False shame is a close relative to false guilt. However, in false-shame scenarios the abuser is seeking to control you by letting you know that you *as a person* fail to meet a standard, as opposed to your behaviors which is the characteristic of false guilt. *You* are at fault, not your behaviors. It would be a healthy shame to suddenly have a "wardrobe malfunction" in public. For the manipulative, they seek to expose you figuratively by determining that you as a person, your personality, intelligence, skill set, education, or some other such thing inherent to your personhood are simply not up to the standard required, and, as in the case of false guilt, the standard is *their subjective standard* of what is acceptable.

Using sarcasm, putdowns, and language to demean your character, those who false-shame are letting you know that *you* just haven't got what it takes. Done persistently this can make the victim question their worth and value. It is cruel and abusive.

Blaming the Victim

Blaming the victim is another classic tool of abusers and it is flat-out wicked. It is commonly seen in rape situations where the rapist will defend his actions by declaring "It's not my fault, did you see what she was wearing?," or with a knowing glance and a sneer, remark "Everyone knows what kind of girl she is." This is a specialized form of shifting the focus (another manipulative tactic). The abuser has committed a terrible crime, but, like a magician using sleight of hand, wants to divert your attention to somewhere else. This immediately puts the victim on the defensive, distracting from the real problem—the rape itself.

I had an experience where I and another elder were often told to leave the "difficult people" (those who were really engaging in covert aggressive abusive behaviors) to others who had the skills to deal with them, because we did not have the skill set to deal with such people. Here we have both false shame (you aren't up to it) and blaming the victim (if you had the skills, they wouldn't act this way). It is akin to being beaten with baseball bats and then being told the problem is you for not wearing a helmet. You end up so busy trying to defend yourself from those who are blaming you for the way you are being treated that the real abusive behavior itself is ignored.

Playing the Victim

Once again this is a shifting-the-focus tactic. This manipulative technique is intended to work on the conscientious nature of people who by nature are nice and want to be kind to others. This describes church people exactly. This tactic is used when the perpetrator has been caught out in some unethical or abusive behavior and can't avoid the fact that they did it. But it isn't really *their* fault. They are the victim of circumstances beyond their control. "I am poor," "My wife just left me," "My child was sick" or whatever. The idea is to get you to think, "Yeah if I were in their shoes, I would act like that too."

A classic form of it is when a church seeks to discipline a member for their abusive behavior and they declare they are under attack from cruel, unloving, and graceless Christians who don't know how to forgive. This is a very powerful tool to get "persecutors" to back off. Jennifer Freyd, a psychology researcher, author, and educator at the at the University of Oregon first introduced the acronym DARVO[20], standing for Deny, Attack and Reverse Victim and Offender. She demonstrates that abusers play the victim by denying the behavior, attacking the character, mental health or credibility of the accuser, and then declaring themselves to be the innocent victims of their accuser and their baseless claims. When done well it will both discourage others from coming forth and isolate the real victim.

Lying

Not much needs to be said about this tactic as truth be told (pun intended) most of us do this from time to time. It is a means of attempting to put ourselves in the best possible light in order to avoid the shame of being found to be wanting in some way.

A more manipulative technique is lies by omission, where some of the truth or shades of the truth are told. This is more devious because the stories being told, or the excuses being made, have just enough of the hint of truth about them as to appear plausible. No one is likely to question the half-truth. For instance, an employee of a company may be suffering severe mental health issues as a result of relentless bullying and the management's failure to address it appropriately. The poor employee finally has enough and explodes, has a serious meltdown, and is admitted to a mental health facility. The management tells the other employees, "So-and-so has mental health issues" (true) but no mention is made of them actually being complicit in failing to provide a safe environment for her. By being open about the employee's issue, it looks like openness and forthright honesty, but the real issue (bullying and management failure) is never addressed. It is an image management technique, and it is manipulative.

Triangulation

Triangulation is a means of obfuscation by dragging a third party into a conflict and confusing the issues, to get someone else on your side and

---

20. Freyd, "Violations of Power"; Harsey et al., "Perpetrator Responses to Victim Confrontation."

to back your argument. Imagine a circumstance where your daughter has married a man with a narcissistic personality. They have a child together and after some years she finds the strength to leave him. He has lost his ability to directly affect, abuse, control, or manipulate his ex-wife. So, instead, he inserts his child into a triangle. "Tell Mommy I miss her," "Tell Mommy I'm sorry," "Tell Mommy I have a new girlfriend," "Tell Mommy she is mean for destroying our family."

Or you might be in conflict with an abusive individual whom you refuse to allow to run a ministry because you have serious doubts about their character and behavior. She will gladly inform you that you are the only person who has any problem with her, that everyone else thinks she's great. In this case the ubiquitous *everyone else* is triangulated. If this person has offended most in the church this is harder to do, so the triangulation then might become "Every other organization I work with, or volunteer with, etc., has no problem with me. It is only this church that has a problem." The point of the triangulation, like all manipulation, is to attempt to control your perceptions or your own behaviors in order to attain what is wanted. "Well, I guess we should let her do the ministry if nobody else has a problem with her. The problem must be me."

Minimization

This is exactly what it sounds like. One of the classic ways it shows up is in reporting of child sexual assault and rape cases. The press will report that a teacher had sex with their 13-year-old student. In reality, the teacher raped the 13-year-old student, by action as well as by definition of the law. To suggest the two had sex is to minimize the depth of the crime.

Or an abuser will be engaging in a pattern of psychological and emotionally manipulative behaviors of the sort I am outlining here, and if you were to complain to a church authority, they would say things like "It's just a difference of opinion, different temperaments, struggling to get along" or "You are just exaggerating and making much out of nothing," rather than naming it for what it really is.

In dysfunctional churches minimization comes in the form of euphemisms like "difficult people" which is a whole lot easier to swallow than "psychological abuser." When I left my church, I read a letter describing the fact I had been both the subject of and permitter of abuse in our church. The next speaker got up and said, "Every church has its ups and downs," or words to this effect, and went on to speak to the church about the next agenda topic. This is classic minimization; abuse is not ups and downs!

Churches will say things like "No church is perfect." True, but in what specific ways is it not perfect? A blanket statement like that is simply a nonstatement which effectively says, "We have no intention of actually checking to see what is going on, because it is probably no worse than anywhere else."

Gaslighting

A particular form of what experts call "crazy making," this is a process whereby the manipulator is seeking to convince you they never said or did the things they actually did, and that it is all in your mind. The term "gaslighting" comes from the 1944 film *Gaslight*, in which a husband slowly drives his wife crazy by adjusting the gaslights in the house and making her think she has done it. She becomes increasingly convinced that she's insane, questioning her own view of reality. Imagine that you and a leader at church decide that a wall in the church needs painting. The leader might tell you "Let's paint the wall green" and then you go and get green paint and start painting. Sometime later the leader walks in sees the green paint and harangues you for painting the wall green. They swear on a stack of Bibles the two of you had agreed on blue, and then, to compound the manipulation, declares that your decision to paint it green is a passive-aggressive attempt to undermine their authority. This leaves you questioning your sanity, hence "crazy making."

Gaslighting is designed to make you question your own perception of reality and you can see how, when done repeatedly, this is a really wicked manipulation tactic. And good manipulators can do this without blinking. I was once in a conversation with a manipulative person who said something, and when they were asked "Why do you always bring up that topic?" looked me straight in the eye and said, "I didn't bring it up, you did." For the next ten seconds or so I was flummoxed as I tried to rewind the conversation in my mind and figure out if that was true. "Did I really bring up the topic?" I was so worried about who said what I lost track of what we were actually saying. Perfect manipulation!

Spiritual Abuse, a Special Case

Although I have no intention of looking at the different forms of abuse in any detail, I do want to make special mention of spiritual abuse, because this is such a relevant topic within the context of a church. Sadly, so too is sexual abuse of course, but the difference is that sexual abuse is kind of obvious when it happens, even if dysfunctional organizations don't actually deal with it well. But spiritual abuse can occur in even the best of churches and it is not always obvious.

It is a special form of emotional and psychological abuse within a spiritual setting or context. In a good starter text on this subject David Johnson and Jeff Van Vonderen define spiritual abuse this way:

> Spiritual abuse can occur when a leader uses his or her spiritual position to control or dominate another person. It often involves overriding the feelings and opinions of another, without regard to what will result in the other person's state of living, emotions or spiritual well-being. In this application, power is used to bolster the position or needs of a leader, over and above one who comes to them in need.[21]

This definition describes elements which are common to all forms of abuse: the misuse of power to control, dominate, and coerce.

In another scholarly work, Lisa Oakley and Kathryn Kinmond expand on this definition:

> Spiritual abuse is a form of emotional and psychological abuse. It is characterized by a systematic pattern of coercion and controlling behavior in a religious context. Spiritual abuse can have a deeply damaging impact on those who experience it.[22]

Spiritual abuse occurs when the covert aggressive manipulation tactics I described above are used by someone in a position of spiritual authority, misusing their power in order for them to coerce or maintain control. The idea of having a God-given mandate to lead, coupled with coercive manipulation, is insidious and can cause great harm.

And this does not need to be an all-of-church thing. I had always thought of spiritual abuse as something that occurred in extreme cults and sects. I saw it as a whole-of-system problem: individuals being judged by their behavior, their dress, and their diet; being conrolled with regard to

---

21. Johnson and VanVonderen, *Subtle Power of Spiritual Abuse*, 20–21.
22. Oakley and Humphreys, *Escaping the Maze of Spiritual Abuse*, 31.

who they call friends; it being mandated that members must attend every service; and families being ripped apart by coercive control from the top down by the church, as they attempt to control everyone and everything. I thought spiritual abuse was an all-of-system, legalistic adherence to the rules, and a total attempt to control the thoughts, beliefs, feelings, and behaviors of those in the system across the board.

But it needn't be this way. It can be isolated to one person in one ministry in isolated circumstances. An elder in a church, for instance, because of his position, carries a certain authority. When this is used in conjunction with covert manipulation techniques in order to get his way, to coerce others to toe the line about an issue, or to keep people quiet about a sin that may have been exposed, all of these things then would fall under the guise of spiritual abuse.

Imagine for instance a pastor who decided that it is the call of God on the church to start a ministry of some sort. As the Senior or Lead Pastor, he declares himself to be in a position of God-placed authority and declares his views, therefore, by extension, are God's views. Knowing the leadership team will be reticent to follow his lead, he starts a campaign of making phone calls to the elders, suggesting they haven't got the mental fortitude to understand the value of his proposal (false shame). He suggests that they should be spending more time in prayer and Scripture reading so as to be better in tune with God's call on the church (false guilt). Some of the elders start to complain about these tactics and start calling him a bully. He then announces to the church that he is being obstructed by an ungodly eldership that is looking to run him out of the church because they are jealous of his gifting (playing the victim).

This is what spiritual abuse can look like in the church. Now the ones being abused in this scenario are primarily the elders, but if the pastor gets away with this the people learn by observation not to question the authority of the pastor. Spiritual abuse has set in. The elders' personhood and faith are questioned by one in authority, all for the benefit of the pastor. The elders were obstacles to overcome and having done so they and the church are now objects for use. Nobody is being controlled in terms of dress or food or the company they keep, so the abuse is far less overt and hence the subtlety of it can go unrecognized as spiritual abuse, but it is very much abusive. And people are being hurt. The church is not safe with this pastor.

SUMMARY

These manipulations I have outlined here (albeit in brief detail) are emotional and psychological forms of abuse that, in church scenarios, when used by authority, are spiritually abusive as well. These things can be done alone or in conjunction with other forms of abuse in a pattern of repeated coercive behaviors which are designed to control. I detail them here because unlike the physical and sexual forms of abuse which are most obvious, these are far more covert and subtler forms of abuse that can go unnoticed or be dismissed in dysfunctional churches.

Any church in which individuals are behaving like this as their *primary* means of maintaining authority or control, or seeking authority and control, or where people are enabled to behave like this, are unsafe environments. They are abusive and dysfunctional. People are being used, misused, abused, and hurt. And the scars can last a lifetime.

A healthy, functional church is a wholly safe environment in which the relationships that exist glorify God by being:

- *Spiritually safe*: Dysfunctional churches are spiritually unsafe, souls are in danger
- *Physically Safe*: Dysfunctional churches are physically unsafe, bodies are in danger
- *Emotionally safe*: Dysfunctional churches are emotionally unsafe, hearts are in danger
- *Intellectually safe*: Dysfunctional churches are intellectually unsafe, minds are in danger

In an unhealthy church where dysfunctions abound, abuse can occur, and by definition abusive organizations are unsafe organizations, even if the abuse is subtle, isolated, or low-level.

But where do these dysfunctional churches come from? How do they start, and how do they continue? What is the genesis of all this dysfunctional and abusive behavior?

These are the topics I will now explore.

2

The Soil
(In What Environment Does Abuse Grow?)

JESUS TOLD A VERY famous parable often called the parable of the sower (Luke 8). It tells of a farmer who plants seeds and gets varying qualities of crops as a result, depending on the type of soil in which they land, ranging from no crop to great crops. Given that the quality of the seed is not in question, it may be fair to better call this the parable of the soils, because the soil is really the only variable in the story.

The soil really does matter. Ask any gardener. I used to get terrible tomato crops every year. I had a great garden bed filled with compost and soil. I used to add organic material and manures and would dust for pests and fungi, and still the tomatoes were small or had a black spot on them that made them rotten. I had given up until I read one day that the problem was a lack of calcium in the soil. The soils around here are poor in that they are missing this vital element. So, I bought the right fertilizer and added trace elements to the soil, and before you knew it, I was growing tomatoes like I knew what I was doing. The soil matters.

Up to this point I have spoken about dysfunctional churches. I have not looked at any specific dysfunction, per se, but just the generalized idea that dysfunctional churches are failing to thrive. I have explored how dysfunctional churches can harbor abuse and abusers, and the generalized form this can take. Now I want to stop and look at how this is sustained. In the next several chapters I will look at the seeds of this bitter fruit, but before I do that, I want to explore the environment in which this seed grows. For dysfunction and abuse to reside in a local church the soil must be prepared for it. So, what does this soil look like?

2.1

Anxiety

ANXIETY CAN BE DEFINED as the response of an organism to a threat, whether real or imagined. It is a process that, in some form, is present in all living things.[1]

> Do not be anxious about anything, but in everything by prayer and supplication with thanksgiving let your requests be made known to God. And the peace of God, which surpasses all understanding, will guard your hearts and your minds in Christ Jesus. (Phil 4:6–7)

I don't know if you have ever suffered from a real diagnosable anxiety disorder. I have been diagnosed with dysthymia (persistent depressive disorder), which can include bouts of anxiety. When anxiety and panic strike, it is absolutely awful. The first time I can readily remember having an anxiety attack was soon after I arrived in Australia in 1984. I can't be certain what triggered the attack, but I do know I was deeply unsettled by the reports and ongoing aftermath of a mass shooting that occurred approximately one month previously, infamously named the San Ysidro McDonald's massacre. I couldn't sleep and couldn't eat. I had this deep sense of dread that my life was going to end at any moment. I have had this kind of thing happen from time to time since, and the best image I can give is that in these episodes, I feel like I am clinging to the end of a rope, dangling over a bottomless pit, with no way up and only one way down. It's just a matter of time, I can't hang on forever. And I can tell you, in those moments, quoting me a verse like Philippians above is useless.

---

1. Kerr and Bowen, *Family Evaluation*, 112.

The anxiety I feel is baseless, irrational, and not focused on anything specific. It isn't a result of doubt or a lack of faith. It is a brain chemical thing, a brain wiring thing, maybe genetics. And it is horrid. I wouldn't wish those episodes on my worst enemy. Those who have experienced similar or worse will know exactly what I mean.

There are also real diagnosable anxiety disorders. The DSM-5 lists 4 anxiety disorders.[2] These are considered disorders because the thoughts of worry and fear can become so intrusive as to affect a person's quality of life. They avoid social situations or are unable to function at work or school. These are real and serious mental health issues, however they are not the forms of anxiety that are the focus of this chapter.

Then there is the idea of anxiety as fret and worry, which is really what the verses in Phil 4 are talking about. Paul isn't saying "Don't have a mental health disorder," but rather "Don't let your life be consumed by worry," or "Don't constantly be concerning yourself and fretting over things over which you have little to no control." In a similar way, Jesus, in Matt 6:25, said:

> For this reason I say to you, do not be worried about your life, *as to* what you will eat or what you will drink; nor for your body, *as to* what you will put on. Is life not more than food, and the body more than clothing?

This is more or less a conscious thing, at the forefront of our thinking; an underlying awareness of the fragility of life and how easy it would be for what we rely on to suddenly disappear, or even more so, to fret about what we need and how it might never be available. We might worry that we will lose our job or if we lost it, we won't be able to pay the bills. We worry about our health and our kids. This is the kind of anxiety Jesus is speaking about here. And these really are legitimate concerns. It can be easy to become overwhelmed and immobilized by this kind of anxiety. The cure for this is to constantly turn our eyes to the sovereign God who calls us his children (1 John 3:1). A really useful CBT (Cognitive Behavior Therapy) type of thing is to do what Paul writes immediately after those well-known verses in Phil 4:6–7, and which is in fact Paul's cure for this kind of anxiety:

---

2. Diagnostic and Statistical Manual of Mental Disorders [DSM-5]. The previous version [DSM-4] also included OCD as an anxiety disorder, but this has now been shifted to its own entry in the latest version (5) of this manual.

> Finally, brothers *and sisters*, whatever is true, whatever is honorable, whatever is right, whatever is pure, whatever is lovely, whatever is commendable, if there is any excellence and if anything worthy of praise, think about these things. As for the things you have learned and received and heard and seen in me, practice these things, and the God of peace will be with you.

This is one important way that Christians through the ages have dealt with the real frets and worries that are part of living in a fallen world—focus on, mediate on, remind yourself of, and trust in the promises of God.

Anxiety has its value, and although unpleasant it is not always a bad thing. It can be a pointer to a genuinely unsettling series of events that need our attention; a life-threatening diagnosis, for instance, or concern for the airworthiness of some airlines after a repeated recent history of disasters. Many researchers of anxiety would call this normal and acute, with no real consensus as to whether acute anxiety should be called fear or not. Regardless, anxiety is part of the warning system inbuilt in the human brain that alerts us to circumstances of which we should be wary.

However, in this chapter I am writing about an anxiety that, when unrecognized, is the fertile soil in which dysfunction can grow and thrive. The etymology of words can be helpful and in this case we can get a sense of where the word "anxious" comes from. It has its root in the Latin word from which we also get "anger" and "angst." The root had the idea of choking or suffocating or throttling.

> Anxiety is emotional pain. It constricts and limits life. At the center of its painfulness is uncertainty. We can neither put our finger on what is disturbing us nor pick out a clear-cut villain who is threatening us. Nothing in specific stimulates it and nothing in particular is its object.[3]

This is the kind of anxiety that I want to suggest is the soil in which dysfunctional churches grow and thrive and in which abuse can occur. Anxious churches are operating with an underlying distress that is often unseen, unknown, and unnamed. In fact, if you were to ask members of churches if their church was anxious, they would almost emphatically say no unless you ask in private, or if you promised not to tell or use their name or record it, or . . . hmm, maybe they are anxious after all.

---

3. Steinke, *How Your Church Family Works*, 16.

They don't know what they are anxious about, and it is not the kind of thing that is preventing the church from going about its business. The church is not paralyzed into inaction, but it is paralyzed into nonaction regarding its dysfunction and possible abuses, because it is blind to the abuses or blind to its anxiety, or both.

Now of course a church is not an entity that has anxiety in some kind of a disembodied way. To say a church is anxious is to say the people within it are anxious, the individuals themselves. So, what are we anxious about? Let's explore some of these topics.

ANXIETY ABOUT THEM

I'm a dinosaur. I came to Christ in the early 1980s. Ronald Reagan was president. *Dallas* and *M*A*S*H* were huge hits, rather than late-night reruns. You could get on board a plane without all this crazy security that makes flying such a nightmare now. There were no personal computers, no email, no portable phones. I wrote to my now-wife in those years by handwritten letter, actual snail mail. It took weeks for us to communicate.

When I first came to faith, I needed a Bible. I went to a book store, just your everyday garden variety book store, to get my first Bible. (Now I'm really showing my age, you have to look hard to even find a book store!) The religious section only had Bibles and Christianity stuff, no Qu'ran, no Bhagavad Gita, just good old-fashioned, American-as-apple-pie Christian stuff[4] . . . but no longer. Go into any book store now and the religious section (if they even have one) is full of every flavor of every belief system you can think of. The religious landscape has changed vastly in the last thirty-five years or so. I don't think the church is at peace with it. Recognize it? Yes. Try to understand it? Yes. They try to cater to it often (seeker-friendly churches, for instance), but are never really at peace with it. Anxious, if you will.

The church these days sits isolated like a missionary outpost of the kingdom in the first world. There is this beautiful monastery in France called Mont Saint-Michel. It sits very close to the coast on a bit of an island that you can walk to when the tide is out, but when the tide is in you can't get to it without a boat. This is kind of like the church. The church was connected to the culture and drove the culture and was the

---

4. Tongue firmly planted in cheek!

culture, but now the rising tide of secularism has cut her off, leaving her disconnected from the shore of which she was once a part.

The church finds herself in uncharted waters. That is, a post-Christian society. Never before in the history of the world has there been such a thing. Unlike earlier missionary endeavors that arrived on foreign shores to proclaim Christ to those who have never heard, today's first-world churches are surrounded by hostile tribes who have the collective memory of the church and its practices and have decided they have been found wanting. In their view, the church is a failed enterprise that needs no longer be seen or heard. Instead, board up the buildings, tear them down, or remagine them as restaurants and wedding venues. The church is tolerated at best, and aggressively dismissed as a danger to our advancement at worst (a la Richard Dawkins and the new atheists), as something that needs to be eradicated.[5]

"Secular" used to mean "of this world," as opposed to the things of the other world, the transcendent world, the heavens, the sacred. The created order was placed nicely into these dual categories and secular was not a thing to be feared, but simply understood as part of God's good creation. But this idea has slowly changed over the centuries. Secularization has come to refer to "the process by which sectors of society and culture are removed from the domination of religious institutions and symbols"[6]

This has been popularized by the concept of separation of church and state, which tends to mean the church and religion are one sphere and the things of the state another. The one should not influence the other. But the idea has grown so that it now affects the totality of all aspects of our life—its culture, arts, movies, television, music, and literature. Secularization is the triumph of science "as an autonomous, thoroughly secular perspective on the world."[7]

And science and empirical testing is the measure of all truth claims. We have come to believe that if a truth claim cannot be scientifically and empirically tested then the claim is invalid.[8]

As the secular West continues to push back on public religion, the church is starting to feel an increasing level of anxiety of what this will

---

5. Not just Christianity, the new atheists are allied against all forms of religion and supernatural thinking of any kind.

6. Berger, *Sacred Canopy*, 107.

7. Berger, *Sacred Canopy*, 107.

8. This in itself is a truth claim that cannot be tested by the scientific method, so it is in fact a logically invalid statement, but that is a topic for another book.

mean for our Christian schools and hospitals and the like. Christian social justice missions of all flavors have always relied upon the willing acceptance and cooperation of the governments for support and protection. Secular governments valued the critical part these institutions played in providing for a stable society. Governments were pragmatic, even if they didn't like the ethos of these places. If Catholic orphanages or Christian private schools did not exist, who would pick up the bill?

But with a more aggressive secularization it becomes increasingly hard for faith-based organizations to run according to their stated faiths and beliefs. Adherence to a traditionally Christian sexual ethic, for instance, is now problematic at best in the hiring practices of these faith-based social justice organizations. What happens when a traditional evangelical church refuses to hire a homosexual pastor? Or refuses to rent their church building for a gay wedding? How long before the secular world prosecutes the church for these crimes against the secular?

In the introduction to her book, *It is Dangerous to Believe*, Mary Eberstadt describes a litany of alarming (for American Christians at least) court decisions and legal precedents that are having a serious impact on the way Christians live their lives. But not just the US:

> These disparate stories taken from recent headlines are examples of a toxic new force now hurtling across the United States and other advanced societies. They are part of the mounting toll of a widespread and growing effort to shame, punish, and ostracize people because of what they believe. This is moral and social change for the worse—and not only in the United States, but across the boundaries of what can still be called Western civilization.[9]

This is an aggressive secularism indeed. Even democracy itself is threatened.

> Secularism acts politically against its competitors and defines them as what it is not. It claims to be the exemplar of justice, neutrality, democracy, common sense, rational argument, tolerance and the public interest. That claim would indicate that the religious is not those things. Though those moves can be fair if appropriate concessions are made to context, "they are not the only moves possible." This is where the problem comes in because most secularists do not concede that nonsecular democratic alternatives can be legitimate versus secularism.[10]

9. Eberstadt, *It's Dangerous to Believe*, loc. 128 of 2879.
10. Baker, *End of Secularism*, 107.

Anxiety

Secularism has become the de facto standard against which all other belief systems are measured. And the church in the first-world West sees this and hears this. Our faith is under threat; our democratic right to speak is under threat and it produces an underlying anxiety in our church communities. I hear it almost every week at church when they open the service for prayer. "Thank you, that we can meet peacefully and openly." We get it. They are coming for us; it's only a matter of time.

Although Christianity today bears the brunt of this push against religion, it isn't the only victim:

> Persecution on grounds of religious faith is a global phenomenon that is growing in scale and intensity. Reports including that of the United Nations (UN) Special Rapporteur on 'Freedom of Religion and Belief' (FoRB) suggest that religious persecution is on the rise, and it is an "ever-growing threat" to societies around the world. Though it is impossible to know the exact numbers of people persecuted for their faith, based on reports from different NGOs, it is estimated that one third of the world's population suffers from religious persecution in some form, with Christians being the most persecuted group.[11]

Christians have all but been wiped out of Iraq and Syria, the cradle of ancient Christianity, and the bad news rolls on. Surrounded on all sides by secularists and anti-theists, and aggressive and even violent oppression from other religions, the church is on the run like at almost no other time in her history.

We try to calm ourselves by reminding ourselves that the gates of hell will not prevail against the church (Matt 16:17–19) but secretly I think we have our doubts.[12]

This rapidly rising tide of secularism and anti-Christian violence has surged in my lifetime. Unlike the proverbial frog in the pot that has no anxiety about the increasing temperature of the water, this rising tide has come in like a tsunami—we can see it and our reaction can be anxious.

---

11. Mounstephen, *Bishop of Truro's Independent Review*, 15.

12. I do know that this verse is saying the gates of hell cannot withstand the assault of the church, that is to say hell's defenses are weak, and not the other way around, but historically the church has misunderstood this. I am using this verse in its commonly misunderstood way. One way to ease the anxiety of the church is to teach this verse properly. "Onward Christian Soldiers," as it were.

ANXIETY ABOUT US

With the barbarian hordes at the door, there is an unconscious anxious reaction to want to pull up the drawbridge, put sharks in the moat, archers on the parapets, and defend. Within the cloistered walls of our faith community, we can find safety with each other. We are motivated and compelled to get in the fight together. In the words of one set of researchers, "External threat seems to increase the tendency to form strong bonds."[13]

We can provide ourselves comfort in times of trial. Community, (our specific brand of church community especially) will keep us safe, we tell ourselves, as long as we can answer well the following three anxiety-inducing questions:

- Do we believe right? Are we believing the right things?
- Do we behave right? Are we doing the right things?
- And perhaps the most anxiety-inducing question of all, do I belong?

I think there is an underlying sense that if we behave and believe in an orthodox way then God will be pleased with us. Let the barbarians tear down those others; we will be safe because we are right. But a little voice inside us keeps asking, "What if we aren't right?"

What if We Don't Believe Right?

What if our theology isn't right? What if we are Armenian and really we should be Calvinist? I mean they have the doctrines of grace, so then what do we have? Or what if we are Calvinist and really should be Armenian? Has God really destroyed our free will? Did we ever really have it?

Okay, most people sitting in our churches aren't asking that kind of question, they are just busy trying to feed the kids and pay the bills. But they are asking about Genesis and six-day creation because their friends are asking (or ridiculing). What if our adherence to six-day creation proves to be logically and cognitively unsustainable? Some people think this is the case already.

This is where the anxiety comes, when we, like an inverted pyramid, rest all of our view of Christianity on a small, parochially specific theology or set of theologies. For example, if you have based your whole church and belief system, your faith as it were, on six-day creation and

---

13. Baumeister and Leary, "Need to Belong," 502.

it could be proven unquestionably to be false, then what do you have? I have heard it said repeatedly that if you don't take a literal approach to these six days, then you basically are saying you don't believe the Bible in its entirety. There's an anxiety-inducing statement right there! So, if there were to be an absolutely unquestionable certainty that six-day creation cannot be the right interpretation (and I am not saying that here) then the entire pyramid collapses under the weight of a belief that could not bear it. Your entire faith system falls to pieces, or at least big parts of it do. This is too much to bear; anxiety-inducing, maybe? If my entire faith system depends on believing the right thing, then I am going to be pretty anxious about any attack on this belief system and pretty wary of anyone who suggests something else. Too much is at stake.

Or take the weight of the pressure of the world to ensure that women are given equal opportunity. What if you have a theology that sees only male elders and pastors? Are you right? Is that position sustainable? Will you have to change? What will it mean if we do?

I think our anxiety to believe the right things, I'd even go so far as to say that a system that *requires us* to believe the right things, drives us to be overly certain about things that we can never be, nor should we be, overly certain about. We have left no room for doubt. And so, if we doubt, it produces anxiety in you and others. Anxiety is uncomfortable and we don't want it, so we seek to eliminate it. In this kind of environment doubters can be viewed with suspicion, especially if you question things which are believed to be the nonnegotiables of the faith and church.

Now of course there are some things that should be nonnegotiables, the things that the church has declared to be the teachings of the orthodox church. Simple things like Paul's teaching in Acts 20:21:

> I have declared to both Jews and Greeks that they must turn to
> God in repentance and have faith in our Lord Jesus.

We need to teach the Apostles' Creed or Nicene Creed, which laid out the teachings of the church for centuries. You might include the sufficiency of the work of Christ and perhaps the five *Solas* of the reformation. I don't want to give the impression that it is a theology free-for-all, far from it. But there are many other things that really are issues of conscience: the role of men and women in the church, for example, or gifts of the Spirit, church governance, dress, the use of alcohol, and the like. We need much grace in these things or we can produce anxiety in our communities.

And coupled with the anxiety to believe the right things is the anxiety of "Am I believing it enough? Maybe my child is sick because I didn't believe in healings enough. Maybe I lost my job because I didn't believe that God is provider enough. Maybe I am being punished for my lack of faith, or inadequate faith, or lack of certainty." We can confuse faith with certainty. We can fall into the trap of thinking that not only do I feel I have to believe what is right, I have to believe it with certainty. Gregory A. Boyd calls this the Idol of Certainty:

> To put it bluntly, I find it hard to avoid the conclusion that, for all its sincerity, the certainty-seeking, doubt-shunning understanding of faith reflects the same religious idolatry that entrapped the religious leaders of Jesus' day. The things that make certainty-seeking Christians feel loved, worthwhile, and secure before God—that is the thing that assures them that they are "saved"—is that they feel confident *they believe the right things with a sufficient level of certainty.* Doesn't this mean that it is their certainty in what they believe about God, rather than *God himself* that is their source of *life?*[14]

If we believe that a lack of certainty in our belief is going to cause us to fall away, or cause God to be angry with us, this can create a great deal of anxiety in us. However, the Bible indicates:

- Faith is a gift (Eph 2:8–9)
- Some have greater measures of faith than others (Rom 12:3–8)
- Having faith and unbelief is biblical (Mark 9:23–25)

As Boyd goes on to say:

> If I am confident that God unconditionally loves me because of what he did for me at Calvary, then wouldn't I be confident that his love for me does not increase or decrease based on how accurate my other beliefs are?[15]

We have more freedom than we realize—freedom to think and freedom to doubt—but if we think there is a specific set of things we have to believe, and of which there can be no doubt about, then there will always be an underlying anxiety. "If only someone will tell me what to *believe* so God will be pleased with me" we bemoan. This is just the kind of thing

---

14. Boyd, *Benefit of the Doubt*, 68–69 (emphasis original).
15. Boyd, *Benefit of the Doubt*, 69.

a toxic leader needs to hear. There are no shortages of unhealthy people who will tell you what you should think. Yes, anxiety is indeed a fertile soil for abuse.

What if We Aren't Behaving Right?

I was reading recently about Multi-Level Marketing schemes (MLMs) which really are thinly veiled pyramid selling schemes. The article was talking about how they get you in by "love bombing" you at the outset. They overwhelm you with telling you how great you would be, and how you are a great fit for the product and the company. They dazzle you with all the wealth that can be yours in just a few short years. They parade a highly successful leader of the company to show you it can be done. And then once you're in, you are their slave.

It's all a bit manipulative and dishonest, as this article indicated 73 percent to 99 percent of all participants in these schemes earn nothing and in fact lose significant thousands of dollars.[16] But people keep at it. And their anxiety levels increase as pressure is put on them to perform. They place pressure on close friends and relatives to buy until finally they quit, but not after a large investment of time and money and stress on their relationships. This article goes on to explain how one woman left, then returned to selling the same products after being convinced she was doing it wrong the first time and just needed to do it right, and this new mentor would help. So, with newfound enthusiasm back she went.

Churches can be like this; they love bomb people. People come to our churches and we are effusive, welcoming, and kind. But before long, either through direct admonition or through subtle unspoken rules, it becomes obvious to any newcomer what is acceptable and what is not. I had one such unsubtle experience at a church I visited in the United States. I arrived just off the ship, in jeans, bearded, and carrying my newly purchased NIV Bible. Looking for a church to attend, someone recommended this place to me, so I went. After the service a very friendly deacon of the church greeted me. He was pleased I was there and told me I was very welcome, but that I would need to shave, wear a suit, and only use a King James Bible if I wanted to continue to come. Like modern-day Pharisees, the rules of behavior were clear.

---

16. Bond, "How MLMs and Cults Use," para. 5.

In dysfunctional churches the right behavior can be very overtly expressed, as in my experience, or more subtly done by just observing what everyone is doing, what is said from the pulpit, or what is written in church bulletins or whatever. But however it is done, whether overtly or covertly, we soon learn the lesson of what is right behavior. This can lead to an anxiety if we do not believe we are behaving right. And as we will see in the next chapter, with the desire to belong being the driver that is, we will soon change our behavior to fit in or leave.

And then there is the "blueprint for my life" view of Christianity. Think about how often this has been said: "God loves you and has a wonderful plan for your life," with the following out-of-context verse used to support this perspective:

> For I know the plans that I have for you,' declares the Lord, 'plans for prosperity and not for disaster, to give you a future and a hope.' (Jer 29:11)

This verse, which is about corporate Israel in a specific time in her history and which has nothing to do with my individual relationship with God, can be used to teach that God has *one* plan for my life, *one* exact blueprint of exactly how it should be built, and it is my job to get on board with that.

Or maybe we see God's will for my life as a maze. One path will get you to the promised land at the end, the rest is just twists and turns that leads to dead ends. We get anxious about questions like, "Whom should I marry?," "Where should I live?," "What career should I take?," "Is this the right path, is this God's wonderful plan?" And if trouble comes, "Is it because I took the wrong path?" This kind of anxiety can lead to one willingly submitting themselves to another who will shepherd them and tell them what God is calling them to. The infamous Shepherding Movement, or Heavy Discipleship Movement, is an example of people willingly submitting themselves to abusive and manipulative leaders partially out of the anxiety of ensuring they were doing God's will for their life. These "shepherds" would tell you where to work and whom to marry, with supposed authority straight from God. "Don't trust yourself," these churches say, "you need an umbrella of protection. I am God's anointed to help you navigate the maze of life, which you can never figure out on your own."

I have always viewed God as being far more generous than this. Christian life is a highway (as the song goes), with the on-ramp, the narrow gate of repentance, and faith in the saving work of the Lord Jesus

Christ. In Christ the options are wide, with many lanes that all are leading in the right direction. I can choose any number of things, but the barrier rails and median strips are the moral boundaries which I should not cross. But within the moral guidelines of God, I can use wisdom to make any number of choices, and can expect God to bless it. Sometimes his will is unmistakably clear: "Take this lane."

We have more freedom than we think, but if we think there is but a narrow range of options for the Christian, one blueprint, one winding path, and if we are always trying to walk it and wondering if we have wandered too far, then there will always be an underlying anxiety. "If only someone will tell me how to *behave* so I don't mess up," we bemoan. This is just the kind of thing a toxic leader needs to hear. There is no shortage of unhealthy people who will tell you what to do and how to behave. Yes, anxiety is indeed a fertile soil for abuse.

SUMMARY

In this chapter I have looked at underlying anxieties that can run unseen, unnamed, and unknown amongst people in a local church community. Like good soil, these anxieties, if left unchecked, provide the fertile soil in which abuses can thrive. These are the anxieties of:

- Do we *believe* right? Are we believing the right things?
- Do we *behave* right? Are we doing the right things?

But there is a third, and, in my view, more important anxiety that drives what happens in the local church, and that is: *Do I belong?* A willingness and a need to belong, and the anxiety which can underlie our doubt that we do, can drive us to engage in beliefs and behaviors, or turn a blind eye to such behaviors, that would in other less anxious environments never be tolerated. This requires a chapter on its own. In the next chapter I will look at this question by delving a bit into the murky waters of social psychology.

2.2

Anxiety: Do I Belong?

As I wrote above, the most anxiety-inducing question of all, and perhaps the root of all of our other anxieties, may be, "Do I belong?"

Social psychology is a field of study which is concerned with the connections between people. Whereas standard psychology is about understanding the hows and whys of individual behavior, social psychology interests itself in how we act corporately and how we act and interact with others. One area of study in this field deals with the idea of "belongingness." Research has shown that a need to belong is a fundamental human motivation.

> We propose that a need to belong, that is, a need to form and maintain at least a minimum quantity of interpersonal relationships, is innately prepared (and hence nearly universal) among human beings.[1]

These researchers reviewed years of data in this field and have discovered what the church has been saying long before its inception; we were made for relationship. It's always nice when science finds empirical evidence to support these things. God, in his triune nature, is a fellowship of love, and as his image-bearers, people too are made for love and relationship.

The analysis of the existing research by Baumeister and Leary also indicates there are negative outcomes for people who have no sense of belonging. This *lack of belonging* would indeed be one good definition of loneliness. The impact of loneliness, or lack of belonging, can have

1. Baumeister and Leary, "Need to Belong," 499.

severe impacts on emotional, mental, and physical health. We need close interpersonal relationships of the sort you would find with a life partner or in a parent-child relationship, for example, but research has shown our need for corporate relationships as well.

A 1996 research paper by Marilynn B. Brewer and Wendi Gardner highlighted that each of us has three sources of identity, or how we define ourselves.[2]

> We may even base our self-concepts not only on our unique traits and characteristics (individual self), but also on the attachments we form with significant others (relational self), and the social groups we identify with (collective self), thus, continuously navigating our self-definitions between "I" and "we."[3]

What is being proposed by this research is that we come to define our identity based on three self-concepts:

- Personal traits: e.g., intelligence, hair color, height, etc.
- Roles we have in relationships: e.g., son, husband, etc.
- Prototype of the group: e.g., evangelical, Christian, ethnicity

Our need for belonging is met in the second and third roles above, in both our close interpersonal relationships and in being part of a larger collective, a global collective, if you like. But being part of a global collective (i.e., "I am an evangelical Christian") does not meet the full need of belonging, because we have no unique identity within that larger collective and there are no interpersonal relationships within that collective. I might be an evangelical Christian and identify this way, but I am faceless and have no connection, per se, with that group. It is a depersonalized connection although still important as part of the source of my identity. The research shows that we also have an innate need to be in relationship with a local collective of individuals:

> The need to belong is something other than a need for mere affiliation. Frequent contacts with nonsupportive, indifferent others can go only so far in promoting one's general well-being and would do little to satisfy the need to belong.[4]

---

2. Brewer and Gardner, "Who Is This 'We?'"
3. Brewer and Gardner, "Who Is This 'We?,'" 84.
4. Baumeister and Leary, "Need to Belong," 500.

To fully meet the need to belong we must be part of what I am calling a local collective, which in the church's case would be the local church community. And not just attending on a regular basis, but with healthy interpersonal relationships within it. This is vitally important for our sense of self and identify. In the global collective we might have a common identity but within the local collective a common bond.

> In other words, individuals seek to define themselves in terms of their immersion in relationships with others and with larger collectives and derive much of their self-evaluation from such social identities.[5]

A second important part of Brewer's research is what she has described as optimal belonging. Brewer's optimal distinctiveness model was developed to describe a motivational theory of social identity and attachment to large social groups. In this model, we derive our social identity:

> from a fundamental tension between human needs for validation and similarity to others (on the one hand) and a countervailing need for uniqueness and individuation (on the other).[6]

We seek to define our social identities by trying to achieve a balance between the need to be included as part of a local group (inclusion motive) and yet maintain our own unique self (differentiation motive).

Each of these motives serves to keep the other in check. As we become more immersed in one social group, the need to be included in other social groups declines, but the motive to be a unique self increases. Conversely, if an individual starts to move away from a social group, the need for differentiation is met and decreases but a drive for more social inclusion increases.

APPLICATION TO CHURCH

Now this is where anxiety raises its ugly head. In a community where belonging becomes paramount it can become possible for people to become overbalanced, prepared to sacrifice their own identity for the sake of the group identity. I become the church and its people, and they become me.

Extreme cases of this are cults like Peoples Temple (founded by Jim Jones) or The Heaven's Gate millennial cult. So convinced were people in

---

5. Brewer and Gardner, "Who Is This 'We?,'" 83.
6. Brewer, "Social Self," 477.

those communities of the need to behave right and believe right, and so desperate were people to belong to those that did so, they were prepared to sacrifice everything, ultimately their lives. They lost themselves in the group identify to the detriment of their own individual selves.

As will be seen in the next chapter, being too closely connected to a community and being an undifferentiated unique self is an anxiety-inducing experience. The more we lose our sense of self in a community, the more anxious we become. In the same way, the less we are connected to a community that we see as vital to our well-being, the result is also anxiety. We must achieve an optimum balance. For some people in unhealthy, dysfunctional organizations this balance is tipped too far into immersion of self in the community.

Now what Brewer and Gardner also go on to describe is that if we, as a local collective, place our collective identify at the forefront of what identifies us as a people, then those who are in the "in-group" (us) and those who are in the "out-group" (them) becomes the determining and most important factor of how we evaluate others. If I am in the global collective of Catholicism, and being Catholic is elevated in my local community as being of great importance, then I am always evaluating others as non-Catholics. Now this in and of itself is not bad, but if we assign negative values to terms like "non-Catholic," then we can discriminate against, be derogatory towards, and actively get anxious about non-Catholic others. Denigrating others has the effect of lifting our social self-esteem.[7] When being part of the group is magnified as being most important, or nearly so, then those things that differentiate those who are not in the group—the others—are the means by which we evaluate them. The evaluation need not always be derogatory, but we will evaluate them based on what they are not or what they are as opposed to us. When this becomes malevolent is when to be the other becomes an effective pejorative.

Extreme cases of this kind of thing is xenophobic nationalism of the type found in Nazi Germany in the thirties and forties. My contention is that when churches actively and intentionally elevate their uniqueness about their brand and place this at the forefront of what it means to belong to that particular local church as opposed to the others, it automatically increases the anxiety level in a church. We don't even have to actively denigrate others; constant praise about how good we are can have the same effect. If we are this good, we infer that everyone else must be that bad.

---

7. Brewer and Gardner, "Who Is This 'We?,'" 91.

In my church experience we frequently told ourselves we were doing church better than the other churches nearby. I actively stated this and agreed with this sentiment when it was expressed by others, and by doing so I unknowingly, automatically, and *necessarily* increased the underlying anxiety amongst us. Doing this can cause many people to have an uneasiness of what would happen if they didn't belong. Now I say *necessary* because if the need to belong is such a strong motivator, and we place our uniqueness at the vanguard of our identity, then needing to belong to *our* brand necessarily will be a source of anxiety. In the same way that drinking or eating are strong motivators and failure to be sure where these might come from can cause us to be anxious, so too a failure to be sure we can belong or do belong will be source of worry and anxiety.

You might be familiar with the acronym FOMO (Fear of Missing Out). It is a social media thing, where a person can become anxious if they feel that some socially important event is occurring somewhere else and they are not part of it. So too we can have this FOMO about our church. People will fear missing out on the blessing God has for them or their family if they are not part of *that* church doing *that* thing in *that* way. We chase the latest trends, do the popular things, copy the successful churches, all so we don't lose people. Or we go to the opposite extreme and denigrate the latest trends as not biblical (thus inferring that we are).

When a church amplifies its uniqueness, its superiority in some way, its adherence to biblical doctrine and teaching and ministry, when a church decides it is doing things better than others, and openly discusses this, it is easy to passively devalue the *others*. When a person is caught up in such a church the innate social pressure and motivation to be part of the *we* as opposed to the *them* is strong. A general anxiety exists just under the surface.

Couple this with the potential rewards that can be given to the inner circle of the we, things like ministry positions, power, authority, money, and influence. There is great pressure to blur the lines between self and the collective. Too easily, "I" can become "us."

I am aware of this in my own experience. Over time I became more and more immersed in my church community, ultimately ending up in a full-time position as a preaching and teaching elder. My job, friends, social network, and worshipping community all depended on this place. My identity was the church and the church was me. I lost sight of myself, or maybe more correctly, not having a real understanding of who I was in the first place, this church gave me identity. This is unhealthy, and not necessarily the fault of the church. This is my stuff.

There can be a very strong push within anxious churches for individuals to be enveloped in the entire ecosystem of the local church and its ministries. Any person in such an organization who has other church affiliations is considered suspect.[8] For instance, most churches have their own cross-cultural overseas mission programs. These are good programs supporting missionaries all over the globe. If, however you refused to support the missionary your church was helping, in preference to a missionary another church was supporting, this might be viewed as not really being committed to the church. This failure to fully buy into everything the church is doing can then be greeted with the suspicion that you are not really one of *us*. This suspicion would be further amplified if the missionary you supported was not part of the global collective. A Protestant evangelical supporting a Catholic missionary would be considered very questionable. Why support "them" and not "us?"

In this kind of environment, when the social and even financial rewards can be very high for belonging, a great deal of anxiety can exist just under the surface. "Will I be accepted?," "Will I get a position?," "Will I belong?" When believing right and behaving right become the entry cards to belonging, the human motivation to belong can even cause us to sacrifice our individuation for group belonging.

This increases the anxiety in the individual who has chosen to violate her own sense of self for what she told is the common good, which is fine until the organization engages in behaviors that violate her own personal ethic. Then a real cognitive dissonance sets in. *Me* or *them? I* or *we?* People in these churches can see what happens to those who choose to believe differently or behave differently. When they are onboard, they are showered with love and affirmation, but question the leaders and immediately their loyalty becomes suspect.

People are taken aside and counseled for their lack of loyalty. Using the whole range of manipulations described previously, the anxious member is soon brought into line. "If we are that unique, and I am now at risk of not belonging," (so the internal dialogue goes), "then I better keep

---

8. This however does not always include para-church organizations, as long as they are part of the global collective to which the church identifies; if they are Catholic enough or evangelical enough, then volunteering in those kinds of organizations is applauded.

my mouth shut." These loving/condemning tactics are powerful reinforcers to keep the flock in line.

Being heavily motivated by an innate sense of a need for relationship can, in dysfunctional churches (churches that exploit this need), make us susceptible to abuse:

> The unwillingness to leave an abusive intimate partner is another manifestation of the strength of the need to belong and of the resulting reluctance to break social bonds. The fact that people resist breaking off an attachment that causes pain attests to how deeply rooted and powerful the need to belong is.[9]

Given the high levels of "need to belong" anxiety that can exist in dysfunctional churches it comes as no surprise that when abuse or dysfunction is highlighted, those within the community will tolerate, minimize, excuse, or ignore it. To call it out might mean losing the right to belong.

There is another closely aligned reason why it can be hard for people to recognize or call out dysfunction and abuse in their community. Churches can often uncritically conflate themselves with a good God of justice, mercy, and love. Pattison highlights how this conflation, or what he calls "idealization" of the church, can make it very difficult to accept the shaming behaviors of dysfunction and abuse.[10] A cognitive dissonance can be created in the community that places a high value on not only belonging, but belonging to something that they have determined is clearly God-ordained. When abuse is highlighted, this can be too painful to comprehend:

> It is difficult for an idealizing community to recognize that it has a part in creating and maintaining shame. If the church sees itself mainly as an instrument of a reconciling gospel and divine salvation, the fact that it may help to nurture and maintain alienation will be a very hard truth to accept. The temptation may be to reject or ignore this threatening and potentially damaging insight.[11]

Churches metaphorically can fuse themselves to this good God, and for someone to have the chance to belong to this community is enticing. Language like "We are doing what is best for the church" can be the unwitting code for "We are doing what is best for God" in such idealizing

9. Baumeister and Leary, "Need to Belong," 503.
10. Pattison, *Shame*, 282–85.
11. Pattison, *Shame*, 285.

communities. Belonging to such God-ordained communities, serving God, and doing God's work are concepts that can be intoxicating, which can then make confronting abuse and other shaming behaviors all the more difficult.

Here are a few ways to recognize the heretofore unrecognizable anxiety in your community.

High levels of control by the leadership team are evident

For instance, if the leadership team absolutely cannot be questioned or there is limited or no transparency in the major decision-making in the church, this is a sign of an anxious leadership team. If you find yourself saying "I don't really know what is going on," this may point to an anxiety-riddled church and leadership (Behaving right).

Another example is if the leadership group is refusing to allow different beliefs about things that it declares to be core beliefs, but which historically have always been viewed as peripheral (i.e., if there is no place for any differing view on the gifts of the Spirit, or you have to believe in six-day creation or male-only elders, and dissention from any of these views is frowned upon openly, through public rebuke or continual admonishment from the pulpit—Believing right).

If the case for theological views is couched in terms of shaming you for not believing the right things or for not believing them enough, this is a sign of an anxious community. For instance, as a woman you are publicly shamed as having a "Jezebel Spirit" because you hold to the view that gender should not preclude a person from eldership or pastoring a church (Believing right, Do I Belong?).

If there is an underlying sense that God needs us, that we are indispensable to his salvation kingdom plan because of our great ministries, not only is this breathtakingly proud, but a pointer to several anxieties at work. Stop and ask yourself, "What if we changed course, either in theology or ministry? What if we stopped a particular ministry today?" How would you feel about it? Anxious? (Believing right, Behaving right).

If the leadership team will not allow open conversations about major conflict in the church; must maintain control of conversations; engage in and demand secret confidential meetings with only one or two people (a form of divide and conquer in the cases of conflict "resolution"); then this would be a sign of an underlying anxiety in the leadership group (Behaving right).

Unwillingness or inability of the community to question the leadership

Related to the above is a community of believers who have learned by example that there are some questions which should never be asked, some people who should never be questioned, and some things which should never be talked about. Or, at best, questions can be asked, but there is no tolerance for questioning the answer. People see problems, but they are told to trust the leadership. So, instead, grumbling occurs behind closed doors:

> Since it is not all right to notice or talk about problems, people form conspiracies behind closed doors and over the telephone as they try to solve things informally. But since they have no authority, they solve, and solve, and solve—but nothing really gets solved. And all the while, building God's true kingdom is put on hold.[12]

If you find yourself in a church where there are secret car-park meetings among a small group of you following every church meeting this is a pointer to an underlying anxiety (Behaving right).

Keeping secrets from each other

A leadership group that is factionalized is a clear indication of an underlying anxiety. This was true in my ex-church. As a leadership group some of us knew some things about really major issues that other leaders had no idea about. We had, for instance, a convicted pedophile in our church. I was aware and so was another elder, but we kept it from the rest of the leadership team. Why? It was told to us by this individual in confidence and we didn't want to break the confidence. I never questioned the foolishness of this (Behaving right).

Or you may have some elders dealing with a pastoral issue with someone in the community, but they are keeping it from the others for the same reason(s): confidentiality, privacy, not wanting to gossip, etc. It all has the veneer of compassion and pastoral care, but really at its heart

---

12. Johnson and VanVonderen, *Subtle Power of Spiritual Abuse*, 78.

is anxiety; anxiety stemming from the fear of losing control, because information is power. Control the flow of information and you maintain control (Behaving right).

Now yes, there are some things that should be confidential, but might I suggest that if you have elders in your church with which you cannot trust confidential information, then they should not be elders in the first place? I don't care what the sensitive nature of the information might be, open honest transparency in all forms of pastoral information amongst the elders is a good means of preventing abuse, and allowing secrets amongst the leadership group is a sign of an anxious and dysfunctional leadership group.

Similarly, some members of the church may be let into certain secrets by the pastor or leadership group and told to keep them from others. This is a manipulative tactic designed to control the other by making them feel special and included, part of the in crowd (Do I belong?). Now that you know this secret you can be controlled by being threatened with exclusion from the in-group if you spill the beans.

But ultimately all the secret-keeping in churches comes from those in control and the anxiety they have about losing that control. If I have secrets, but I control the flow of information, I can be in control. People will have to come to me and I get to decide who is in and who is out. It is intoxicating to be the one in control, and those of us out of the loop crave to be in the know (Do I belong?).

What will happen if I leave, or can I leave?

Really good diagnostic questions to ask yourself about the level of anxiety in you and your church are the following: "What will happen to me if I leave?," "Am I allowed to leave?," or "Where will I go if I leave?" Ask yourself those questions. This is not the same as asking, "Do I want to leave?" Let's assume for this exercise that your church is healthy and you love it there. But stop and ask yourself, "What would happen if I left? How would I feel?" Sad is good, loss is understandable, but if the answer is you feel afraid or worried or anxious, something isn't right. No church should ever have that kind of hold on you. In my ex-church I had no shortage of people tell me they wanted to leave. They knew something wasn't right. They could feel the anxiety, but they asked, "Where would we go?" The answer is easy—anywhere else.

If you feel you can't leave (which is different than not wanting to leave), if you feel you are bound in some way, that your salvation or your faith or your personhood in some way is in danger if you were to leave, this is a real pointer to anxiety in you and in the church (Do I belong?).

The "ins" and the "outs"

Have you been at your church for a long time and yet still don't belong, don't fit in? Are there those who are in while you feel out? There are the cool kids and then the rest, among which you are a part? You attend everything you can attend, you give, you commit, you volunteer, and yet you feel like the whole church is moving in a certain direction while you're hanging onto an inner tube being towed behind a speed boat. You are hanging on behind, hoping you aren't about to be thrown off. You have gifts, but they aren't being used. You have something to offer but it isn't being accepted (although they will always want your money). The same people, whether officially leaders or not, seem to make all the decisions, get all the attention. This would be both an example of anxiety in you (Do I belong?) but also in the church itself.

WHY THIS MATTERS

George K. Simon, in his very helpful book *In Sheep's Clothing: Understanding and Dealing with Manipulative People*, describes people as being on a continuum from neurotic to character-disordered.[13] Only a small percentage of the population would find themselves as diagnosably neurotic or character-disordered, but all of us fit along this continuum to one extent or another. But what is interesting is that both of these types of personalities (at the extremes) are described by Simon in their relation to anxiety:

> A common saying among professionals is that if a person is making himself miserable, he's probably neurotic, and if he's making everyone else miserable, he's probably character-disordered.[14]

A church with unnamed, unseen, and unrecognized anxiety is a sitting duck to the character-disordered, manipulative, and abusive

---

13. Simon, *In Sheep's Clothing*, 35–38.
14. Simon, *In Sheep's Clothing*, 35.

individual. They can smell this kind of neurotic anxiety a mile away. The more anxious the community, the more neurotic the community. This is why I call anxiety the soil in which dysfunction and abuse grows. Dysfunctional churches are churches that are unaware of their anxieties, and which are therefore unaware of how and why they act the way they do.

We as people and churches full of people operate on three levels: the cognitive, spiritual, and emotional. We can think what we think and express it and have our theologies and believe it firmly, but when some form of crisis hits a church, it is the unresolved, unseen, and unknown emotional system stuff, the anxieties bubbling under the surface, that will ultimately determine how we act. In the words of Edwin Friedman:

> In order to imagine the unimaginable, people must be able to separate themselves from the emotional processes that surround them before they can begin to see (or hear) things differently.[15]

Dysfunctional organizations are those in which the leadership lacks imagination. Unable to imagine a better way, they remain locked in old ways of reacting and behaving. And in so doing, abuse can be enabled, often for generations.

SUMMARY

In these last two chapters we have looked at three major areas of anxiety in the church. The anxiety that comes from a hostile environment outside of ourselves, and the anxiety-inducing issues of:

- Behaving right
- Believing right
- Belonging

These anxieties are a soil tilled and ready for a seed to be planted. The seed is the unresolved family-of-origin issues of the "influencers": the founding church families or the current leadership group.

---

15. Friedman, *Failure of Nerve*, 35.

3

The Seed
(What Is Its Origin?)

3.1

The Seed

What has been said about cultural history is true of individuals: If we do not know our familial history, we may be doomed to repeat it.
—John Bradshaw[1]

Walk into any church. It doesn't matter what flavor: Catholic, Orthodox, AME, Baptist, Pentecostal—the rainbow of possibilities seems endless. And each has a distinct air about them, something that separates them from each other. Maybe it's the liturgy, or the ethnicity of the congregation, or the style of worship, or the buildings or whatever, but each has a culture. Some churches are like McDonald's franchises, each church a clear copy of the main campus. Other churches are unique in their own right.

The cultures of our local churches are a complex mix of the individual cultures we bring as well as the local culture of the people from which we come. This is readily seen if you go to other countries, in Africa or South America or into rural areas of third-world countries. The cultures of those people groups show up in those churches as well. It is easy to see another culture but it is only seen in relief to our own. Only when we see another culture have we got something with which to compare it. If the whole world was colored in shades of blue you would never know it until something in a shade of red came along. So too with culture. We need to see our culture in contrast to another to really comprehend it.

1. Bradshaw, *Bradshaw on*, viii.

And this is an important thing, because as I have been saying, dysfunctional churches which can enable and allow abuse have a culture within them, of which the members that attend are too often completely unaware. A healthy church will be prepared to step back and look at themselves and critically analyze what they do and why.

Many years ago, I preached a sermon with the absolutely clumsy and easily forgettable title: "The Wise Weigh the Ways Before the Ways Get in the Way of the Whys." What I was suggesting is that if we are wise, we will weigh up and think about what we do and the way we do it, before what we do and the way we do it starts to get in the way of why we are doing it in the first place.

For instance, if a church started out as a people who were all about the gospel, and over time behaviors and practices developed and entrenched themselves to the point where the gospel is either polluted or forgotten, then they would be wise to repent of those things and return to the solid foundations of the good news of Jesus.

Or maybe it started badly in the first place. The goal may have been one thing, but now over the course of time they realize that goal was not a destination to which they ought to have set sail. Churches should be prepared to go back and rethink what they do. It's easy to allow the stuff that gets done, the busyness of church if you will, the programs and settled-upon theologies, to become so forefront in the church that they can, as we have seen, fail to be a responsive church to Spirit and word. The ways and whats get in the way of the why.

As I have explored, churches can be anxious places and a culture which breeds anxiety or maintains anxiety comes from somewhere. It doesn't just appear. Our churches are full of people who bring their own strengths and weaknesses into the mix. A culture forms that attracts or repels. We bring our stuff, our clichéd baggage if you will, into every relationship we enter, including and especially church.

Who we are as people and where we come from informs what we are and what we do. A critical analysis of this can help to kill the bitter fruit of dysfunction that can enable abuse. My contention in this chapter is that the dysfunctional, unresolved family of origin stuff in the life of the senior leaders, pastors, or founding families of a church is the seed that, if left to grow, creates a church culture that reflects the originating familial dysfunctions. The anxieties in these people become the anxieties of the church. As the leadership goes, so goes the church. If the head is sick, the body suffers.

Unresolved family-of-origin issues in the leading families replicate themselves in the style of the leadership group. If there is familial dysfunction in those leaders it will become the dysfunctional style of the leaders in the church as it is all they know. These are the seeds of dysfunction and abuse in the church.

It is what causes the system to be dysfunctional at a leadership level, but a corollary is that unresolved family-of-origin issues in the members allows for this dysfunction to continue, as these members are subconsciously responding to the unresolved stuff in their families that makes them "warm" to the dysfunction of the church. It feels like home. The emotional maturity of a church never raises itself above the maturity level of the founding families or the senior leadership. Emotionally immature leaders are enabled by emotionally immature members.

It has often been said, "Almost all problems in the spiritual life stem from a lack of self-knowledge." I think this is right and this is also my experience. It was only as I matured emotionally that I was able to mature spiritually. Unrecognized emotional wounds are an undercurrent that drives our behavior.

Take, for example, a person who was raised in an abusive environment. Deep emotional wounds may exist under the surface, but in many ways the person can be highly functioning and successful in many aspects of their life and career. However, as a leader of a church they may reenact this abuse or neglect because they do not see it themselves. This form of emotional immaturity can then unwittingly make the church an unsafe environment as neglect and abuse is reenacted in the church community. Leaders who have not dealt with their own issues of abuse and neglect as children will have no name for it. And even if they are not personally engaging in abusive or neglectful behaviors, they will be unable to see it or name it when it is happening in their community.

Churches are emotional, spiritual, and familial systems. It is easy to understand the idea of a spiritual system. This is at the surface all the time at the conscious level; the familial concepts are a little less conscious, but when pointed out they become obvious. Churches are frequently described as families, it's common language, but the emotional system is below the surface, unrecognized, unseen, and unnoticed as the real driving force in what is actually happening in the church. In the end, in dysfunctional churches it is the underlying emotional energies that are driving behavior, not theology, regardless of what is said or believed. The reality is, in dysfunctional churches in which abuse is enabled or thrives, there is a lack of awareness on the part of the church as an emotional system that is ultimately a reflection of the dysfunction of the leading families or leadership group, and which is enabled by the dysfunctional emotional systems in the families that attend.

Church communities are reacting in a natural subconscious way to unresolved emotional issues regardless of what they say or think they believe about God and Christ. When a crisis hits, it is the unresolved emotional system energy that causes a knee-jerk reaction, an emotional energy that determines how they react and respond to this perceived threat.

This reactive behavior can be pointed to later after calm has returned, and apologies can be given as the guilt or shame or the Bible causes them to recognize, "Oops, that was not very Christian of me," but until they recognize and root out the emotional basis for what caused the reaction in the first place, the behaviors will repeat, often for generations.

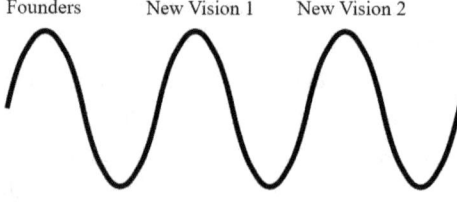

Figure 3

The above figure crudely demonstrates the life cycle of a culture of a church. The initial culture for good or for bad with all of its life and dysfunction is a copy or reflection of the founding families, the original church planter, or its pastor. Their issues become the church's issues. If it is grossly dysfunctional and abusive, then the church will be grossly dysfunctional and abusive. Churches like this rarely survive the first major crisis (the death of the founder, for instance). But if the dysfunction exists to a lesser degree (that is, the church *seems* mainline, healthy, and functional on the surface, not a cult or sect) the sons and daughters of the founders can continue the work, and the grandchildren as well, continuing to replicate the original culture and keep it alive. The culture can last for generations. But eventually over time the strength of the founder's familial influence starts to wash out. A new pastor comes along with strong visionary leadership (and a host of his own baggage to go with it.). The members buy into the vision and the old culture is replaced with a new one. If this new leader is relatively healthy then the church starts to reflect this healthier outlook. Abuse and dysfunction (if it existed in the past) fade away. If, however, the new pastor has his own unresolved issues, then the old dysfunctions will simply be replaced by new ones, and this cycle can continue for centuries.

THE SEEDS OF DYSFUNCTIONAL CULTURE

To understand the origins of this dysfunctional behavior, it will be helpful to briefly look at some of the historical work done by family psychologists. Their insights into the dynamics of child-rearing and family systems can be easily transferred into understandings of how churches work.

Alice Miller

In 1980, in a groundbreaking work, *For Your Own Good*[2], Swiss psychologist Alice Miller outlined the impact on children when raised within families that she describes as being categorized by a *poisonous pedagogy*. In this text she relates centuries of child-rearing advice given to parents (in a German context) which is designed to help them create obedient children by breaking their will. Some of these tactics were manipulative and cruel, but to some extent are still used by parents to raise *obedient* children, with the emphasis on *obedient*. There is no doubt that parents need to be in control of their children, but not *to* control them in the absolute, abusive sense. These are two different things.

> I can only state that a very small child needs an empathic and not a "controlling" human being (whether it be father or mother) as care giver.[3]

The difference between controlling and in control is that parents that are in control are in control of both themselves and their emotions, as well as the needs and understanding of the growing emotions and well-being of the child in their care. Controlling parents however, will use all forms of manipulative and physical outbursts and punishments to obtain the obedience being sought, with no recognition of their own

2. Miller, *For Your Own Good*.
3. Miller, *For You Own Good*, 6.

selfish needs driving this controlling behavior. Her argument is that this kind of parenting violates the rights of the child. Children know no better and the impacts can be serious.

> If there is absolutely no possibility of reacting appropriately to hurt, humiliation, and coercion, then these experiences cannot be integrated into the personality; the feelings they evoke are repressed, and the need to articulate them remains unsatisfied, without hope of being fulfilled.[4]

For young children there *is* no possibility of reacting appropriately. They haven't got the resource. Parents who raise their children in controlling ways are responding to the unknown issues within themselves and are trying to meet their own needs by taking it out on their children. Anxiety, shame, helplessness, and insecurities unknown and unseen in the parent are being used to control the child and are then reproduced in the child. All of this is done in order to raise good, obedient children. Her conclusion is that traditional, controlling parental techniques teach:

1. Parents are the masters (not the servants!) of the dependent child
2. They determine in a godlike fashion what is right and wrong
3. The child is held responsible for the parent's anger
4. The parent must always be shielded
5. The child's life-affirming feelings pose a threat to the parent
6. The child's will must be "broken" as soon as possible
7. All this must happen very soon at a very early age, so the child "won't notice" and will therefore not be able to expose the parent.[5]

Now as I look at this and listen to the countless stories of those who have come out of dysfunctional churches there is an eerie correlation between the above list and the culture of these churches. Simply replace "parent" with "pastor" (or another church authority figure, such as a bishop, deacon, etc.) and "child" with "church member" or "congregant" and you are describing the kinds of things evident in controlling, abusive organizations.[6] For instance, the pastor must always be shielded, or in a godlike fashion the elders determine right and wrong.

---

4. Miller, *For Your Own Good*, 7.
5. Miller, *For Your Own Good*, 59.
6. To a lesser or greater extent, depending on the level of dysfunction in the place.

The Seed

Now of course Miller is talking about Germans in a eighteenth-, nineteenth-, and early twentieth-century context, and parental techniques which are recommended by secular thinkers. Surely those of us who are Christians and who were raised in Christian homes and by Christian parents who are motivated by the love of God are not influenced by this kind of poisonous pedagogy. You cannot (one might argue) correlate Miller's thinking with the church as simply as I have done here.

But Julius Rubin explores the seeds of modern American evangelicalism[7] as being the pietist behaviors and beliefs of the early American church up to and including the Second Great Awakening of the early 1800s.[8] These early American church groups put a great premium on personal piety and established an effective if not literal theocracy.

> Bound together in a church covenant, collective discipline, and *caritas*, churches kept their members free from sin and devoted to executing God's will. Church discipline, together with the strict patriarchal discipline of family government and the civil government, promoted orderly relations for saints and the unregenerate alike.[9]

The strict patriarchal discipline described, with the husband/father male authority figure to which submission by the children and women should be given, is still a very strong sentiment in many Christian homes.

Rubin goes on to describe the pietistic behaviors encouraged, demanded, and enforced by these strong paternalistic homes, whose cultures were replicated in the churches as well.[10] Fastings, "mortifications of the body," putting to death the sins of the flesh and the like, all in an attempt to maintain a close, warm communion with God himself, were common features of these puritanical churches. According to Rubin:

> Indeed, the evangelical personality was created out of a deliberate trauma—the parental declaration of war against the willful toddler. Evangelicals spent their lives in a futile attempt to prove themselves worthy of parental love through acts of total submission and obedience.[11]

---

7. And, by extension, all Western evangelicalism, due to the weight of the American culture on the West and its missionary venture in the last 300 years.

8. Rubin, *Religious Melancholy and Protestant Experience*.

9. Rubin, *Religious Melancholy and Protestant Experience*, 43.

10. Or maybe better, the culture of the church was replicated in the home.

11. Rubin, *Religious Melancholy and Protestant Experience*, 49.

And there it is: at the heart of the evangelical movement in America is a form of poisonous pedagogy, only this time with an American, biblical, Christian twist on it. And in my experience, this form of parental, male-dominating control exists even today in homes and churches, especially those in which abuse is enabled. All for the good of the child, in obedience to Christ and the Bible, as they see it. "Raise up a child in the way he should go, and in the end, he will never depart from it," (Prov 22:6) is the biblical mandate for this kind of thinking. And the ever-popular spare the rod, spoil the child, readily comes to mind (Prov 13:24).

This thinking is still prevalent in some circles today. A recent essay on a popular conservative website enjoins the use of physical and other forms of strong discipline to teach our children "the muscle memories of authority, obedience, relationship, and blessing—things they'll still be a part of when they're adopted children of God."[12] My issue here is the strong emphasis on obedience to authority figures. It is easy to exercise these muscles in such a way that our children become unthinking pawns, obeying autocratic rulers, because this was taught as children by too-authoritarian kinds of parenting.

Raised by parents using a system of rules that includes the idea (amongst other things) that to question is disobedience, it is easy for some to transfer this thinking to their understanding of the role elders, leaders, and pastors take in their churches. They misinterpret Heb 13:17 to mean "Don't question your elders, they are appointed by God so just obey." Or how often has abuse been perpetrated in churches, with the leader being considered sacrosanct with the misapplication of this verse "Don't touch the Lord's anointed" (1 Sam 26:9)?

This close correlation suggests the parenting styles of the parents of the leader of a dysfunctional church were of Miller's poisonous type. Being unaware of the paucity of emotional intelligence that this kind of upbringing can produce, they now run their church the only way they know how. John Bradshaw highlights the impact on such child-rearing when he says:

> Children raised by patriarchal parenting rules quickly learn that the way to get love is to give up their authentic self and develop a self that meets the demands of blind obedience and duty. When

---

12. Dillehay, "How the Rod Can Point Children to God," para. 11.

the core of self is covered up with a false self, true self-love and self-esteem are impossible.[13]

Miller also describes how being raised in this kind of environment produces a range of false beliefs:

1. A feeling of duty produces love.
2. Hatred can be done away with by forbidding it.
3. Parents deserve respect simply because they are parents.
4. Obedience makes a child strong.
5. A high degree of self-esteem is harmful.
6. A low degree of self-esteem makes a person altruistic.
7. Tenderness (doting) is harmful.
8. Responding to a child's needs is wrong.
9. Severity and coldness are good preparation for life.
10. A pretense of gratitude is better than honest ingratitude.
11. The way you behave is more important that the way you really are.
12. Neither parents nor God would survive being offended.
13. The body is something dirty and disgusting.
14. Strong feelings are harmful.
15. Parents are creatures free of drives and guilt.
16. Parents are always right.[14]

Again, if you have come out a dysfunctional and abusive church organization you will be able to see some of these things being played out to a lesser or greater extent by simply replacing "parent" with "church authority figure" and "child" with "church member." Think about how the evangelical church traditionally has dealt (or not dealt) with the issue of sex and sexuality. The body is something dirty and disgusting indeed, it would seem. And I have seen more than my share of number 11. Spiritual hypocrisy runs rampant in some churches:

---

13. Bradshaw, *Bradshaw on*, xviii.
14. Miller, *For Your Own Good*, 59–60.

> As adults, people act the same way their parents acted in an attempt to prove that their parents behaved correctly towards them—i.e., really loved them and really did it for their own good.[15]

It is simply too painful to accept that our parents may have been wrong. Instead, these undealt-with truths in the lives of the leadership and in its membership are the seeds of dysfunctional churches.

So why would church members warm to this kind of controlling leadership behavior? Because it feels right, it reminds them of something they cannot name or place. It just seems like home, and for many that is because it was exactly like home. We are going to feel comfortable, often for reasons we can't articulate, when we find ourselves enveloped by a culture and people that replicate our family of origin:

> A child cannot acknowledge the negative sides of his or her father, and yet these are stored up somewhere in the child's psyche, for the adult will then be attracted by precisely these negative, disavowed sides in the Father's substitutes he or she encounters.[16]

Speaking to the question "Why Hitler?," Miller observes:

> And so, when a man comes along and talks like one's own father and acts like him, even adults will forget their democratic rights or will not make use of them. They will submit to this man, will acclaim him, allow themselves to be manipulated by him and put their trust in him, finally surrendering totally to him without being aware of their enslavement.[17]

In a similar way, church members that see a controlling individual with all the attributes of Dad may readily set aside their normal reservations and submit themselves to such a pastor or church authority. Long-embedded generational mandates to obey, submit, and rely on the Bible, God, and the church, elders, and pastors can breed a dysfunctional community that is enabled by people who are not aware of what it is they are surrendering to. This can be particularly prevalent in churches that are full of second-, third-, and even subsequent-generation Christian families, especially if they are strong patriarchal families. People

---

15. Bradshaw, *Bradshaw on*, 75.
16. Bradshaw, *Bradshaw on*, 72.
17. Miller, *For Your Own Good*, 75.

tend to rely on the word of the pastor or the leader and to suspend their critical thinking to support the Lord's anointed.

People are prepared to give up themselves, their true authentic selves (see chapter 6.2) because, as we have seen, failing to do so may result in being excluded or marginalized from a family group or church. This is a pain and anxiety too great to bear.

It may seem paradoxical, but in fact it is quite understandable when we think about it, that churches run by controlling individuals may be attractive to those for whom this was not their family-of-origin dynamic, but in fact the opposite. If your parents emotionally or physically neglected you and you arrive at a community that is the exact opposite, it can be extremely intoxicating. Here is a community that seems to fill the void of what you thought family should be. Churches can lovebomb new members and very quickly adopt new people into church. Soon, however, the church tells you what to do and how to do it, what to believe and how to believe it. But you don't mind. "Finally," you say to yourself, "I'm home. I have a place to belong."

Bowen Family Systems Theory

Not only is understanding how we are raised an important pointer to the seeds of church community dysfunction, but so, too, is comprehending how our churches operate as familial systems.

Murray Bowen was an American psychiatrist. His ideas have transformed family counselling theory by moving past the didactic ideas of Bowlby's attachment theory[18], which were focused primarily on mother-child relationships, to seeing the family as a unit.[19] His therapy models address not just the individual who comes to therapy, but seeks to address the entire family system, of which the client is but a representative. The family as a system, according to Bowen, can be described as a series of eight interconnected concepts which include:

- Triangulation
- Differentiation of Self

---

18. Bowlby focused on the importance of the child's social, emotional, and cognitive development relationship with their mother. His observations helped shape his belief about the link between early infant separations from the mother and later maladjustment in adult life.

19. Kerr and Bowen, *Family Evaluation*.

- Nuclear Family Emotional System
- Family Projection Process
- Multigenerational Transmission Process
- Emotional Cutoff
- Sibling Position
- Societal Emotional Process

All of these concepts are important and speak in some way to how our churches operate.[20] I want to focus primarily on differentiation of self, because amongst all these concepts its absence is readily apparent in dysfunctional churches. Leaders with poorly developed self-differentiation lay the seed for much dysfunctional behavior.

Bowen suggests that there is an:

> ... instinctually rooted life force (differentiation or individuality) in every human being that propels the developing child to grow to be an emotionally separate person, an individual with the ability to think, feel, and act for himself. Also assumed is the existence of an instinctually rooted life force (togetherness) that propels child and family to remain emotionally connected and to operate in reaction to one another. The togetherness force propels child and family to think, feel and act as one. The result of these counterbalancing life forces is that no one achieves complete emotional separation from the family.[21]

A healthy and mature individual is someone who balances the tension of closeness and separateness well. What Bowen describes is that anxiety is created in families by the perception of being too close (enmeshed) or too distant (separated) in key relationships.

In healthy functional families, individual emotional maturity can become an attainable goal, because a person is learning to balance these tensions well:

> Self-differentiation is characterized by the ability to separate thinking from feeling, affording a person the ability to think about feelings and to feel about thinking. Self-differentiation reduces the amount of reactiveness and irrational behavior in a family.[22]

20. See Steinke, *How Your Church Family Works*, for a clear description of Bowenian theory at work within a church.
21. Kerr and Bowen, *Family Evaluation*, 95.
22. Bradshaw, *Bradshaw on*, xix.

Differentiation of self is a key idea here. It describes the ability to make decisions based on one's intellect, processing information using reason and not emotional and felt responses. Don't let this language fool you. Going off the handle or panicking in the face of a crisis is no more an emotionally driven response than a cold-hearted decision to emotionally cut someone off who disagrees with how the crisis should be handled. Both reactions stem from anxiety, both are emotionally driven.

The anxious person is a person who is either too closely fused or too far removed from others. If we are anxious about closeness, we disengage. If we are anxious about separateness, we enmesh. Anxious people are either an "I am a rock; I am an island person" or an "I can't live without you" person. Healthy, well-differentiated individuals maintain a balance between these two poles. Our anxiety about closeness or separateness in nonfamilial situations derives from how well we resolved (and are resolving) these tensions within our own families of origin.

> Well-differentiated people are able to be themselves, to do and say what they want, think, and feel without undue concern about whether others will criticize them, and without a need to either flatter or criticize others inappropriately. They can be open about themselves and accept the differences of others without reacting when others try to get them to change in some way. Yet they are open-minded about the possibility of change and are able to rethink their position when new information comes in. They do not think that change is an admission of inadequacy.[23]

Well-differentiated people are flexible and adaptable. They are aware of their own feelings and the feelings of others but are not driven by them. They don't react instinctively from subconscious, unresolved emotional ties to family members, ties that resemble their current relationships, though they are subconsciously unaware of this:

> It is one thing to be consciously reminded of someone from the past by the way a person speaks, acts or whatever; and quite another to find we have strong feelings about a person—or they about us—which seem to come out of the blue. What may be happening is that a feeling from childhood which could not be processed or dealt with is triggered by the current situation, and may be hard to deal with in the present unless we understand where it is coming from.[24]

23. Richardson, *Family Ties That Bind*, 36.
24. Rose, *Psychology for Pastoral Contexts*, 22.

Inflexibility is a hallmark of dysfunctional families full of poorly differentiated people. Rigid walls or boundaries are established (separateness) or the walls don't exist (enmeshment). Overall, the system is closed. Closed systems are rigidly opposed to change, with individuals within it either firmly enmeshed or determinedly separate. This is opposed to open, healthy family systems:

> An open system is one in which the parts interconnect, are responsive and sensitive to one another, and allow information to flow between the internal and external environments.[25]

Closed systems are, by definition, closed off to new information from external sources. People within it respond in unhealthy, reactive ways to changes in circumstance or events beyond their control that impact or affect themselves or others within the system.

Virginia Satir lists the underlying beliefs of the closed dysfunctional family system:

- People are basically evil and must be continually controlled to be good.
- Relationships have to be regulated by force or by fear of punishment.
- There is one right way, and the person most powerful has it.
- There is always someone who knows what is best for you.[26]

All systems seek balance, whether closed or open, healthy or dysfunctional. This balance point, this place where everyone feels comfortable, even if the comfort is dysfunctional, is known as the homeostasis, or steady state of the system. All systems seek to maintain homeostasis and to resist change. Healthy systems can detect this resistance and, in emotionally healthy ways, can accommodate the change and establish a new homeostasis. However, in dysfunctional, closed families, change is seen as a threat to the power base and to the system in general. The whole system will react to the threat of change by seeking to resist it and restore everyone and everything back to its original, albeit dysfunctional, place. For instance, a child who leaves home as a young adult is surely going to upset the homeostasis, and although an anxiety-producing event, in a healthy family this change is seen as good and natural. The family can and will accommodate this change in meaningful and healthy ways. In an

---

25. Satir, *New Peoplemaking*, 22.
26. Satir, *New Peoplemaking*, 130–35.

unhealthy family this change is seen as a threat, and the ways of interacting with the leaving child can become aggressive or the family can simply emotionally cut off from the child, reflecting, in an emotional way, the sense of abandonment his leaving is causing the family.

There is one last idea from Murray Bowen that I would like to address here and then I will tie it all up with application to churches, and that is the idea of *anxiety "binding."* In healthy families, if an anxiety-inducing event should occur, the system becomes unbalanced but members within it are able to understand their feelings, recognize their reactions, and deal relatively rationally with the situation. They communicate, seek constructive solutions, and establish a new homeostasis if necessary.

Unhealthy families, however, are in a state of perpetual anxiety. In these families the anxiety-inducing event is far less serious a problem then their chronically anxious reactions to it. Our anxiety just rubs off on everybody else. As an example, I might have a car accident, a bit of a fender-bender in my wife's car, but fearing that she may react badly I will seek to hide it or downplay it. This means I might come home sullen and angry. Picking up on these cues other family members may start arguing about unrelated issues at home. The whole system becomes destabilized.

One way families with chronic anxiety can seek to reduce the overall anxiety is by binding it to a family member. In chronically anxious families the anxiety can become symptomatic in that a person will exhibit emotional, social, or other dysfunctions. For instance, your teenage son may have a drug and alcohol problem which, although serious in its own right, may really just be an outward manifestation of the dysfunctional relating occurring in the home.

The teenager becomes the "identified patient," and all the energy of the family is focused on helping or enabling his behavior. This dysfunctional way of behaving maintains the homeostasis in the family.

The parents might bring the child to therapy, but what Bowenian theory would suggest is one of the ways of helping the child deal with his issues is to fix yourself. As individuals begin to become emotionally healthier, self-differentiated people, the overall anxiety in the family is reduced, and the underlying motivation for the teenage son to continue to abuse substances is reduced.

HOW THESE THINGS TRANSLATE INTO THE CHURCH

If the process of becoming one's own self was not developed well from within their families of origins, then this lack of differentiation will appear as a hallmark of the leadership style in its leaders. The poor lack of differentiation will inform and become the primary method of interacting within the church. The church culture starts to look like the dysfunctional families of origin that have congregated to form the church community.

If the lack of differentiation appears in the form of separateness, the church really can't function at all. It is, by definition, dysfunctional. If people are quitters, nonvolunteering, or just failing to commit due to their own unresolved family of origin anxiety that they are now bringing into church relationships, then no meaningful church activities can occur. This type of dysfunctional church is unlikely to exist, or exist for long, because those who exhibit unresolved forms of anxiety which result in them seeking isolation from others are unlikely to plant churches.

More common is a dysfunctional church founded or led by individuals whose lack of differentiation comes in the form of enmeshment. In these types of chronically anxious churches, the lack of self-differentiation appears as an anxiety toward those who don't belong, the outliers, those that don't behave or believe the way we need them to behave and believe. This need stems from the anxiety within the leadership, but also increases the anxiety of those who don't belong and feel the pressure to conform. These churches may be happy for new members to come and attend, but also need these new members to assimilate quickly.

The more dysfunctional the leadership, the more the pressure to enmesh. This is designed to deal with the unresolved anxiety in the leadership whose greatest fear is losing control. Obsessively controlling leaderships in dysfunctional churches require their members to be enmeshed. It is a key marker for abuse. As I said previously, controlling is different than being in control. The more controlling the leadership, the more likely some form of abuse is occurring. The too-closely enmeshed church copies the emotional system of the families of those that lead:

> Feelings . . . blur self-boundaries because they have difficulty in discriminating between self and other in close relationships. Because they blend into the other, they ordinarily see differences as liabilities, i.e., "because I am this way, you should be this way too." In the process of diffusing into others, they seek certain reactions in response and cannot accept the other person the way he is.

This sets up a struggle with the other and difficulties in direct proportion to the intensity and closeness of the relationship.[27]

Take again these false beliefs from Virgin Satir below. In dysfunctional churches, with poorly differentiated individuals leading them, the false beliefs can become the basic underlying assumptions of the church, whether consciously spoken and acted on or subconsciously driving the culture.

- *People are basically evil and must be continually controlled, to be good.* The more dysfunctional the church, the more the people are reminded in pejorative and shaming ways of the depth and wickedness of their sin. Grace may be spoken of, but often rarely seen. Sin and your propensity to fall short are ever at the forefront. Given your wickedness you need someone to control and lead you. The leadership team (of course) is the given answer.

- *Relationships have to be regulated by force or by fear of punishment.* The more dysfunctional the church, the more closed they are to outside influence. Those that are not us are viewed with great suspicion. People can become isolated from their own family members as increasing demands for service, attendance, and money place an ever-increasing demand on the member.

- *There is one right way, and the person most powerful has it.* The more dysfunctional the church, the less input the members have in the direction of the church. The leadership makes all the decisions, with little input from others, or with token input from others that is then ignored, all while giving the appearance of having been consulted. Any questioning of those in authority is immediately crushed, and the questioner soon outcast. No public dissension is tolerated.

- *There is always someone who knows what is best for you.* And it is never you. The more dysfunctional the church and its members, the more the members are prepared to lay aside their own judgments for the advice, mentorship, and discipleship of the leaders.

Now these things are all on a continuum. The more of these beliefs that are present and the stronger the beliefs, the unhealthier the church becomes and the more sect- and cultlike it becomes. Here, in these false beliefs, these seeds, we see the anxieties of *behaving right, believing right*

27. Fogarty, "Family Emotional System," 85.

and belonging, starting to bear fruit. The more dysfunctional the church, the more closed it is to responding to the stimuli of the word and Spirit. The undealt-with and often unnamed anxieties within the leading group require the church to be tightly controlled, and thus the Spirit is quenched (1 Thess 5:19).

Abusive behaviors in churches like this can be enabled and tolerated. Controlling, manipulative, and narcissistic bullies or sex predators are pastorally cared for (see chapter 5.3). It has the appearance of being gracious, but the energy driving this care is anxiety. By tolerating and pastorally caring for abusers in the community, the abusers become the identified patient. They are a symptom of a dysfunctional, poorly differentiated leadership group. The anxiety of the leaders is bound in the abuser. By focusing on the abuser, the leadership team's anxieties are reduced. This is one of the reasons abusers are not dealt with properly. They become a requirement of the system. Having an identified patient who is abusive within the community maintains the homeostasis, albeit a dysfunctional one. To come face to face with why this individual was enabled would require the leadership to come face to face with their own unresolved needs for this behavior. If the behavior is illegal then they become culpable. Better to manage the individual and bind their anxiety than to deal with it openly. This is the very definition of dysfunctional emotional behavior.

SUMMARY

I have covered much in a very short space and it can seem overwhelming. It took me years to come to an understanding of some of these concepts, and I still learn new things every day.

- My primary contention for this chapter is that the dysfunctional, unresolved family-of-origin stuff in the life of the senior leaders, pastors, or founding families of a church can create a church culture that reflects this originating dysfunction.

- Being raised by parents that used the kind of child-rearing ideas that Alice Miller calls *poisonous pedagogy*, ideas used as means of creating obedience in children, seems to correlate into the kinds of controlling people that can end up as church leaders in dysfunctional churches.

- Bowenian Family System Theory is informative to understanding how church families work.

- Abuse is enabled in dysfunctional churches because it helps to bind the undealt-with anxieties in the leadership group onto the abuser. This "identified patient," who is abusive within the community, maintains the homeostasis, albeit a dysfunctional one.

Church cultures don't just appear:

> Cultures originate out of the choices individuals make within the bounds of their specific experiential history. The criteria by which people make these choices explain the origins and evolution of specific cultures.[28]

The unseen hands of the families of origin are one such major criterion. It is the seed planted in a soil of anxiety that can grow to become abusive. Much bitter fruit comes from this. But if the choices being made can lead to dysfunctional cultures, then it must be possible to make new choices that would change the culture. Sadly, and too often in dysfunctional churches, this never happens. Instead the dysfunctions are nurtured. What helps the bitter fruit of dysfunction and abuse grow?

I will explore those ideas now.

---

28. Handwerker, *Origin of Cultures*, 12.

4

The Trellis
(What Supports It?)

EVERY SUMMER FOR YEARS now, I have had this love-hate relationship with the summer vegetable garden. I have these grand ideas of growing a great crop of vegetables, but about two months in, pests and diseases, issues of too much or not enough water, fungus, you name it, have had their way with the patch. It rarely produces well, particularly with resspect to tomatoes; I have never had much luck growing them well. Then one year, determined to do it right, I bought a tomato-growing kit. It included the ready-started plant, fertilizer packets, and a trellis (which consisted of three long bamboo sticks that were to be shaped over the plant in a tepee fashion) on which to support it. It is well known that three-legged objects are the minimum number of legs required to support a stable strong structure that can support weight, be it a stool or a trellis. Given this support, the plant was able to thrive and do well. The air around the leaves reduced its susceptibility to fungal attack, and the support kept the weight of the fruit from breaking the branches and off the ground.

In the same way this three-legged trellis can support a tomato plant, so too a three-legged trellis of dysfunctions can lead to and support abuse in the local church. Now not all three of these things need be present in the local church for abuse to occur, nor need all three be as equally strong as the other. And just because these things exist does not mean there is abuse present in the church. But with this structure in place, with these dysfunctions, it is easy for abuse to occur, to be stable, and to be supported by the system.

These things exist on a continuum. For instance, there can be a very strong dysfunction of *Unquestionable Power and Authority*, but little of the *Unity above All* dysfunction. This means that the abuse that might arise is less stable and in a less pronounced way, but abuse is still abuse and is still unacceptable.

These three dysfunctions often exist in a dysfunctional organization and can either lead to or support abuse in the local church. Other dysfunctions can and do exist in other abusive organizations, but these three will frequently be present. Let's explore them. They are:

Unquestionable Power and Authority.
Unwanted Conflict.
Unity above All.

4.1

Unquestionable Power and Authority

Authority is mainly a moral power; therefore, it must first call upon the conscience, that is, upon the duty that each person has to contribute willingly to the common good.
—Pope John XXIII[1]

You know that the rulers in this world lord it over their people, and officials flaunt their authority over those under them. But among you it will be different. Whoever wants to be a leader among you must be your servant.
—Jesus (Matt 10:25)

What makes the temptation of power so seemingly irresistible? Maybe it is that power offers an easy substitute for the hard task of love. It seems easier to be God than to love God, easier to control people than to love people, easier to own life than to love life.
—Henri Nouwen[2]

---

1. John XXIII, *Pope's Caress*, 20.
2. Nouwen, *In the Name of Jesus*, 77.

Mr. Smith has been a member of First Church since it was planted by his good friend who was the founding pastor more than forty years ago. Although the friend moved interstate and is no longer the pastor, Mr. Smith remained. Over his time at First Church, Mr. Smith has become its biggest financial backer. He is devoted in both time and treasure. He has worked with many pastors over the years, through good times and bad, helping to mold the church into the successful church he and others believe it to be. He was an elder and leader for years, but recently he has retired from such roles and now he has no official influence in the church.

But the church knows and whispers and gossips about the fact that Mr. Smith really runs the church. Nothing important ever gets done without his approval. No one can think of any time in the past where any decision was made, at least not any big decision, that he disagreed with and for which his opinion was not sought after and followed. And even though he is retired and not on the board, he is involved in every discussion about every important thing. Why? Because all the leaders go to him for advice. "We just want his wisdom" say the other leaders.

But privately these leaders fume. This retired man is calling meetings and putting forth proposals for policies and programs that some of them do not want. But the unspoken rule "Don't go against this retired man's wishes," is understood loud and clear. The board and current pastor meekly give in. "Peace, you know. Unity."

This works wonderfully for Mr. Smith; he gets all the authority and respect and power of decision-making without any of the responsibility. And should it all fall in a heap? He can say with a clear conscience "I wasn't on the board; I didn't make this decision."

This power base also has the added benefit (as far as Mr. Smith is concerned) of keeping the lead pastor sidelined. Not that he is necessarily consciously doing this, but really. Can some brought-in paid staff really run the church as well as a founding member? Someone who knows all the history and mission and vision of the place? And if the pastor is good-natured enough, he is willing to defer his authority to the retired elder to maintain unity and peace. He has learned through painful scoldings and veiled threats that you don't question the decisions or opinions of Mr. Smith. Lose Mr. Smith's support and you lose the pastorship. History at First Church has demonstrated that. But the pastor salves his conscience with the thought "At least good ministry is getting done."

Does any of this sound familiar? It should, because it is a common dysfunction in churches that can abuse: an ambiguous locus of authority, coupled with the unspoken rule of "Don't question the *real* authority," that is, those with the power.

But sometimes the locus of authority is not ambiguous. The lead pastor or his acolytes are in charge and you better well know it. Take the Westboro Baptist Church in Topeka, Kansas for instance. In the early years of the church Fred Phelps was in charge. He held all the power authority and everyone knew it. His words, his teachings, his ways were THE rules, THE teachings, and THE ways, and everyone one knew it. Over time this transferred to others, but the people in the church knew full well where the authority lay. And it lay with these people, without question. Read through the memoirs of some of the family members that left and this is a recurrent them. For instance, here are the words of Libby Phelps Roper:

> I was sick of the constant paranoia and the unending anxiety. I suddenly realized why the church had been so adamant about keeping us from spending time with friends outside of the church. They wanted me to have as little contact as possible with anyone who might question what the WBC was doing—what I was doing. They figured as long as they kept me contained, I wouldn't have cause to question my surroundings, to question their authority.[3]

In the case of the Westboro Baptist Church, power and authority reside with the leadership and there is no ambiguity about this at all. Compared to the Smith Church you might think, "Well this is good, right? No ambiguity, no hidden power factions, clear ideas of power and authority in the church."

But the dysfunction (one of many!) in the Westboro case is the same as the Smith Church, and that is, no matter where it lies, power and authority are to be unquestioned and followed to the letter at risk of dis-fellowship (which can happen frequently).

But it needn't be a whole of church thing. The dysfunction can reside in the little fiefdoms that some ministry leaders are allowed to run within the context of the local church. Youth ministries tend to be a haven for this kind of thing over most other kinds of ministries, although they haven't got an exclusive lock. It might be that because we so value working with children, we will tolerate anybody willing to do the work. Who knows?

---

3. Phelps, *Girl on a Wire*, loc. 1964 of 2687.

Take Mrs. Green's Annual Easter Cantata program, which she has been running for as long as people can remember. Musicians and singers have come and gone, but she is one constant in this church. This is *her* ministry and everybody knows it. She has a wonderful story of how God called her to this role and this church just in case anyone questions the ministry. "I am God's anointed servant for this task," she'll quickly let anyone know who dares question her role. "I'll pick the material. I'll select the musicians. I am in charge." She has this passive-aggressive way about her, asking for forgiveness being easier than permission, that has made life hard for every pastor and elder assigned to that ministry since it began. And in a dysfunctional organization she gets away with this because, "Look how good the ministry is and at least someone is doing it." It's her ministry and the pastor, elders, and everybody else just needs to get on board or get out of the way.

Whether it is ambiguous or clear, all of church or just some ministry-based things, in dysfunctional organizations the dysfunction that can lead to abuse is the dysfunction of *Unquestionable Power and Authority*. Usually residing in one person or a very small select band of people, this dysfunction can lead to abuse, because no matter what the authority says or does (even if illegal), it isn't questioned. The followers have been trained to turn the other eye and keep their mouths shut, usually out of fear.

AUTHORITY VS. POWER

When we are talking about authority in the local church the first question worth asking is "What is it?" Robert Paul Wolff describes authority and more helpfully helps us contrast it with power:

> (Legitimate authority) is a matter of the right to command and of the correlative obligation to obey the person who issues the command.[4]

It is important to distinguish this from power, which is the ability to compel compliance. This can take the form of the threat or actual use of force, but one not need have authority to use power.

This is an important distinction to observe, because in dysfunctional organizations there can often be confusion about the difference between

---

4. Wolff, *In Defense of Anarchism*, 9 (emphasis original).

authority and power. For instance, in the example of the First Church, the elders had authority, but Mr. Smith had the power.

So where do power and authority come from? Authority is always conferred; power is innate or autonomously assumed. Authority is granted and hence a gift, as opposed to power, which is inherent.

Authority in the simplest terms is power legitimately exercised[5]

Authority is also at times called instrumental power and is designated as such to differentiate it from influential power. Instrumental power is the power inherent in the authority which has been conferred upon the one who holds it. Influential power, on the other hand, is the power to influence without necessarily having the authority to exercise this power. Mr. Smith in the above situation would be the influential power, although the pastors and elders were the instrumental power.

We need to understand one other definition, and that is the role of the *Conferring Authority*:

> *Conferring Authority*—The organization or individual which has within themselves the right to relinquish and delegate some of their own authority to another individual or organization.

It looks a little like this. A police officer has the authority of the state (the conferring authority) to enforce the laws of the land. He is not born with this authority; it is not innate to him in any way. It is an instrumental power. As he stands along the side of the road, he has the authority, the right if you will, to stop traffic in the name of the state and its laws. A car however has power. Just because the officer stands and requests the car to stop does not mean he has the "power" to stop it. The car can run him over quite easily. The car has influential power. So why does the one with the influential power (car) choose to submit to the authority? Because the driver (hopefully in a law-based society anyway) has been socialized to relinquish his power for the sake of the common good. Recognizing you are speeding in violation of the law of the land endangers others, and so power, although innate, is surrendered to authority, for the good of all. This is a humble act, surrendering your innate power for the common good.

In dysfunctional organizations one of these two dysfunctions can exist which can lead to abuse:

---

5. Leeman, *Political Church*, 61.

- The influential power *does not* rest with the institutional authority, or does so in inadequate amounts, *and* the power base is unquestionable; or
- The influential power *does rest* with the institutional authority and the authority is unquestionable.

But either way, power and authority are unquestionable in these organizations. Consider how this functions within the context of the local church:

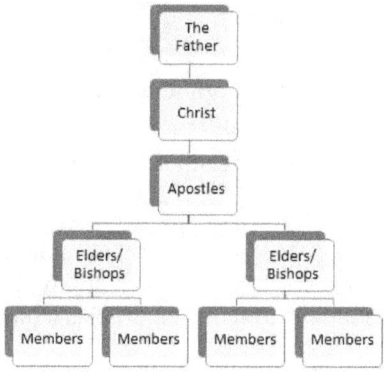

Figure 4

Firstly, with respect to Christ. Matt 28:18 informs us that all authority in heaven and earth has been given unto him. He is the head of the church, but his authority has been conferred to him by the Father. Jesus is also all-powerful, yet he, in humility, divested himself of his power and became man. Again, we see the humility in this act, surrendering his innate power for the common good.

Then the resurrected and victorious Savior, Christ, the head of his church, conferred some of his authority and power (*charismata* or *spiritual gifts*) through the Holy Spirit to his apostles who became the foundation of the church. And in turn the apostles divested themselves of some of their authority and power by the laying on of hands (*charismata*), conferring it to bishops/elders at the local church level. This divesting-conferring process continued through deacons, ministry leaders, etc., with each subsequent lower level receiving their power and authority from the level above, but ultimately from Christ himself.

Here we see authority as being conferred, not taken, and as such not earned; it is a gift. So, too, the spiritual powers; neither the power or the authority of the apostles or the elders/bishops is earned or deserved. They are gifts given, says Paul in Eph 4:12, to serve the church, to equip the saints. In a healthy organization the power and authority reside together.

There is something interesting to note here. There are two kinds of power in the church:

- Natural power-that is, people with innate skill sets, gifts and talents if you will, leadership qualities, money, family influence or position to name a few
- Supernatural power-*charismata* gifts of the spirit.

What I am highlighting is that in a healthy church those with authority are those with the spiritual power, and not *necessarily* natural power. Compare the apostles with any modern book on leadership and leadership skills and the apostles would not fare particularly well. The apostles, for instance, where not natural-born leaders. They did not have great organization skills or financial skills; they were not great motivational speakers. Heck, they were uneducated country rubes from Galilee. But they were spiritually gifted and hence spiritually powerful, which explains the miraculous growth of the church. In unhealthy organizations, those with little or even no spiritual power or gifts can still end up in authority because they are good managers, have greater leadership skills, are good looking or charismatic, run their own businesses, their dads were the founding pastors, etc. We can confuse natural power (talents and giftedness) with spiritual power and gifts.

Wisdom and good providence of course can make it so that those with natural gifts and spiritual gifts are given authority, but the point I am making is this: better a person with spiritual gifts and minimal natural gifts to run the church than a person with great natural gifts and minimal spiritual ones. By and large leadership skills are just that, skills that can be learned and taught. Maybe not to a level of competency of someone with these natural talents, but give me a humble person who can learn the skills of leadership over an arrogant person who has these skills innately anytime.

Secondly, please note: not only do power and authority reside together as gifts in the church, but those that hold these gifts hold themselves accountable to two parties: the authority above them and those they serve below. Take the case of the apostles. As recipients of the gospel, they were answerable to the authority above them, that is, Christ himself, but they also held themselves answerable to those below them, that is, the church. They were prepared to be examined or questioned by both Christ himself and the people to whom they ministered.

Paul was always doing this. In Gal 1–2, Paul opens himself up for examination. "The gospel I preach is the same as the other apostles," he declares, "Even though I never saw them. I got it from Christ himself" (Gal 1:12). "Check and see," Paul essentially says. "Examine my teaching."

In 2 Cor 10:8, he declares that his authority is evident because of the sacrifices he has made for the sake of Christ and them, and that the authority is not for his purpose but for them any way:

> For if I boast somewhat more about our authority, which the Lord gave for building you up and not for destroying you, I will not be put to shame.

And here we see the reason authority is given as a gift. Not so the powerful amongst us can lead, but so they can sacrifice for those they serve. In an unhealthy, dysfunctional organization, authority is used to build or prop up the one who holds it. Those with authority use it to control and manage, rather than sacrifice and serve. "Godly authority, without exception, nurtures and cultivates whatever is placed under it."[6]

Paul makes appeals to his people to examine his teaching, his life, his service. He is open to question. This is healthy in a church. In healthy churches the power and authority reside together in open accountable people who are willing to be examined by the authority above and those below, because they realize that the authority they have is a gift, not for them, but for those they serve:

> If authorities are not accountable, then you have built a system that is in opposition to the freedom that is in Christ. You are ignoring James 3:1, which says, "Let not many of you become teachers, my brethren, knowing that as such we shall incur a stricter judgment." Leaders are more accountable because of their position of authority—not less accountable. Why? Because if you are a leader people are following you, behaving the way you do. You are spiritually reproducing after your own kind.[7]

You see a similar thing in injunctions to elders:

---

6. Bloomer, *Authority Abusers*, 26.
7. Johnson and VanVonderen, *Subtle Power of Spiritual Abuse*, 69.

> Obey your leaders and submit *to them*—for they keep watch over your souls as those who will give an account—so that they may do this with joy, not groaning; for this *would be* unhelpful for you. (Heb 13:17)

Here we also have the recognition that elders are accountable to the authority above them, that is, God himself. Now sadly this verse is often used by authoritarian leaders to abuse and mistreat people. "I am not accountable to you" they will command. "I am accountable to God, do what I say!" Yet the point of this verse is to let people know that a man (or woman) who knows he is really answerable to God ought to demonstrate in his life and actions the kind of fear and trembling this accountability to the Holy One of Israel, the Lord of heaven's armies, the great I AM, really should invoke. As the parable in Luke 12:41–48 indicates, a manager that fears and anticipates the coming of his God is unlikely to beat his servants.

So, what is the measure we are to use to measure our elders? Their adherence to the authority above them of course, and that is the teachings of the apostles and ultimately Christ. As the primary differentiator between the two offices of the church (elder and deacon), elders are apt to teach. The best way to question and test the elders is in their adherence to the doctrine of the authority above them, that is the biblical foundation of the church, the teachings of the apostles. Both orthodoxy (right doctrine) and orthopraxy (right behaviors) are to be assessed. In the church, members are to be like the Bereans (Acts 17:11), testing the teaching of the leaders of the church to see if the things they say and do measure up with the truth, freedom, gentleness, love, and mercy we have in Christ. This lays a responsibility on the members to thinking and learning and understanding for themselves, and not fully relying on the teaching of the pastor or elders. Does the word of God really mean those things? And does the life of the leader measure up?

In dysfunctional organizations, the word of the pastor or other leader is regarded as sacrosanct. It is never to be questioned. This can lead to abuse. In dysfunctional organizations, these pastors turn a disapproving eye to anyone who dares listen to any other teaching the pastors disagree with.

And how does the lifestyle of the elder or pastor measure up to the life of Christ? It is the right and responsibility of the flock to know. And what if it doesn't? Well, two or three witnesses to this can bring an accusation against an elder (1 Tim 5:19), and if found accurate he is publicly rebuked. This is how healthy churches are run.

In healthy organizations, those with power and authority recognize:

1. They get their power and authority from Jesus Christ as gifts and are answerable to him with all that means; and
2. They are accountable to the people they lead and all that means.

Which is why humility should be the primary and first trait you should look for in your leadership group. Humility is the act of knowing your power and setting it aside for the betterment of those without it. This is Jesus. The problem with power, says W. Penn Handwerker, is:

> Power corrupts because it elicits a sense of entitlement. Power elicits violence to avoid the loss of entitlements.[8]

The culturally and religiously accepted form of violence in dysfunctional churches when those in power are threatened? Scapegoating. Those who speak up are seen as a threat to the leadership system and driven away in active and often emotionally and spiritually cruel ways. The sins of the leadership, never articulated, are projected onto and metaphorically placed upon the shoulders of one that speaks up and they are driven away.

In dysfunctional organizations, those with power and authority are either not held accountable and are never questioned, or have limited self-imposed levels of accountability. This is a dysfunction that can lead to all forms of abuse. "Don't ask" and "Don't tell" become the unspoken rules of the system. This supports abuse because nobody is prepared to speak up when intolerable behaviors become evident.

WHY TRUST AUTHORITY?

In my old church all of our office doors were fitted with a small glass window. It meant that it was not possible for me to be in my office even with the door closed and for me not to be seen by someone if they chose to look in. Who could look in? Anyone, and that was just the point. It was a measure designed to ensure the safety of both me and the person in the office with me.

Now think about what this means. This window into my office existed in order that trust *need not* exist. Read that again. *This window into my office existed, in order that trust need not exist.*

---

8. Handwerker, *Origin of Cultures*, 119.

Now this does not mean that I shouldn't be trusted. I am not suggesting that repeated patterns of ethical behavior over time should not establish a level of trust between me and those whom I serve. It absolutely is important this occurs. But because systems of transparency are in place, I am accountable to anyone and everyone. It seems that the way we ensure that authority is working is not by blind trust, but rather transparency.

SUMMARY

In dysfunctional churches, the real authority and power bases are frequently informal, unelected, and unaccountable. Concerns for the character and behavior of the leaders are held behind closed doors in confidential meetings, without the full transparency of the church. Decisions are made by a small clique of the powerful, and the layperson is kept out of loop. Often the behaviors of the leaders do not measure up to biblical standards. Their authority is lorded over people. People are abused, controlled, and managed, rather than loved, released, and supported. This should never be trusted.

This leg of the trellis helps to maintain a dysfunctional environment that can enable abuse. So, too, does the second leg: *Unwanted Conflict*.

4.2

Unwanted Conflict

What is causing the quarrels and fights among you? Don't they come from the evil desires at war within you?

—James, the brother of Jesus (Jas 4:1)

Peace is not absence of conflict; it is the ability to handle conflict by peaceful means.

—Ronald Reagan[1]

Peace for our time.

—Neville Chamberlain

It is one of the news reels that I remember very vividly from documentaries about World War II. (Do we use Roman numerals about our wars to make them somehow more grand, important, meaningful?) It is September 30, 1938. Stepping off the plane, having just arrived back from Germany and waving a document in his hand, there stands Neville Chamberlain—triumphant. "Peace" he declares. It was the Anglo-German Declaration, a document which ceded the Sudeten German territory to Germany. What makes this scene so memorable for me is how

---

1. Reagan, "Address at Commencement Exercises at Eureka College," para. 24.

quickly it all went south for Europe from there. Less than a year later, World War II was on for young and old alike.

This declaration is given as a classic example of appeasement, that diplomatic process of making concessions to a bullying aggressor nation in the hopes that, by conceding now, it will prevent war later. History has not been kind to Mr. Chamberlain. There have been recent attempts to let him and the other politicians of his day off the hook a bit[2], but by and large appeasement, as a way of keeping the peace, is seen as a failed strategy. There is good reason for this. Bullies and aggressors do not respect meekness. "If you back down now, you'll back down later, so give me Sudetenland now, and I'll take Poland later. What are you going to do about it!?"

"Blessed are the peacemakers," says Jesus, and I think too often, for far too many churches, this is translated to mean "Blessed are the peacekeepers, it is more blessed to appease than oppose."

And I understand why this is the fact. We are the church, the people of God, loving and forgiving and kind and nice. We don't argue, we don't yell, we don't have conflict, because if we did it would look bad. We have Jesus and the gospel and hope. People wouldn't think we loved Jesus if we were having conflict. If they thought we were angry with each other they wouldn't stay. And in the evangelical church there is this enormous unspoken pressure that comes with being self-proclaimed evangelicals. We *have* to win people to Jesus. I kind of liken the pressure we put on ourselves subconsciously to win people to Jesus to the pressure I had when I was working as a travelling sales representative for an electronics firm. You know the ABCs of sales: "Always Be Closing." I was under constant pressure to be making the sale, presenting my products and my company and my service as being better than that of the other guys. If my customers or my competitors knew that our company was having internal conflict and turmoil this would hurt sales. So, keep the peace, rather than make it. Don't air your dirty laundry. Put on a happy face, no matter what. Too often I fear this is also the case for churches.

Then there are the words of James 4:1:

> What is the source of quarrels and conflicts among you? Is the source not your pleasures that wage war in your body's parts?

---

2. I.e., appeasement in those days gave the British time to prepare for a war they never could wage in 1938 for instance.

I think some Christians believe that to argue or fight or have conflict or even differences of opinion is somehow a sin. Imagine I want the sanctuary carpet blue and have a pretty good reason for it, and Mr. Jones wants it grey and he has a pretty good reason for it. I can suppress my natural inclination to argue my point out of a misguided understanding of that verse in James, which has me thinking my desires are sinful and so I should always give in. I have kept the peace; I look humble, but can be seething on the inside, because once again Mr. Jones got his way. (There is a Mr. Jones in every church who always gets what he wants!)

We tend to avoid conflict because we think it makes Jesus look bad, or we avoid conflict because we think standing up for our differing opinions is sinful, but in a culture where conflict is avoided, this dysfunction can prop up abuse and abusive leaders.

But being conflict-averse is really just an attempt to avoid the reality that in a world full of diverse people with diverse opinions, conflict is inevitable and can in some cases be profitable. Often, in some sorts of conflicts, the negotiating process of coming to a solution is beneficial in terms of personal growth, understanding, and empathy, character traits that may not develop without this conflict. As the Proverbs say "iron sharpens iron" (Prov 27:17), and not without a few sparks along the way.

And I honestly don't think anyone is buying the conflict-averse, peace-at-all-costs, appease-don't-oppose kind of culture that can exist in our churches. It stinks of phoniness, and you can smell it a mile away. People are just as repulsed by the fake peace that exists in our churches as they would be by full-scale war. It's just that we think appeasement looks more like Jesus than the other, so rather than be honest with our conflict we play these foolish games.

It isn't the conflict that is necessarily the problem, but the way we handle it (or fail to handle it) that is the real issue. Conflict resulting from evil desires, then handled badly by full-scale war, is evil, edifies no one, and grieves Jesus. However, there may be other conflicts that are not the product of evil desires, but the result of natural differences of temperament and personality type. Sweeping these differences under the carpet in a conflict-avoiding attempt at peace benefits no one either. This is equally dysfunctional for a church, and can prop up abusive systems and keep abusive people in power. Let's see how that can happen.

Consider the hypothetical example of Bob, who leads the music team at church. Bob is what we would call a difficult person. He speaks aggressively with people and is in constant conflict over his actions and language with people. He has a seemingly obsessive need to be in control of everything he touches. His common interaction with people is the manipulative tactic of false guilt.

Using this tactic, Bob is constantly letting people know how they are failing to live up to *his* standard of musicianship, failing to play the music the way he thinks they should, criticizing people when they are brave enough to offer suggestions that might improve the music for the day because *he* is in charge and you should not be questioning him. Any suggestion he didn't come up with is seen as attempting to undermine his authority. People walk on eggshells around him. Conflict exists because his behavior *is* abusive.

Dealing with someone like Bob can leave people feeling anxious and guilty all the time; often offended, but they choose to stay silent and just take it. Why?

Firstly, because abuse is being used by Bob as a conflict management strategy. Differences of opinion about music and style is legitimate conflict. Abusing people to get your way is not a legitimate means of dealing with it. Bob is objectifying others seeing them as objects to use or obstacles to overcome. In dysfunctional organizations there is no language for, understanding of, or a willingness to deal with abuse. It too easily gets confused with conflict.

And secondly, these people have a history with Bob that tells them that they can never win an argument with him. They just conclude they should be humble and submit to his authority. And the music ministry is really good and people don't want to upset that. The music team has learned that if they say something, they might get kicked off the team. For them it is easier to appease than oppose. What they really are doing is avoiding conflict to avoid the inevitable abuse. They"ll just keep the peace. Failing to face conflict well or call out abusive behavior props up an abusive leader.

PEACEKEEPING VS PEACEMAKING

What is the difference between peacekeeping and peacemaking? It is easy to think they are the same thing because on the surface, they both are producing the same outcome—the absence of war. But in reality, the difference is like night and day. In simple terms, peacekeeping is about law and fear and latent anxiety, and peacemaking is about grace and love and peace.

In peacekeeping, both parties cease hostilities, or choose to not enter into hostilities because of fear of retribution and adherence to a set of declared (or undeclared) truce agreements (laws). Take the United Nations peacekeeping forces in conflict zones around the globe. Those troops are there because real peace isn't. Both parties are in a state of unresolved conflict, a Cold War if you will. They get a neutral party to stand in between them because they know that without the troops, they would be at each other all over again.

Peacekeeping is what is going on in North and South Korea. The two nations are officially still at war, but have chosen to keep the peace by submitting to a UN-sponsored cease-fire. A DMZ separates the two countries, laws are in place to prevent violations, and each party has sufficient arms and powerful friends (in the case of South Korea, the US; and in the case of North Korea, China and a nascent nuclear program) to keep the other guy honest. Fear and the law keep the two parties apart, but there is no real peace.

So with the case of Bob, people keep the peace because of how he might retaliate (fear), or because the leaders of the church told you that you have to submit to authority (law). Or in a classic form of (mis)using Matthew 18 to keep the troops in line, you are told, "If he offends you, go speak to him privately." But personal history has shown that just leads to further abuse by Bob. "He always has a way of using false guilt to make me feel like I am at fault for feeling offended. I'd rather avoid seeing him one-on-one. (Quite frankly I'm scared of him. He is, after all, a bully!) I'll say nothing and keep the peace."

Peacekeeping, therefore, is about the law and fear. In this case the law with Bob is *Unquestionable Power and Authority*, and the fear is what he will do if you speak to him. You have come to a truce. Here we see two parts of the trellis working beautifully together, *Unquestionable Power and Authority* and *Unwanted Conflict*. There is no arguing and fighting, everybody "gets along" doing their ministry for Jesus, the veneer of peace is on display, the abuser is propped up in his abuse, and nobody is doing anything about it because it might look bad. But at least we have kept the peace.

There is also the potential of conflict as a result of someone coming along with new ideas, creative approaches to intractable problems, or just stepping out of the groupthink and proposing things be viewed differently. "Time for a new vision, a new mission," someone might say. This can threaten the homeostasis and the *Unquestionable Power and*

Authority, especially if the person in charge disagrees or if it's not their idea in the first place.

Edwin H. Friedman, in his book *A Failure of Nerve*, observes that organizations that have a peace-at-all-costs approach are ultimately run by what he calls peace-mongers. He has observed the following as a universal law of leadership:

> In any type of institution whatsoever, when a self-directed, imaginative, energetic, or creative member is being consistently frustrated and sabotaged rather than encouraged and supported, what will turn out to be true one hundred percent of the time, regardless of whether the disrupters are supervisors, subordinates, or peers, is that the person at the very top of that institution is a peace-monger. By that I mean a highly anxious risk-avoider, someone who is more concerned with good feelings than with progress, someone whose life revolves around the axis of consensus, a 'middler,' someone who is so incapable of taking well-defined stands that his 'disability' seems to be genetic, someone who functions as if she has been filleted of her backbone, someone who treats conflict or anxiety like mustard gas—one whiff, on goes the emotional gas mask, and he flits. Such leaders are often 'nice,' if not charming.[3]

"Nice people," "terrified of conflict," "risk-averse," or "peace-mongers" do not sound like qualifications for leadership, and yet often these are temperaments that are found in leadership teams. Now "risk-averse" does not mean that nothing gets done, but only that the things that get done are what the *Unquestionable Power and Authority* wants, what Friedman calls the person at the very top. The rest are not prepared to challenge or propose anything different because of an observed history of what happens to anyone who steps out of line. They learn their lesson soon enough. The *Unquestionable Power and Authority* is risk-averse to anything they don't want, or which wasn't their idea, and the people are risk-averse to challenge those at the top.

The self-directed "disrupters," as Friedman calls them, do not have to be a person as such, but it can be a position in the church. For instance, in dysfunctional organizations the role of pastor itself, no matter who fills it, can be seen as disruptive, so every time a new pastor is called, the position is sabotaged. If he/she becomes (or is) too well differentiated and creative this can be seen as a threat to the system. It is common for

---

3. Friedman, *Failure of Nerve*, 14–15.

new pastors in new roles to be full of enthusiasm, vision, insight, new ideas, and ways of moving the church forward. In dysfunctional organizations, the *Unquestionable Power and Authority*, the peace-monger, can feel threatened, be risk-averse, and then act in ways that sabotage the new pastor. It's not long before the new pastor is declared to be "not a team player" or "not one of us." Any church that is constantly churning through pastors might be evidence of just this thing that Friedman is talking about.

This helps explain why the person at the top, the ultimate power and authority, puts up with the abuse of someone like Bob. Bob is getting things done. Bob is not threatening the homeostasis. He isn't innovative or a disrupter. He is playing within the rules of the game, that is, doing what the *Unquestionable Power and Authority* approves of (great ministry). And the fallout of the abuse? Just a minor hiccup that can be managed. Bob isn't a threat to their power base so Bob isn't sabotaged. Bob is enabled. Abuse thrives.

Peacemaking is an entirely different proposition. As opposed to peacekeeping, it is the path of blessing, which by definition must mean that, as we have seen in the case of Bob, peacekeeping is the path of cursing. No group of abused people can be called a blessed people, I don't care how big or glorious the ministries of the church might look.

> Peacemakers are people who breathe grace. They draw continually on the goodness and power of Jesus Christ, and then they bring his love, mercy, forgiveness, strength and wisdom to the conflicts of daily life. God delights to breathe his grace through peacemakers and use them to dissipate anger, improve understanding, promote justice, and encourage repentance and reconciliation.[4]

Now what I like about what Ken Sande is doing here is that he is recognizing the reality that conflicts exist in daily life and that the Christian response to conflict is honesty:

- An honest recognition that conflict exists and is inevitable;
- An honest admission that I often have a part in the conflict (the proverbial log in my own eye); and
- An honest recognition that we spend a lot of time peacekeeping when we are called to peacemaking.

---

4. Sande, *Peace Maker*, 11.

I want to explore that last idea for a moment, because contrary to what we think we are doing by appeasing (we think we are making Jesus look good), what we are really doing is saying that God's ways of honest confession, repentance, forgiveness, and reconciliation don't work and we have to come up with a solution that does. Failing to call out abusive behaviors or handle the conflict that often accompanies it according to God's principles is insulting to him. It makes Jesus look bad. It fails to glorify him and speaks volumes to those who observe. You are more likely to win people to Christ by open, honest, authentic conflict resolution, which includes all the graces just listed, than by pretending we are all getting along when the place stinks of the fact that we aren't. Ask any church member who is prepared to be honest about what it is like to be in a church that has swept conflict under the carpet in the name of peace and Jesus. The pride of it all just stinks.

And then just imagine what it would look like, if people who have been abusive or in severe conflict stand up publicly, and deal with their conflict openly, confess, repent, and forgive one another openly. This humble expression of truth and transparency gives God all the glory and rips pride out of the conflict. The sad thing is I have seen open hostility in secular organizations handled better than in the church, and that should never be so.

Here is where pride raises its ugly head. Ken Sande helpfully looks at three different responses to conflict when it arises. Fight (attack), flight (escape), or glorify God. Obviously, you know the one he is arguing for. However, pride sits at the heart of both other responses.

In conflict-averse organizations, the fight response is avoided at all costs. Open conflict could not look any less like Jesus, we say, so we bury and suppress any form of fighting. Fighting and arguing aggressively for our positions (as we have seen from Jas 4:1) is seen as akin to pride. If I use slander and gossip, or even worse, physical intimidation or whatever, these are seen as clear and evident signs of pride. "I'll take you to court if I have to," someone might respond. Or, "I am right and I will fight to the death anyone who is going to argue against me." Certainly such responses lack humility, and this behavior surely is unbecoming of a Christian or a church, and so we suppress this form of response (and rightly so) to conflict in most churches. But we still can be aggressive. Since overt aggression is clearly inappropriate, the fighting can take the form of manipulations via passive-aggressive or covert-aggressive behaviors in an attempt try to hide what is really going on. This enables people who use these tactics to get their way (see the example of Bob above), leaving a wake of hurt and disgruntled people along the way.

Or we can simply suppress the urge to fight and just flee. But fleeing in the face of conflict requires just as much pride as standing your ground aggressively, and this seems counterintuitive. Wasn't Jesus a lamb led to the slaughter? He opened not his mouth; isn't this what we are called to?

C. S. Lewis said a humble person "will not be thinking about humility: he will not be thinking of himself at all."[5] Jesus kept his mouth shut for others, not himself. When we flee conflict rather than face it well, it has the appearance of humility, but it is really all about us. I want to deny the existence of my legitimate concerns, or, like Jonah, we will run away rather than face our own shortcomings and biases—both of the responses are self-preservation responses, which are ultimately about us. We are still thinking about ourselves and not the glory of God, which is found in real peacemaking and real, honest, authentic airings of grievances and opinions. Perhaps I don't push my point because I don't really want people to see what I have to say. "What if I'm wrong?" you might ask. "I don't really matter anyway." Suggesting my opinion does not matter is as much about pride as demanding my opinion is all that matters, because it is still focused on self—self-relief or self-preservation.

In healthy churches, we understand that a realistic recognition of the existence of conflict eliminates the ability for abusers to get off the hook. An honest, open, transparent airing of conflict aids others as well as ourselves. It leaves abusers with nowhere to hide. In a healthy organization, all opinions are welcomed and heard, modified and changed if incorrect, or accepted and used if correct; and regardless, our identity and purpose are not wrapped up in what we think or what others think of us. If I am being abused and it is aired publicly, others are protected. Beware of any church or group of church leaders that wants to resolve allegations of abuse or important and major conflicts behind closed doors in confidential meetings. This has more to do with control and fear of conflict than it does resolution. Beware of the church that says (or acts like) it either has no dirty laundry or refuses to let it out to air. This is a sign of a conflict-averse organization that provides the prop for abusive behaviors to continue. Dirty laundry is meant to be aired, otherwise it simply festers and rots.

---

5. Lewis, *Mere Christianity*, 108.

Can you imagine Jesus telling the leaders of the church to keep conversations about a potential wolf or a real wolf in the flock a secret behind closed doors? Failing to adequately address wolves in the church props up abuse, does a huge disservice to the flock, is in direct contradiction to the clear teachings of Jesus (Luke 12:25–48), and is dysfunctional sin. There is an unhealthy agenda going on in such churches which has more to do with control, fear and, peacekeeping rather than peacemaking.

In peacekeeping churches, there is an undercurrent of never-ending anxiety, fear, and turmoil bubbling beneath the surface. Every so often it raises its head in full-blown conflict, but this is quickly swept away with appeals to Matthew 18. Consider the example of Bob. His behavior is abusive and controlling. It needs to be named as such and dealt with. He needs to be honestly confronted with his sin as well as the possibly sinful reactions that we may have had to it. But too often none of this occurs. In the dysfunctional church, *Unquestionable Power and Authority* (his and the leadership who refuse to face reality) and *Unwanted Conflict* are working in tandem to keep an abuser in control and the sheep cowering. Reaching healthy reconciliation gives glory to God. It is what the church is actually called to.

SUMMARY

In this chapter, I have considered how being a conflict-averse community is a leg of a trellis that props up dysfunctions that can enable abuse. Conflict is inevitable and unpleasant, and yet the potential for a community to grow into Christlikeness in the midst of conflict is an opportunity and a grace which can be exercised by wise people. Sweeping conflict and conflicting issues under the carpet or clamping down on conflict out of fear, anxiety, and/or the need for control sets up a community to be abused.

There is a third leg of this trellis that can set up a community to allow abuse to thrive: *Unity above All*.

4.3

Unity above All

UNQUESTIONABLE POWER AND AUTHORITY and *Unwanted Conflict* provide two important parts of a trellis that will support abuse in the local church. The third is equally important in sustaining a stable abusive organization and that is *Unity above All*.

Now what you will find interesting about churches that are big on unity is that they will never (or rarely) openly declare that unity is above all. They might declare unity is as important as everything else, but never better than everything else, and yet what they say and what they do become pretty obvious as soon as conflict raises its ugly head.

Let's go back to our beleaguered Bob again for a moment. His behavior is abusive, he mistreats people, and they get hurt. But the system props him up. His authority is unquestionable, as is the conflict-averse leadership group who keeps him there. No one wants to bring up the issue because that would cause an ugly conflict with not only him and the leadership group, but those people who think "He's doing a good job, so just let it be. Forgive and forget and all that. Besides if we have a big argument it will break the unity of the church and the ministry might end. We all have to be united, so you'd better get in line."

Here you see how *Unity above All* is a close relative to *Unwanted Conflict*. Often the reason we don't want conflict is precisely because it would show we have no unity, and unity in dysfunctional churches is the top of the tree.

Now let's think about this for a moment because unity *is* important. In fact, it is so important that Jesus prayed for it. This tells me two things: one, it matters to Jesus that we have unity, and two, it is always going to

Unity above All

be under threat, otherwise, he wouldn't have been praying for it. Unity matters. Then there are the obvious words of Amos 3:3—"Do two walk together unless they have agreed to do so?" And that weird and wonderful word picture of Psalm 133:1–3: "How good and pleasant it is when God's people live together in unity!" The psalm is full of rich metaphors, with oil, Aaron's beard, and dew on Mount Hermon. Even if you don't understand the cultural images, they must be something good because the writer is so effusive about them. Whatever it means, it is good and it is the place of God's blessing. Unity is really important and we as church people should strive for it and seek it as the place of the blessing of God.

Frequently well-meaning and sentimental leaders of churches encourage their people to unity because they are told it makes the gospel look good and Jesus look good, and if we can have unity it shows the world that the gospel is powerful, because all these disparate types of people are all getting along. The opposite is then mentioned to also be true. If we have no unity within our church, Jesus looks bad, the church looks bad, and the gospel looks ineffective and people won't see love. This is a powerful motivator for good people who don't want any of that. And to some extent this is in fact true. Unity is a good look for a church, no doubt.

Most often when a church speaks about unity, they mean, basically, getting along with each other, where "each other" is interpreted to mean those who call that particular local branch of the church home. It means agreeing with the purpose of the mission and vision of the church and just doing what it takes to get along with everyone so that the mission can be achieved. Unity means everybody rowing together, even with people you don't like, even difficult people. You have to have unity with *those* people. This shows love. Unity does mean this, of course, and it really is vital if a church wants to achieve it missional goals. But did you ever notice how this idea of unity rarely extends to those outside the building? The world outside of the church (the unsaved, if you will) see little and care even less about disharmony in the local church despite what we tell ourselves. What they do see however is all those churches that don't get along. If what we say is true for those within our walls, and if we place such a high premium on unity, and if having unity is about love and Jesus and the gospel, as we tell ourselves, then why does it not extend to those outside our walls? For instance, why isn't the local Baptist church in unity with the local Catholic church? I would like to suggest that intra-church unity would do more for the gospel and love and Jesus than inter-church unity ever could.

Now this isn't some call for ecumenicalism, because the reason there is no unity between churches, who in their own walls place such a high premium on it, is because unity, whether we mention it to ourselves or not, is more specific than that. We have to have a certain type of unity and we know it.

We know truth, love, and unity are important, but although love and truth are absolutes, unity is not. Churches choose (and rightly so in my view) to have no unity with cults and sects. The church has no unity with Mormonism or Jehovah's Witnesses because truth matters, it's an absolute. The church chooses to break unity with those who deny what we see to be inviolable truths. And why? For the sake of Jesus and love and the gospel, the very reasons we tell ourselves within our walls why we should not have disunity! And surely, to break unity, or never have unity, with those who trample truth is an act of love, is it not? Isn't it loving to our flock to protect them from untruths, and loving to those who believe a lie, to let them know so that they might have the hope of walking out of darkness into light (2 John 6)?

It can be a loving thing to do to break unity (or maybe even better to acknowledge the lack of unity in the first place) for the sake of truth and love and Jesus, because the unity we are called to for love and Jesus and the gospel is a unity around truth and love *first*. To have unity within a church we must have a unity that is filtered through the ideas of inviolable truth and absolute love. Love, truth, and unity do not stand on equal terms.

Love everyone, stand for truth, be united in those things. Do not be united with those who do not love, nor be united with those who hold to untruths. In fact, there is, by definition, no biblical unity without absolute love and truth. Not, *it is unloving to have disunity*, but rather disunity exists when you are not walking in love, and, by definition, those who abuse are not walking in love and hence not walking in truth (1 John 1:6–7; 3:15). The abuse *is the dis-unifying behavior,* not the unwillingness to tolerate it or to name it and call it out. Too often in dysfunctional churches that are enabling abuse they get this backwards.

Unity is a noun that has no meaning without an adjective. Take the word quality for instance. There was a time when the word quality on its own used to mean something good. You might purchase quality furniture, or a quality vehicle, and you would be talking about products with fine, old-world craftsmanship, fine stitching, and which were engineered precisely. The word quality meant "good" quality, with the "good" being inferred. But the word "quality" doesn't really mean "good," it just means the attributes or standards of a thing. To know what those attributes are requires the use of an adjective, like "good," "poor," or whatever.

So, too, with unity, because without an adjectival qualifier we don't know what kind of unity we are talking about, and this makes a world of difference. Nazi Germany had unity (by and large) around race and destiny and the Fatherland. But I don't think this is the kind of unity we want in our church. And the Pharisees had unity around purity laws and the resurrection and legalism and their opposition to Christ. Surely we don't want that kind of unity.

The adjective I think we should be using when it comes to unity in the church is Biblical Christian Unity and this means a specific set of things:

- Unity around the gospel
- Unity around truth
- Unity around love

UNITY AROUND THE GOSPEL

The reformers could not have unity with the Catholic Church because as these reformers read their Bibles their understanding of the Scripture caused them to understand that the authority in the church rested not with men, but in Scripture alone. The 5 Solas are how we describe their rallying cry and the thing around which they were united: salvation by Grace Alone, through Faith Alone, according to Scripture Alone, in Christ Alone, to the glory of God Alone. The gospel is a precious treasure, entrusted to the church, because the simple propositional truths of the life, death, and resurrection and soon return of Jesus Christ for the sin of mankind is mankind's only hope. It is the power of God unto salvation and it is important that we preserve it, keep it, and remain united in proclaiming it and protecting it.

UNITED AROUND TRUTH

By truth I don't just mean the Bible as the core of God's revealed truth, or Jesus as the way the truth and the life (which absolutely we must believe), but truth in the sense of living lives of honest, authentic, transparent accountability, keeping and having no secrets. In some churches, leadership is prepared to sacrifice truth for the sake of unity; not outright lies so much as partial truths. Out of fear that they might spook the horses (the community of believers) if they knew the full truth of one thing or another, they might from time to time gloss over the real truth, put a spin on it, to make them look good. It's the behavior of politicians, spinning the truth to maintain the veneer of a unified government, and calling that leadership. Lies by omission to keep the peace and maintain unity, which means that, rather than telling the truth about abusive behavior amongst themselves, they will speak of difficult behavior, bad decisions, and other such partial truths. These things have the veneer of telling the truth, but really were designed to manipulate, control, and manage the image and impression the church has of them as a community, and the leaders as a group. This is dysfunctional and abusive.

We should be united around the truths about our failings and foibles, our weaknesses and wants, our joys and our sorrows, our doubts and questions. Too often the unspoken rule of a community is that once you are a Christian all of your problems have gone away and now you have to pretend to be happy and faithful and joyful all the time. No place for doubt, no place for sorrow. There can often be no place to have open, authentic conversations about your struggles with sin or addiction or childlessness or whatever. Put on your Jesus mask and welcome to church. Too often we are united around the portrayal of these false selves.

UNITED IN LOVE

This is a topic for a book in its own right, and can be rightly argued to be the most important of the three and the thing that ties the other two together. The most loving thing I can do is be honest with you. The most loving thing I can do is to bring the gospel to bear on the pains and trials of your life.

Jesus, in John 13:34–35, says our love for one another is the distinguishing mark of the disciples of Jesus:

> I am giving you a new commandment, that you love one another; just as I have loved you, that you also love one another. By this all *people* will know that you are My disciples: if you have love for one another.

Notice we will be known by our love, not by our unity. Unity is an example of love, but not the fullness of it. And it isn't a suggestion, it's a command: "Love one another." It would have been easier I think if Jesus had commanded us to flap our arms and fly. We are commanded to be Nike lovers—just do it. Given its importance and given how hard I can be to love, it is clear that this is something that the church should be united in fighting for—a community of people that love one another.

Now what is remarkable about this is that Jesus is effectively giving us the authority to determine who his disciples are. Love will mark them; love will distinguish them. "Love in a certain way and you will be clearly marked as my disciple," says Jesus. "Fail to love like this and it is right to question." But united in loving how? Romans 12:9–13 is good place to start:

> Love *must be* free of hypocrisy. Detest what is evil; cling to what is good. *Be* devoted to one another in brotherly love; give preference to one another in honor, not lagging behind in diligence, fervent in spirit, serving the Lord; rejoicing in hope, persevering in tribulation, devoted to prayer, contributing to the needs of the saints, practicing hospitality.

Sincere love looks like those things above at a bare minimum. What is interesting to note are a couple things that Paul says here.

Firstly, when I live my life in the fullness of devotion to God it enables me to love *you* well.

1. I love you well when I serve God with zeal;
2. I love you well when I rejoice in hope;
3. I love you well when I endure tribulation; and
4. I love you well when I am a prayer warrior.

I am empowered to love you well, and you are empowered to love me well, despite the relative unloveliness of each other, when we are walking in close service with and in zeal for the Lord. Through the practices of prayer, in the light of the hope of eternity, and through patient endurance in suffering, Christlike character is developed in me, which enables me to become the genuine lover of others that God calls me to be.

Secondly, note that it is loving for me to abhor evil (Rom 12:9). And make no mistake about it, abuse of any form in the church is evil. The most genuinely loving thing I can do when it comes to abuse is to call it out and deal with the trellis that supports and enables it. Too often we hold fast to the trellis that enables abuse rather than holding fast to what is good. We are called to be united in dismantling systems that support abuse. This is loving, to you and each other, and demonstrates we are the disciples of Christ.

Finally, there can be no unity without humility, united around the gospel, truth, and love in humility. This is Biblical Christian Unity.

These are the words of Paul in Phil 2:2–3:

> make my joy complete by being of the same mind, maintaining the same love, united in spirit, intent on one purpose. Do nothing from selfishness or empty conceit, but with humility consider one another as more important than yourselves.

Notice how many times he emphasizes unity in this passage: "same love," "same mind," "full accord," "one mind." Do you think he has a point?

What Paul is calling his church to is unity in purpose and mission. Not a uniformity where we all look and think and act the same, but like rowers in a scull we are all pulling together with the same goal and purpose in mind, with Jesus as the coxswain calling us and urging us forward.

Like I have said before, unity is important. It is an imperative, it does matter, but notice his point: a biblical Christian unity has its basis in humility, as demonstrated by Jesus himself. No selfish ambition, no conceit, considering the other person of greater value than yourself. This is the mind of Jesus. And there is no biblical Christian unity without it.

There can be no real love without humility. The self-emptying person becomes the person who, abandoning the focus on themselves, now has room to allow others to enter, not to use for their own self-gratification, but to nurture, care for, empathize with. In a word: love. Only the self-emptying have room in themselves to love well. The more of you that you find in you, the less room you have to love. Self-emptying is the exact antithesis of the abuser.

Those who abuse fail these two unifying tests. They do not stand in the truth, nor do they live lives of self-emptying sacrifice. The narcissistic tendencies within the abuser by definition mean they are not empty of the self, but rather are full of self, full of themselves, and as such they cannot love and therefore cannot be in unity with the body of believers. There can be no unity, says Paul, without humility.

The abuser is only in unity with him/herself. He/she is not in unity with Christ, and not in unity with the church. They fail the tests of unity. They fail to love the Lord with all their heart and their neighbor as themselves. They don't walk in truth and they don't walk in love, and therefore, by definition, are not in unity with the body of local believers. Calling that out did not break the fellowship—there was no fellowship in the first place.

Humility is recognition of your own power and strength and choosing to lay it aside for the betterment of others. This is what Jesus did, this is love. He who had it all laid it down for those who had nothing. True biblical Christian unity starts with this: people humbly laying down their lives for the sake of the gospel, speaking and living out truthful, authentic lives together, all in the name of love. This is the church in which we are called to have unity, and this is what we call the fellowship of the saints. These are the things around which we should be united.

But in dysfunctional organizations that enable abuse, the leaders lead with an iron fist, they have *Unquestionable Power and Authority*, and those that are abused refuse to speak up because of the fear of *Unwanted Conflict*, and by keeping quiet, *Unity above All* is achieved. This is an unhealthy trellis of dysfunctions that keeps and supports abusive leaders and others within a church. It is not loving, it is not honest, it is not humble, and it is definitely not Jesus. Church should never be like this. Too often, because of the trellis, it is.

Churches will often say exactly this, that unity is as important as truth and love. What I have hoped to show is that when we inadvertently elevate unity it ends up exalting itself above the other two, and truth and love end up being sacrificed for the veneer of unity and peace. Unity as an idea cannot support the weight of increasing its importance like that. It gets a little pride in itself and unity then exalts itself over everything.

But there is no real unity, just a group of disgruntled, mumbling, murmuring people, feeling the oppression of the dysfunction but often unable to name it, afraid to raise their heads above the crowd lest they have it bitten off. And as I have also said before, this need not be all-of-church stuff. It need not be the elders or pastors. It can be the ministry head or gardener or one of the ushers on a power trip. But in the church, where these dysfunctions exist, this trellis supports and maintains abuse in all of its forms. It must be dismantled.

If there is no commitment to biblical Christian unity, but just a "We are all going to get along" kind of unity, because Jesus prayed for it and it looks loving, then we will be prepared to sacrifice truth, the gospel, or love on the altar of unity. Abuse is allowed to continue and people remain hurt.

Too many churches use the biblical concept of unity too sentimentally. When we ask people to tolerate the intolerable, without passing the nature, actions, and character of those who abuse through the filter of love and truth, we enable the abuser. John Murray has said, "Where there is disloyalty to Christ, tolerance is not love but perverted sentiment."[1] People may be well-meaning, yes, but this is still dangerous.

Worse still is the linking of unity to love, Jesus, and the gospel such that the unity card is used in a spiritually abusive way by those who seek to maintain unity at all costs, even at the cost of banishing, not the abuser, but the whistleblower themselves. Sometimes this is done intentionally, other times naively, but abuse in any form, be it spiritual or otherwise, is still abuse and must be named as such in the church. Unsuspecting good pastors may be unwittingly spiritually abusing their flock by demanding they remain united with one whose very actions and character demonstrate they were never part of us in the first place, all in the name of unity, love, Jesus, and the gospel.

We are to care for, love, and serve one another, even the difficult and unlovable amongst us, and the primary way we do this is by constantly applying the tests of truth and love. Calls to unity for the sake of misguided sentiment leads to further disunity, abuse, and harm. The loving, unifying thing for the church is to see, name, and deal with abuse in all its forms.

SUMMARY

In this section I have looked at the three major dysfunctions that can enable abuse. The first is *Unquestionable Power and Authority*, where leaders of the church are not held to account in any meaningful way by any overseeing body with any teeth to act, and/or the members are cowed into thinking it is not their place to hold the leadership accountable. This is most common in autonomous churches, even if they are part of a larger denomination.

The second is *Unwanted Conflict*. In dysfunctional churches which enable abuse, conflict is avoided at all costs because to be in conflict is deemed to make the church look bad and bring dishonor to Christ.

Lastly is *Unity above All*. This is a close relative of *Unwanted Conflict*. When unity is elevated to the level of being as important as love and

---

1. Murray, "Love and Its Correlatives," para. 12.

truth, when unity is seen as a principal issue with respect to the gospel, then out of fear of breaking unity people are prepared to keep abuse and abusive behaviors quiet, swept under the carpet and ignored.

These three things will most likely exist to some extent in the dysfunctional church which enables abuse.

5

Shallow Roots
(On What Does It Rely?)

GOOD SOIL, VIABLE SEED, and a trellis on which to grow the plant are all vital ingredients if you want to grow a good crop. Arguably the most important part of any plant is its root system. Some years ago, I planted a native tree in my back yard. It grew quickly and put on healthy leaves and shoots. It was a model of health. But the soil around here is rocky, and the tree grew taller than its roots could sustain. All it took was one big wind one summer and over it went. Shallow roots were the tree's undoing,

What I want to demonstrate in the next few chapters is that like a shallow-rooted tree which is at risk, there are a range of shallow theologies that leave churches at risk. Dysfunctional churches that enable abuse can exhibit these shallow theologies, theologies that can leave churches susceptible to abuse and abusers.

These are shallow theologies of

- Forgiveness
- Character Assessment
- Pastoral Care
- Discipline

5.1

Shallow Theology of Forgiveness

To be a Christian means to forgive the inexcusable because God has forgiven the inexcusable in you.

—C. S. Lewis[1]

Be kind to one another, tender-hearted, forgiving one another, as God in Christ forgave you.

—Eph 4:32 ESV

It is axiomatic to say that Christians are to forgive. It is part of the new command of Jesus to love one another, or to be, as Paul puts it, "tender hearted." The church and its people should be noted for their forgiving of one another. It should stand out as a hallmark of the church, be a beacon of light to an unforgiving world, and stamp us as God's children, representing his kingdom in a kingdom of darkness. And the motive, says Paul, is humble recognition that Christ has forgiven you.

He, the Savior of the world who knew no sin, is prepared to forgive the most heinous of crimes against his divine majesty. How then can we—fallen, failing, feeble, and fallible—refuse to forgive others who have sinned against us? Our crimes against Christ are of an infinite magnitude greater than any sin against us. If Christ can forgive us, shall we not

---

1. Lewis, *Weight of Glory*, 108.

forgive others? Is this not the meaning of the parable in Matt 18:23–35? Are not his words, "My heavenly Father will also do the same to you, if each of you does not forgive his brother from your heart" (Matt 18:35) sobering reminders of our responsibility to be a forgiving people?

Loving people learn and become ready to forgive even the most heinous of offenses. Loving people, however, do not overlook. If the church should be known by its love and forgiveness (John 13:35), it also should be known by its ability to apologize well, repent, and seek to make amends when harm has been done. Sadly, too often those latter graces are often lacking. We as church people emphasize love and forgiveness (and rightly so) as hallmarks of our faith. So, too, should we emphasize repentance and apologies as equal hallmarks of our faith. The church should be seen to be the kinds of people who know how to say "I'm sorry, how can I make this right with you?" and repair the damage our actions can cause. That would demonstrate the kind of love by which, says Jesus, we will be known. To demand someone forgive without concomitant repentance by the offender is not loving to the offender or the offended, and the world sees it.

What I want to explore here is that, given that forgiveness is so core to our lives as Christians, how is it that it can be used to sustain a dysfunctional and abusive organization? If we have an incomplete, shallow theology of forgiveness it can lead to the enabling of abuse. This can be seen in three important ways:

- A theology that requires no repentance;
- A theology that is self-centric; and
- A theology that forgets justice.

A THEOLOGY THAT REQUIRES NO REPENTANCE

It starts with two little words: "Just forgive."

How many times have you heard this from a pastor or pastoral carer or someone in the church? You have been hurt and offended against, you complain about it to others, and the advice you are given is, "Just forgive."

What is often meant by this is the idea that since we are all sinners and nobody is perfect, you have to give people leeway. "Don't you remember that Jesus loves and forgives you? So, you have to love and forgive; put it behind you and just move on. 'Judge not lest ye be judged' (Matt 7:1). It is not your job to change people, it is God's business."

Matthew 18 says that if the offender doesn't repent treat him like a tax collector. And how did Jesus treat tax collectors? He just loved on them more. I want to say to you that you don't have to "just forgive." In fact, this shallow or inadequate idea of forgiveness is often at the root of many abusive systems. Yes, we are to forgive, but there is also a concomitant requirement for demonstrable, habitual, character-changing repentance on the part of the offender as part of that process.

Biblical forgiveness is something offered to the offender by the offended party. However, the unrepentant never enters the blessings of forgiveness. Just because forgiveness is offered does not mean the offended party is actually forgiven. To suggest otherwise is to misunderstand the gospel. The very words of John the Baptist and Jesus himself during their ministry started with the words "Repent, for the kingdom of God is at hand." To demand that we "just forgive" without the equal command to repent is to hold too shallow a view of forgiveness. It gets it half-right, and when we hold to this shallow view it helps to keep abuse alive. In fact, to demand the abused and offended forgive the unrepentant compounds the abuse. It is spiritually abusive in itself. Much pain and hurt is caused by this.

Why do I say this? Take, for example, the countless numbers of women who, when approaching their pastor about their abusive husband, are told to submit, love, and forgive. They are frequently counselled, "His behavior is a moral failure, but it is your duty to forgive." Often no requirement is made on the husband to repent of this behavior and she is told to return back into this abusive environment, to continually take a beating and forgive.

Rachael Denhollander, that brave and strong advocate for the rights of the abused, said it well in her victim impact statement at the sentencing of her abuser, Larry Nassar, the US Gymnastics doctor who also mistreated hundreds of other young girls over the course of twenty years:

> . . . if you have read the Bible you carry, you know forgiveness does not come from doing good things, as if good deeds can erase what you have done. It comes from repentance which requires facing and acknowledging the truth about what you have done in all of its utter depravity and horror without mitigation, without excuse . . .
>
> I pray you experience the soul crushing weight of guilt so you may someday experience true repentance and true

forgiveness from God, which you need far more than forgiveness from me—though I extend that to you as well.[2]

She gets it right about forgiveness, the abused that are healing and have healed usually do. Forgiveness must come this way, graciously given, never deserved, and only received by the broken and crushed, to those who feel the weight of their sin.

Placing a requirement on the offended or abused individual to forgive, without the offender confessing and repenting and acknowledging the impact of their sin on the offended party, is to place the onus of fixing the broken relationship solely on the victim, not the offender.

You may have heard it said from time to time that we are to forgive *unconditionally*, which is another way of saying *just forgive*. But although this is a very generous kind of sentiment, it has no biblical merit. It is based on misplaced sentimentality, a desire for everybody to just get along.[3] This requirement is common in churches, as we have seen, that place a high view on unity and peacekeeping. "Forgive, the unrepentant or you'll make Jesus look bad," they are told.

It takes about one second of reflection to realize how unbiblical this is. Does God forgive everyone unconditionally? Does he forgive *you* unconditionally? The answer is, of course, no. There is a condition for forgiveness; it is called repentance. To be told by well-meaning sentimentalists and conflict-averse peace-mongers that you have to forgive unconditionally is asking you to live up to a standard to which even God does not hold himself.

Jesus' interaction with Peter is telling here. When Peter asks how often he has to forgive (Matt 18), and Jesus, using hyperbole, tells him seventy times a day, it is under the proviso that your brother *repents* (Luke 17:3–4). We often forget that last bit, and focus only on the forgiving bit. Jesus never teaches unconditional forgiveness, just boundless forgiveness, and we must not confuse these two things.

This requirement to *just forgive*, in some cases, becomes spiritually abusive. Well-meaning, risk-averse, conflict-averse individuals may seek to control you by asking you to live up to a standard that exceeds biblical standards in order to demonstrate love. And if you don't forgive unconditionally, you are then deemed to be in a state of bitterness and sin and

---

2. Denhollander, "Read Rachael Denhollander's Full Victim Impact Statement," paras. 60–61.

3. See ch. 4.3.

and lacking in love. For the one caught in this trap, it is a painful abuse indeed. Tolerate the intolerable and give a free pass to those who don't repent or risk being seen as un-Christian. We must hold firm to the biblical theology that repentance is vital for forgiveness to occur.

True repentance is seen in not only a change of mind (the literal meaning of the word) but in demonstrable, long-term changes in behavior as a result of this changed thinking. And this takes time. For someone to say they have repented is one thing; to see the long-term changes being effected by this repentance is another. It does not happen overnight. A man who says he has repented of beating his wife demonstrates this by not beating her anymore and taking all the necessary steps required to do the internal heart work that helps him to understand why he chose that path of coping behavior, as well as seeking to make amends for all the harm caused to her and those who surround her. The truly repentant takes ownership of their part in the harm they have caused.

In a dysfunctional and abusive system, sin is never really repented of, apologies are given too easily, and the real weight and impact of sin and its offense on the offended is never really appreciated, sought, or understood. There are no empathetic attempts to understand ("How has my behavior impacted you?"), but simply the injunction "Just forgive." Failure to do so is considered a sign of bitterness, a lack of love, or some other such thing. Suddenly the offended is the offender. This is also abusive. A dysfunctional organization has then used a shallow view of forgiveness to perpetuate and maintain abuse.

A SELF-CENTRIC THEOLOGY

Frequently, popular ideas of forgiveness are focused on what it does for you, the forgiver, how it releases you from bitterness and contempt. For instance:

> The only way to heal the pain that will not heal itself is to forgive the person who hurt you. When you release the wrongdoer from the wrong, you cut a malignant tumor out of your inner life. You set a prisoner free, but you discover that the real prisoner was yourself.[4]

Or this oft-quoted sentiment:

---

4. Smedes, *Forgive and Forget*, 133.

> Unforgiveness is like drinking poison yourself and waiting for the other person to die.

And another:

> Human forgiveness is an internal series of decisions to release your own animosity, hatred, anger, fear and the desire for revenge against another, replacing these emotions with more benevolent feelings, including love.[5]

The problem with these ideas is they are so self-centric, as if forgiveness is *primarily* about us and what it does for us. But forgiveness is not primarily about us, the offended. It is primarily about the offender. It is primarily about releasing an offender from the debt they owe for the offense they have committed.

Imagine if I had run up a large number of traffic and parking infringements, and never bothered to pay the tickets. Finally, one day I am hauled before a judge, and he decides to let me go, to forgive me of the debt, and not require I pay it. Who would this benefit: The legal system, or me?

See, this is what forgiveness is about. When we sin or offend against God or man, we are in their debt, and forgiveness is about releasing us from the debt. The Greek word *tetelesti* is translated in our Bible as "it is finished" and are the words our Savior spoke from the cross. It was also the word written across business documents or financial receipts back in the first century to indicate the debt had been paid in full; the debt had been forgiven. This primarily benefits the debtor because it releases them from what was owed. A debt was owed and payment was made to settle the account—finished.

Here is what makes the gospel such good news! What the gospel reveals is that Jesus pays a debt we owe to a holy God whom we could never repay, and so our release from debt is entirely an act of grace, motivated by love. Think about God's forgiveness of us in Christ. To suggest that God is wounded by our sin, can't heal from it unless he forgives us to free himself of bad feelings, and sends Jesus to die on the cross in order that he might feel better is not only unbiblical, it is (dare I say it) blasphemous. No, God, motivated by love, forgives us in Christ for our benefit, to release us from a debt we could never repay. Forgiveness is first and primarily about releasing the indebted.

---

5. Ball and Puls, *Let Us Prey*, 155.

There is certainly a secondary benefit to us to become forgiving people. Countless books and articles on the subject can be found by just a quick internet search, but to make it about us primarily helps to maintain dysfunction and abusive systems. Why? Because it goes back to what I was saying about repentance—it puts the burden on the offended party to make things right and leaves the perpetrator unaccountable and still in their sin.

OFFENSE

To think biblically and fully about forgiveness requires us to forensically understand the nature of the debt incurred when I offend you. For instance, if I were to steal something from you, you would be offended against and the debt incurred would be the cost of the goods plus perhaps pain and suffering as a judge may determine. Or, in the example of the traffic infringements, the debt owed is obvious. If, however, I verbally assault you or physically assault you or insult your children or some other such thing, you are right to be offended and hurt by these behaviors. But what debt has been incurred? What debt is being forgiven?

To understand this, I am going to take a little detour through the idea of *shalom,* but bear with me. I will tie all this together shortly.

Let's go back to what we know about mankind as revealed in Gen 1:27. This is the foundation of all Christian human ethics. We are not just some amorphous blobs, or self-determining entities, but are created in the image of God, and as such, a dignity and worth exists in all people. In their prefall state, Adam and Eve reflected in perfection the glory of God in his new creation.

The world was in a state of "good" and "very good" (Gen 1:31). The Hebrew and biblical concept for this is *shalom,* which in English we typically translate as "peace," meaning an absence of conflict; but it is a word with far richer meaning than this. Strong's defines the word as not just peace but:

> completeness, wholeness, health, peace, welfare, safety, soundness, tranquility, prosperity, perfectness, fullness, rest, harmony, the absence of agitation or discord.[6]

---

6. Strong, *Strong's Exhaustive Concordance,* word number H7999.

All of mankind's relationships were whole or complete, without fault or separation, without mar or distortion. Mankind's relationship with God, their relationship with others, and their relationship with the created order in which they lived were in a state of *shalom*.

But as we know all too well, mankind fell and now fall short of the glory of God (Rom 3:23). This fall destroyed *shalom* and ushered in evil. All of mankind's relationships now are incomplete, lacking peace, wholeness, tranquility, or rest. Evil enters into all of our relationships to some extent. One of the great apologetic questions asked is "Who is the author of evil?" But this understanding of *shalom* answers this question. In the same way that darkness is the absence of a thing, not a thing in itself, so evil is the absence of a thing, not a thing in itself. In the case of darkness, it is the absence of light. In the case of evil, it is the absence of *shalom*.

Although fallen, the image was not obliterated, just marred and distorted.[7] The dignity of man and his close association with his maker is seen in this verse:

> One who oppresses the poor taunts his Maker, But one who is gracious to the needy honors Him. (Prov 14:31)

And perhaps his dignity is seen no more emphatically than in this:

> the word became flesh and dwelt amongst us. (John 1:14)

He, Jesus, took the form of a man, not a horse. Yes, we may be fallen, and evil may have entered our relationships, but we still bear the unmistakable thumbprint of God on our beings. All mankind—the *imago Dei*.

We tend to use the word "broken" when we speak about our relationships with God and man and the created order, but a more appropriate biblical idea would be "incomplete." "Broken" is a more therapeutic word which is popular these days because it encourages us with the idea that we can be fixed. But, if we are incomplete, then nothing within us can ever complete us, and despite the schmalzy sentiments of Tom Cruise in *Jerry Maguire*, no person can ever complete us either. Every person you ever met, including you, is incomplete is some important way. Our emotions, our intellect, our physical frailties—they all point to an incompleteness that affirms the fall, what the Reformers called total depravity, evil, if you will. All our faculties incomplete; image-bearers, but with holes.

---

7. Gen 9:6 and Jas 3:9 affirm the image-bearing nature of man postfall.

Figure 5

Why this is important to understand is because what mankind is so adept at doing in this incomplete state is looking for anything and everything to fill what is lacking. Drugs, alcohol, sex, money, power. You name it, all the idols of this life are used as means of trying to fill what is lacking within us—including each other.

When I offend you, I seek from you, an image-bearer, something that will fill what I feel is missing in me. I feel out of control, so I seek to control you. I feel a lack of material good, so I take yours. I feel lonely, so I demand that you meet my loneliness. We seek to take from the other what is lacking in us. The problem is we, as image-bearers, are only a poor reflection of the one who is able to meet those needs—God himself. This explains why all sin is ultimately against God. The famous story of Joseph and Potiphar's wife in Gen 39 is one of offense and sin. She seeks from Joseph what only her husband should give, but it also points to a deeper need in her that only God can meet. Joseph sees and knows this and declares, "How can I do this sin against God" (v. 9)? This is his way of saying "How can I take the role of God to meet the need in you when he alone is the font of all good?" This also demonstrates that all offense against another is in some sense a form of idolatry, seeking from the created order something that only God can give.

Herein highlights the insidious nature of child abuse. Abuse in a child takes from the child what he/she has no capacity to replace. The child has no ability to understand what is happening to them or why. That which is taken can take until adulthood (if even then) to heal, and the scars are permanent.

This is why that detour through *shalom* is so important when it comes to the idea of forgiveness. For forgiveness to be about the offender first is to notice that when I offend you, I have used you, I have treated you like a little god, and I have sought to take some of your dignity and worth. This is the debt that is owed and this is the debt that needs be forgiven.

When I forgive you, I release your demand on me to be God, and this is vitally important because this is firstly about the offender. It seeks to show the offender that what you sought in me, the thing you felt I could provide, the dignity and worth you sought to take from me, is not yours to take and is not in any way able to meet your need. I release you from seeking this from me and I point you to seek it from the one who alone meets all our needs.

If, however we make forgiveness primarily about us, a self-centric view as it were, it helps to keep dysfunction and abuse alive because we never point the offender to the God of all good. Sure, we may meet our own need, the offender may no longer be on our books, and the bitterness and self-damage that this can cause us is released, but she/he is still free to continue to seek their needs in us or someone else, and so the abuse and dysfunction continue.

A self-centric view of forgiveness theology also does not address the equally important idea of justice associated with forgiveness. And this is a vital thing that is often overlooked in a shallow theology of forgiveness—justice.

A THEOLOGY THAT FORGETS JUSTICE

With justice being such a massive and important idea in Scripture I sometimes wonder how we miss it. But having detoured through the idea of *shalom* it starts to become obvious how proper forgiveness must include the idea of justice. When offended, I have three choices:

- Seek revengeful justice;
- Seek retributive justice; or
- Seek restorative justice.

God chooses the third option. The third option reveals the heart of God, is the only option to restore *shalom*, and only happens through a deep and biblical understanding of forgiveness.

The Failure of Revenge

Once, when I was a child of perhaps seven or eight in the cold of a New Jersey winter, I made a snowman. It was not very a good one, but it was mine and I was proud of it. Some neighborhood kids, known to be the troublemakers, older than me and no doubt from difficult families (although the subtlety of that was lost on me at the time), came and knocked the head off the snowman. I complained to my mother, who just told me to fix it, which I did, and again they came and knocked off its head. This repeated itself a few times until my mother, exasperated by my inability to deal with the situation told me, "Well go knock the head off their snowman!" So, I did, and not only the head, I smashed the whole thing to the ground. And then ran like crazy and hid in the house lest they find me and mete out some revengeful justice of their own. Ah revenge—a dish definitely served cold in this instance.

Revenge of course is the easy option, easy at least in that it takes the least amount of thought, although it takes an enormous amount of energy. Its energy is emotionally driven, based on a real sense of injustice of the crime committed, and seeks to get back its own in an "I'll show you" kind of attitude (plus a bit more because, let's be honest, it feels good to give back just a bit more than we got).

But all revenge really does is continue to escalate the war. God does not take revenge on us for our sins, although honestly he has every right to do so.

The Failure of Retribution

Retributive justice is the kind of thing our prison systems are engaged in. Not necessarily by design, they have the honorable idea of imprisonment with the hope of rehabilitation and many programs are run in prisons to effect just this kind of thing. Sadly, as evidence too often shows, this happens all too rarely despite the best intentions of our systems.

Retributive justice is a system of punishment for the crime. An eye-for-an-eye kind of thing. There is no vengeance involved, just a dispassionate recognition that for each offense there is an appropriate penalty, and it is meted out by an implacable judge, who is unmoved by any kind of emotional plea.

This is the kind of thing that shows up during many election campaigns where the party not in power vows to go hard on crime, ridiculing the bleeding hearts of the party in power who they say are letting so many criminals get away with murder. But Mirsolav Volf highlights the inadequacy of this form of justice:

> What would be an adequate punishment for Joseph Stalin, Lenin's evil and dictatorial successor in the old Soviet Union between the two World Wars? He not only ruined his own country and invaded many neighboring ones, but in the process exterminated some 20,000,000 people. If we are after justice, his crime will have outstripped any kind of punishment we could devise for him . . . Punishment alone falters before the enormity of such crime.[8]

You often hear this kind of thing after a court case where someone has been sentenced to life in prison for a crime and the family of the victim say, "Even execution would be too good for him. There is no justice. Nothing will bring our daughter back."

As Volf declares, revenge simply escalates and multiplies evil (the loss of *shalom*); retribution, at best, contains evil.[9] Only forgiveness restores *shalom*. This is the heart of God; this is restorative justice.

The Glory of Restoration

Restorative justice is at the heart of true biblical forgiveness, and if we have too shallow a theology of forgiveness, we will fail to recognize that the whole point of forgiveness is justice, but not just any justice, restorative justice. Any view of forgiveness, therefore, that does not fall under the umbrella of restoring *shalom* is inadequate and leads to or continues the maintenance of a system of abuse.

In the Bible, the words "justice" and "righteousness" are two closely related words. Justice is about setting things right, or perhaps you might say justice is the energy or force that makes things righteous. The below illustration (Figure 6) can be helpful here.

God's holy standard is the measure of things that are right, *shalom*, if you will, the absence of evil. It is the standard against which all things are aligned. The plumbline represents that old building tool, now obsolete, that helped determine the straightness of a wall or structure. Mankind, however, is not right, and his relationships are not right. There is no

---

8. Volf, *Free of Charge*, 135.
9. Volf, *Free of Charge*, 161.

shalom, evil exists, we are a crooked line which does not measure up to God's standard. As the Bible says, all have sinned and fall short.

But God in Christ justifies us. Justice is done and justice is applied externally to us. As Paul says, we are made the righteousness of God in Christ (2 Cor 5:21) We, the crooked lines, could not straighten ourselves, we needed the external application of justice in Christ to do this for us. This then restores us into right relationship with God. We are declared righteous. We *aren't* righteous, just declared right, the righteousness of Christ imputed to us. This is restorative justice, God restoring us to a right standing with him, and in so doing, by the power of his Spirit, making it possible for us to be right in all our other relationships. Justice is done to make us right, to restore *shalom*.

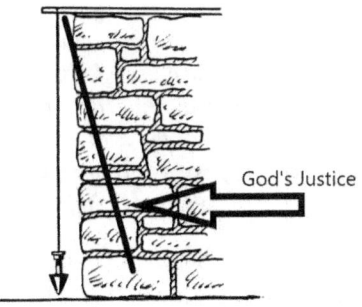

Figure 6

This is what God's forgiveness of us does. It restores *shalom*. God does not simply overlook the offense, but rather he has dealt with it in Christ. A shallow view of forgiveness wants us to overlook or minimize sin and offense even in the face of nonrepentance, but this is not how God forgives. His justice was satisfied, the penalty is paid, and this justice is then applied to us in order to make us right.

Therefore, any theology of forgiveness and understanding of forgiveness in person-to-person relationships that does not include the idea of the restoration of relationship as its goal, the returning to *shalom*, is inadequate. Now whether or not that actually happens is another thing, but it is the goal.

In order for justice to be satisfied, and in order to restore our relationship with God, the price paid for our sin against an infinite God is the infinite worth of Christ. In person-to-person relationships, the price paid for offense in order for justice to be satisfied is confession, repentance, and restitution. There is no justice and no forgiveness if we simply overlook the offense without these ideas.

THEOLOGICALLY RICH FORGIVENESS

If we make forgiveness about us primarily, or don't require repentance, or fail to consider the concept of restorative justice, we create a very shallow, inadequate, and unbiblical concept of forgiveness. When this then is exercised and enforced in dysfunctional churches it can lead to, or perpetuate, abuse.

So, what is a proper view of forgiveness? Given the previous discussion I would like to define forgiveness this way:

> *Forgiveness is a social transaction that is entered into by two parties, one offending and the other offended. It is a totally gracious gift, undeserved, given by the injured party, to the offending party, releasing the offender from the debt that is owed. Motivated by love, the offended party graciously offers this gift with the hope of restoring* shalom, *a shalom that the offense has served to break.*

Now what I am doing here is making a clear distinction between what we commonly call forgiveness, that is being *willing, able,* and *ready* (WAR) to forgive, and the state of forgiveness, which never can occur without two parties doing their part. And the reason this is helpful is because often we are told we have to forgive someone who has wronged us even if they never own their part in the conflict, and to do so seems as if somehow they have gotten away with something. What I want to show is that even though we own our part and are *willing, able,* and *ready* to forgive, the other party is not actually forgiven without repentance and confession. Let's explore this.

The below illustration will be useful here. Forgiveness always requires two parties: the offender and the offended. Much has been written[10] to help deal with whether or not something is or should be an offense, whether we should let it go or not. But for the purposes of this illustration we will assume the behavior of one party is legitimately offensive to the other. The offender is in a state of unforgiveness and the offended has not forgiven. In order for forgiveness to happen, both parties must do their part. The top arrow is the work of the offended (accuse, rebuke, and go

---

10. See Sande, *Peace Maker,* ch. 4.

to war for forgiveness) and the bottom arrow is the work of the offender (repent and confess). Only when both parties do their part and restitution is offered has the state of forgiveness been achieved. The difference is that the offended party, commanded by Christ, *must* do their work. It is the law of love. The offending party can choose to stay unforgiven, but the offended party is called to go to WAR for forgiveness.

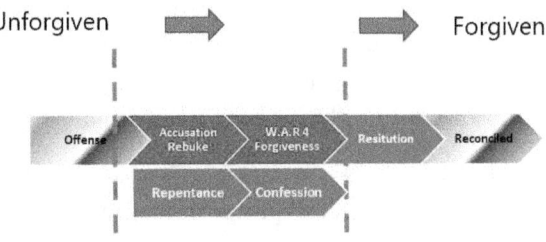

Figure 7

WAR for Forgiveness

The W stands for "Willing."

This is the hard part and quite frankly in the worst of cases (i.e., sexual assault, murder of a loved one, etc.) the bit that will take the most work. To be willing to forgive means to have a heart attitude that is expressed in the words of Christ "forgive as you have been forgiven," and given what we have said about *shalom* and evil in the human heart, nothing short of a miracle by the Spirit of God doing his work in us can make us willing. Which is why the acronym WAR is so apt—we may have to battle hard for this.

A willingness to forgive is a unilateral one-sided decision. It is not dependent upon anything the other party does, although their ownership of the hurt will go a long way towards making this easier. Forgiveness does not forget that the offended has been hurt and that this hurt has bred a desire for revenge. The offended has the high moral ground, which is voluntarily relinquished by the act of forgiveness. Being willing means being:

- predisposed to something; open-hearted; magnanimous
- willing to decide to let go of your anger and right to revenge

- willing to be patient. If you love a person, you are willing to wait, to be both longsuffering and willing to wait for a repentance that may actually never come.
- willing to accuse or rebuke. A willingness to express the truth in love. Speaking truth about the impact the behavior of the offending party has had on you is a kindness that may lead to repentance (Rom 2:4).
- willing to reconcile. If you love the person, you want them to be in relationship with you. You desire a restoration of *shalom* between the two parties. Reconciliation may not always be possible or even safe, but we must be willing to consider it and work towards this end, if possible.

When Jesus says we are to forgive he means this. As you look at the above list, is this not how God is willing to forgive us? Motivated by love, patient, knowing our frame, knowing we are dust, in kindness describing and rebuking our sin? We, as forgivers, are called to reflect this standard with one another. We are call to do all the heart work in ourselves that puts us in a position where we offer forgiveness, and if the offending party does their work, they become forgiven.

The A stands for Able.

How are we able to forgive others? The gospel, of course. This is the point of the parable in Matthew 18:21–35 and Paul's admonition in Eph 4:32. We are able to forgive because God in Christ has forgiven us. The penalty for my sin—and just as importantly (and maybe more so in this context) the sin of the offender—is paid for and borne by Christ. This is something I think we often forget. Jesus died for the sin *and* the person who committed it against you. He loves them and hates their sin as much as, and in fact more than, you ever could.

Here is where empathy can play an important role. Knowing and understanding the frailty and fallenness of the one who so badly offended you does not excuse them of their behavior but helps in some way to level the playing field in your understanding of the impact of sin on them and on all of us.

And this is also why the diversion through *shalom* was so important. Although you may have been horribly sinned against, grievously so, ultimately the sin is against God. You have been used and your dignity taken in order to meet some unmet need in another. This not only offends you, it offends God, and he is willing and able to forgive the other in Christ and offers you this grace to forgive as well:

> And you, who were dead in your trespasses and the uncircumcision of your flesh, God made alive together with him, having forgiven us all our trespasses, by cancelling the record of debt that stood against us with its legal demands. This he set aside, nailing it to the cross. (Col 2:13–14)

God is able to forgive us because his wrath is satisfied in Christ. Nobody is getting away with anything: not you, and not your offender. This is the power of the cross. This is the wisdom of God.

The R stands for Ready.

Only when we accuse and rebuke, confront our offenders with their sin, and only when we do the hard work of letting the gospel and the Spirit of God transform our hearts so that we become willing to go to WAR for forgiveness, will we be ready.

The work of getting ready may take years, a lifetime even, but Jesus makes it clear: we need to forgive as we have been forgiven. To be willing and able and ready to forgive is what it means to forgive another. But the other does not enter the blessings of this state of forgiveness without a willingness to do the hard work on their part, to confess and repent and seek to make amends. You may have forgiven them, but unless they do their part, they are not forgiven.

God is willing, able, and ready to forgive the contrite in heart, the repentant sinner. He is willing, able, and ready because of the work done in Christ. But not everybody enters into the blessings of forgiveness. Only those who repent and confess and lay down their lives at the foot of the cross know real forgiveness, and are released from the burden of the debt they owe.

How do I know I am ready to forgive? Thomas Watson says it well:

> When we strive against all thoughts of revenge; when we will not do our enemies mischief, but wish well to them, grieve at their calamities, pray for them, seek reconciliation with them, and show ourselves ready on all occasions to relieve them.[11]

---

11. Watson, *Body of Divinity*, 581.

This may take time, much time but a key marker in yourself is the growing compassion and empathy within you for those that may have hurt you; to be able to place yourself in their shoes, imagine the hurt, anger, and pain that may be driving their hurtful behavior; to attempt to understand what it may have been like to have come from an environment where (perhaps) abusive behaviors were not only the norm, but have become the other's primary method of coping with interpersonal relationships. To imagine and understand their dysfunctional background, to see the broken wounded sinner that is the other, to see them as Jesus sees them, this levels the playing field.

This is not some sentimental attempt to absolve them of responsibility, but a sign you are ready to forgive is the compassion in your heart that arises as you recognize that they, like you, need a Savior. It is at this point that you are able to hand them over to Christ—to his wounds, his cross, his blood—and let Christ be the justice that must be sought and given.

Being willing, able, and ready to forgive is what I believe the Bible means and what Jesus means by "forgive one another." This does not mean the offending party is forgiven, as I said this would require work on their part, but by doing our part as the offended, we fulfill the law of Christ. Making this distinction between what we the offended are to do and what the state of forgiveness looks like is important because it releases the offended party from having to seek justice or feeling that justice will never occur. Whether the offending party ever acknowledges or repents or not, whether the offended see justice in this life or not, the offended are able to hand the offender over to Christ and release them from their debt to his, and for the offended to be in a place to do this is a great grace. This may take time, this is a WAR, but by the grace of God it can be done.

And let's not make the mistake of thinking that forgiveness absolves the offender from the ramifications of behavior. If it is criminal behavior, the law still must play its part. If it is unethical or immoral behavior that violates a Christian *ethos*, then removal from positions of influence should be mandated, or church discipline enacted as necessary, and appropriate remedial actions taken to ensure the safety of the church and the emotional and spiritual growth of the offender. This is part of restorative justice.

SUMMARY

If we do not have this systematic view of forgiveness, then it is easy for us to act in ways that appear Christian. We will "just forgive" actions that effectively sweep offense under the carpet and enable offenders and their supporters to continue to offend and abuse for years. This is dysfunctional and this shallow view really is at the heart of many abusive systems.

A shallow view of forgiveness is at the root of the bitter fruit of dysfunction and abuse, but other things are as well. A shallow judgment of character also aids this dysfunction. How? Let's look at this next.

5.2

Shallow Judgments of Character

Judge not lest ye be judged.
—Jesus (Matt 7:1 KJV)

Better to be a man of character than a man of means.
—Irish Proverb

Charisma is no substitute for Character.[1]
—Eddie Gibbs, Leadership Next

One thing that is common in the modern church is a commitment to ministries that go beyond the simple things that we do on a Sunday morning. Churches these days are a miasma of ministries: children's ministries of all kinds running on all days, youth ministries, Bible studies, small groups, craft groups, really the list is only limited by the imagination of people who feel led by God to run such things and the number of people in your church willing to attend such groups. These activities, by and large, have wonderful redeeming value. The gospel is preached, community is created and strengthened, young people and children come to Christ, and the faith of people grows in the word. The church is called to this.

---

1. Gibbs, *Leadership Next*, 128.

But coupled with the burgeoning number of ministries that a church operates is the equally burgeoning number of people that are required to lead and run these ministries. It is one of the tasks and responsibilities of the pastors and elders of the local church to appoint the right people to these roles. The question is "Who are the right people?" There are a range of Cs that describe the kinds of characteristics that are important when looking to fill roles in churches.

- Capability: the skill set required to do a task (*Talent*);
- Capacity: the resources, both time and physical assets, required to do a task (*Treasure*); *and most importantly*
- Character: The settled disposition of one's nature

Now as I discuss the judging of character in this chapter, and in the context of dysfunctional and abusive organizations, I am primarily concerned with assessing and judging the character of individuals, particularly when it comes to the leadership's role of appointing people into positions of authority in the church. If the leaders of a church are going to confer some of their authority onto another, then *they must judge character first*. This is done to protect the church and the individual placed into a position of influence. If what we euphemistically call a "difficult person" is placed into a leadership role, this can lead to abuse of others or constant conflict and turmoil surrounding the individual. This is not healthy for them, the church, or the ministry they lead.

This assessment of character is not, however, intended to decide if they should be a member of the church or not, or whether they should attend the church or not. It is not an assessment of whether or not they are a Christian. The bar for leadership roles in church, no matter what the ministry, is far higher than for the regular nonleader. Determining that someone has character issues that make them unfit for leadership does not mean they are unfit for church; in fact, just the opposite. Church is the place that God calls disparate individuals together so they can learn from, lean on, and love one another. Church will be filled with people who are completely different from you. This is difficult in itself. There will be, to name just a few things:

- toxic personalities
- differences of opinions
- diversity of preferences

- different levels of emotional and spiritual maturity

One person's difficult person is another's friend. I am and was a difficult person to some people and some personality types, and will always be. But the point is that when the level of difficulty is such that it points to character issues, then it is right and safe for the leadership to measure this and disallow some individuals from leadership roles, no matter how capable they are.

Church leaders must also be empathetic to those individuals within their congregation that exhibit difficult behaviors, and not automatically assume they are connected to character issues. Hundreds of underlying and behind-the-scenes things may be happening for the parishioner: family member illness, loss of a job, children getting into legal trouble, marriage difficulties. These issues may be unknown to those who observe them, but will manifest themselves in the form of argumentativeness, anger, depression, etc. Generous and careful pastoral care can and should get to the heart of the issue, and the pastoral carer can help navigate this season with the person without it necessarily disqualifying a person from ministry.

Sometimes the best pastoral care for someone in a leadership role that is facing this kind of personal crisis is to give them time off, and sometimes the ministry is just the thing to help them navigate this tough season. There is no one-size-fits-all solution. But there is a big difference between difficult people and behavior due to personal crises, and manipulative, abusive behavior used by people as a means of navigating life and coping, which point to serious character issue. Leaders must judge these things well.

For example, imagine Mr. Smith comes to the leadership team with a proposal to run a male teen sporting camp. The goal is to build camaraderie, teach sporting skills, coupled with Bible teaching and evangelism. Should the leadership team allow it? How would they decide? He has been a member of the church for some years. Imagine that Mr. Smith has run this ministry in another church before, has done all the training and is accredited by the overseeing organization. Coupled with that, the church has the space and the time slot to run the ministry, and it fits the mission goals of the church. Mr. Smith says he has sufficient time to run the ministry. He has the capacity (time), the resources (an available campground), and capability (skill set and training) to run the ministry. Is this sufficient to let him run the ministry?

For many churches, particularly smaller ones, this is all they want: capable people with the capacity to do ministry and who voluntarily are willing to do it. After all, churches want to be about the Lord's business, and here is someone God has raised up from amongst them to do it. Surely God is calling the church to this ministry. It is a no-brainer. So the church lets him do it.

Now what if Mr. Smith is one of those difficult people? His interpersonal relationships are fraught; he has no or few noticeable friends within the church. He is in conflict frequently with people, including the leadership team. People walk on eggshells around him. He is manipulative, passive-aggressive, and abuses people verbally. Are these behaviors not a pointer to issues with his character and his walk with Christ? With this extra information now ask yourself: Should the leadership team let him run it? Too often in dysfunctional organizations the answer is still yes.

In these dysfunctional organizations, so-called difficult people, people with great passion, great capacity, and great capability, can end up in leadership positions even though an honest assessment of their character would demonstrate them to be unfit for ministry. Character really matters, but too often in dysfunctional organizations it is left unjudged, or else character is relegated below capacity and capability in terms of perceived importance because the glory and potential of a ministry blinds us.

What happens if Mr. Smith is actually already running that ministry, has been for ten or twenty years, and the ministry is really good, despite the constant turmoil surrounding this person? Isn't the success of the ministry evidence of a person without any serious character issues? Because if Mr. Smith was deficient in character, the ministry would fail, wouldn't it? Do we just overlook character because of the great ministry? Again, in dysfunctional organizations the answer is yes. Character is never judged, or is judged poorly, and therefore, even if he is unfit from a character perspective to lead the ministry he is never removed. And this can lead to abuse, both from the ministry leader himself and the leadership team willing to enable him by clamping down on any complaints about him. People are called to turn a blind eye to the abuse for the sake of the ministry, all to the glory of God.

Too often character is overlooked or undervalued, or assessments of character are forbidden, and it's this failure to judge character that can lead to much abuse in the church. Tim Challlies, in a blog post entitled

"Character Is King," discusses his take on the rise and fall of the ministry of Mark Driscoll and the Mars Hills Church he founded:

> When the Bible lays out qualifications to ministry, it is character that rules every time. The Bible says little about skill and less still about results. It heralds character. And from the early days, Mark Driscoll showed outstanding natural abilities which led to amazing results. He knew and proclaimed sound theology. But he also showed an absence of so many of the marks of Godly character. A hundred testimonies from a hundred hurt friends and former church members shows that what we saw from the outside was only a dim reflection of what was happening on the inside. The signposts were there, but we ignored them.[2]

Abuse existed in Mark Driscoll's church because of the dysfunction of not judging character or judging it too lowly—in this case the character of the lead pastor himself. A failure to judge character first caused no shortage of hurt and pain for a lot of people, pain that was unnecessary if only they would have judged character first. Clearly Mark Driscoll had capacity and capability, far more than most; he was and is highly gifted in many ways. But as Challies says, character is king, and it wasn't measured[3] in Mark's church. This was a dysfunction that led to abuse.

Again, highlighting the willingness to measure capability and capacity but not character, Diane Langberg puts it this way:

> Though rarely spoken about, character and personal history are shaping influences in those who lead. We frequently select leaders according to their gifts rather than their character. Leadership in the body of Christ should be based not on natural abilities but on spiritual maturity and Christlikeness.[4]

The church is notorious for turning a blind eye to character in order to bask in the glory of charisma. So, what is character and what does it mean to judge it?

CHARACTER

The etymology of character is quite telling. The word comes from the Greek *kharakter* for "engraved mark," "symbol or imprint on the soul,"

2. Challies, "Character is King," para. 12.
3. Or insufficiently measured.
4. Langberg, *Redeeming Power*, 129.

and "instrument for marking," and can be traced further back to the words for "to engrave," "pointed stake," and "to scrape and scratch." So, effectively, character is the settled, deeply-etched personality traits of an individual:

> Character is nature and nurture. It is nature cultured and disciplined, so that natural tendencies are brought under the sway of the moral motive. His natural individuality marks off a man from his fellows by clear and specific differences. But this individuality may be nonmoral. To produce character it must be brought under discipline, and organized into the structure of a true moral being . . .
>
> Above all, [character] includes a choice, a settled habit or bent of will, so that it can be seen in its outcome in conduct. Character takes up the raw material of nature and temperament, and it weaves these into the strong, well-knit texture of a fully moralized manhood."[5]

Bruce's understanding of character as being both a product of nature and nurture is helpful, as he highlights the fact that even the most corrupt of natures can, with the proper nurture or environment, be shifted to something that we would call good character.

Bad character is hereditary in that we get it from our first parents: Adam and Eve. However, good character is not hereditary; some people are not born with it better than others. Good character traits are both learned from our environment and our natural parents. For instance, if we have parents that value being a good democratic citizen and instill in us the value of our vote, then we will, over time, develop the character trait of voting at elections even when it is inconvenient, because to not do so would violate our character. No one is born a good, democratic citizen.

A biblical understanding of the fall indicates that the human heart is by nature corrupted, and its inclination is away from God and his good. Our character is rotten to the core. But thankfully, by God's common grace, most of us do not exercise the full corruption that we otherwise might. For instance, Jesus indicates that murder starts in the heart, and hating your brother is just as bad as murder. There are, I suspect, no shortage of haters, but thankfully most of them do not end up murderers in the actual sense. And as Bruce is indicating, it is most likely nurture that prevents this. We are raised (most of us anyway) to respect the life

---

5. Straton, *Formation of Christian Character*, 51–52.

of people even if we vehemently disagree with them. Nurture and culture keep us from killing them even though we might loath them in our heart.

But the character is still one of murderous hatred even if we don't engage in that vile act, and it is here that the Christian relies on the gospel and the sanctifying work of the Holy Spirit to convert us from those who hate to those who love, from those who seek revenge to those who forgive. The corrupted and vile nature of the human being, even the best of us, is brought under the sanctifying work of the Spirit of Christ to those that believe, and so our character is transformed into his likeness.

Character, therefore, is the deeply engrained nature of our heart that leads to behaviors, and character can be formed and changed by our environment, and more importantly by the gospel.

Now the interesting thing is that we, as deceptive individuals, can put on quite a show to hide our true nature or character from others. And so, in order to see or understand the character of another takes time. Someone who walks into your church with a pleasant smile and a handshake can just as easily be a kindly pastoral carer or child predator, and on first glance you have no way of knowing. Or on second glance, or third, and so forth. It can often take a long time to discern this, depending on the level of deceit and the individual's skill in hiding it.

In a brilliant article on the topic at the Catholic Education Resource Centre, Douglas McManaman describes the stealth of the narcissistic character in our churches. Afraid people will see the real person inside, an evil inside that the narcissist actually loathes, the narcissist puts on a likable and agreeable persona instead:

> When it is a question of evil, it is precisely the element of disguise that people tend to overlook. We are wont to assume that evil, character disorder, profound moral depravity, psychopathy, pathological narcissism, etc, are easy to detect and that such people can only intimidate and inspire fear upon a first encounter. But this is only the case with those not intelligent enough to disguise their depravity, like the common criminal. The most dangerous among us are those intelligent enough to appear as paragons of virtue.[6]

What McManaman is describing is, of course, the character-disturbed, clinically diagnosable narcissist, but there is a narcissist to some extent in us all, and as such we desperately try to display the behaviors

---

6. McManaman, "Narcissism and the Dynamics of Evil," para. 29.

and characteristics of a person that will be well-received in the social community in which we find ourselves, including in (and dare I say even more so) in the church. We want reflected back to us the affirmation of what we hope to be, not necessarily what we are. I had always thought of one day making Jesus masks, handing them out to the congregation on Sunday morning, and getting all the people to put them on. This may have been the most honest we had been as people in a long time if I had done that, because in many ways we (and most likely many other churches) were very good at playing Jesus.

Now this is not to say that all people who go to church are phony and hide behind Jesus behaviors, and that there isn't real love and compassion in the community—far from it. But what I am saying is that in some church communities, dysfunctional ones, the behaviors required to fit in, to get power and authority, and to get leadership roles are soon learned and can be put on to great effect. In those dysfunctional communities, the unspoken rule is "Look like this and be accepted; look different and you're not." Human nature being what it is it doesn't take long to conform.

Therefore, the leaders of a church have a great responsibility to ensure that the character of the individuals who lead and run ministries, of those who aspire to authority, are measured over significant time to determine the nature of their character, because although someone can put on a good act for a long time, eventually nature will win out. Clues to the real nature of all us will eventually show. As McManaman goes on to say:

> The clues, in isolation, will suggest only minor imperfections or character flaws. But taken together over a number of years, they suggest something much more ominous. The inconsistencies evident in the behavior of the narcissist prior to his discovery should never be simply accepted, only to be forgotten. Rather, one must ponder the inconsistencies in behavior until they become consistent, that is, until the apparently inconsistent behavior acquires an intelligible narrative that rings true.[7]

Now, again, I know his point is about the diagnosable narcissistic-disordered personality, but he still has something to say to all of us. It has been more popularly described using the metaphor "people are full tea cups. Only when bumped will what is inside us come out." This is to say that the clues to our real nature and character will be on display when the pressure comes to bear. And this only can be observed by those around us

---

7. McManaman, "Narcissism and the Dynamics of Evil," para. 33.

over time. This is one of the reasons for instance, that Paul declares that anyone appointed as an elder to the church should not be a new convert (1 Tim 3:6). Give the sanctifying work of God time to do its work in transforming character into Christlikeness.

In fact, God is not even remotely as concerned about our behaviors as he is about our character. In the famous story of Saul and the Amalekites (1 Sam 15) Saul is rebuked "to obey is better than sacrifice" (v. 22), meaning an attitude of the heart pointing to character is far better than a bunch of religious behavior. It was the main beef Jesus had with the religious rulers of the day: the heart (that is character) first, behavior second.

In dysfunctional organizations, character is either not measured or measured in far too shallow a way. Enthralled by the glory of ministry and the charisma of the leaders, shallow assessment keeps abusive ministers in place.

Now it is easy to think at this point that I am suggesting that the leaders of a church have to be nigh on perfect, with no character flaws. But of course this would then ensure we had no leaders. The proverbial "nobody is perfect" rings true for our church leaders as much as anyone else, which is why the Bible gives us lists of requirements or characteristics of the things that make for a suitable leader in your church. What we should see in our leaders is mature people whose lives are on a clear trajectory towards these things, with the character traits clearly evident in many places and in many ways.

Paul's lists in 1 Timothy 3:1–16 and Titus 1:5–9 are designed to help discover over time the people whom God has called who exhibit the characteristic traits of a leader in your church. Now what is interesting to note in those lists is, at least on the surface, they look like behaviors, but it doesn't take more than a minute to realize they are clearly a pointer to character. Note the ideas in Paul's list are really character traits:

> An overseer, then, must be above reproach, the husband of one wife, temperate, self-controlled, respectable, hospitable, skillful in teaching, not overindulging in wine, not a bully, but gentle, not contentious, free from the love of money. He must be one who manages his own household well, keeping his children under control with all dignity (but if a man does not know how to manage his own household, how will he take care of the church of God?), and not a new convert, so that he will not become conceited and fall into condemnation incurred by the devil. And he must have a good reputation with those outside the church, so

that he will not fall into disgrace and the snare of the devil. (1 Tim 3:2–7)

As Craig Hamilton states, "When it comes to any leadership role, but especially Christian leadership, character is king."[8]

There it is again: character is king. Now one of the things that dysfunctional organizations can do, particularly those that hold to a high view of the Bible, is they tend to get microscopic about things. What I mean is they zoom in intently on this list, see it as behaviors, see someone who can achieve or who achieves these things, and therefore conclude this is all that is required for leadership. But what they don't focus on is other passages of Scripture that are not about leadership, *per se*, but would be the basic common denominator for anyone in a leadership role, and should certainly be evident in any leadership candidate, namely the fruit of the Spirit:

> But the fruit of the Spirit is love, joy, peace, forbearance, kindness, goodness, faithfulness, gentleness and self-control. Against such things there is no law. (Gal 5:22–23)

Notice there are some similarities between this list and the one for elders (gentleness and self-control), but others as well, such as kindness, peace, joy, etc. This fruit must be evident in any leadership candidate, and particularly these individuals, because behaviors can be faked but attitudes cannot. It is hard to fake joy or peace. People with unresolved anger issues in their heart, for example, may manage a ministry perfectly well, but bump them and they snap. It's obvious.

And then there is Paul's description of humility in Phil 2. Should this not also be a trait of our leaders? Perhaps the prime one? But if we focus only on the 1 Timothy and Titus lists, we can end up with some very character-disturbed individuals running the show, a formula for abuse.

JUDGMENT

Now one of the protestations made in dysfunctional organizations about the judging of character is the theology that says we are not called to judge anyone. They say "Look at the words of Jesus in Matthew 7:1–3":

> Do not judge, so that you will not be judged. For in the way you judge, you will be judged; and by your standard of measure, it

---

8. Hamilton, *Wisdom for Leadership*, 50.

will be measured to you. Why do you look at the speck that is in your brother's eye, but do not notice the log that is in your own eye?

"or the words in 1 Samuel 16:7":

> . . . man looks at the outward appearance, but the Lord looks at the heart.

For these organizations, this is proof enough that we are not to judge character, just behavior, as behavior can be managed and should never be linked to character.

I want to test this theology. Let's start with Matt 7.

Matt 7:1–3

> Do not judge, so that you will not be judged. For in the way you judge, you will be judged; and by your standard of measure, it will be measured to you. Why do you look at the speck that is in your brother's eye, but do not notice the log that is in your own eye?

Is this verse of Jesus a blanket injunction about the sin of judging another? The Greek word translated *judge* means:

- to pronounce an opinion concerning right and wrong;
- to pronounce judgment, to subject to censure.

Jesus warns us against doing such a thing, but it is not a blanket prohibition. It is allowable under the circumstance of verse 2, that is, you are prepared to be judged by the same standard and measure that you judge another. Hence verse 3: "get the log out of your own eye first." This is not so much a concern about judging as it is a concern about an attitude of judgementalism, that is, a self-righteous judgment of others without recognition of the sin in your own heart. The classic "people in glass houses" kind of thing. The Pharisees were masters of this.

If this verse means we are not to judge ever, then to take this argument to its extreme, the *argumentum ad absurdum* if you will, then we would be wrong to judge Hitler or Stalin or Pol Pot or any of the other despots of the twentieth century. Clearly it is right for us to judge both the behaviors and the characters of these individuals.

The context of this section is clear. Jesus is calling people to be judges, but not hypocritical judges, not acting like you are superior to the one whom you assess. Motive is key:

> Yet let's be clear. Jesus is not suggesting that we have no right to make moral judgments about human behavior, and he is certainly not suggesting we have no right to hold others accountable. He doesn't condemn mutual accountability and moral responsibility and the need to address sin in the church—he addresses hypocrisy.[9]

But what is it we are judging? When Jesus says "only judge by the same measure with which you are going to judge others," is he talking about behavior or character? Or both?

For instance, let's say that you have committed murder. I judge that you killed a man. A person is dead and your actions caused it, but can I assign motive? Should I? Can this indicate character and heart? Should we judge character and motive in this instance? I say not only should we, but to not do so would be a great injustice. Should we not differentiate between involuntary manslaughter and first-degree murder? Both result in the death of an individual (behavior or action), but contain two very different motives (character, nature). And we must judge rightly—justice demands it.

I would like to suggest that Jesus is calling us to carefully judge not only the actions of others, but also, from time to time, to wisely discern the heart, character, and motive of the actions. But dealing with our own sin first is critical. If I were to paraphrase Matthew 7, I would put it this way:

> Don't judge the intent or motive or character of another unless you are prepared to be judged with the same measuring rod. Get your house in order before attempting to judge another. Once your house is in order you will be able to judge rightly, because the unresolved stuff in your own life is likely preventing you from seeing others rightly.

This is why the leaders of the church need to be mature Christians and why Christians with unresolved issues who go around judging others can cause so much harm in the church:

> The truth of the matter is we should all be grieved about sin in our lives. And when we see it, we should address it, confessing it

---

9. Bargerhuff, *Most Misused Verses in the Bible*, 28.

and forsaking it out of reverence for God. It is only when we are consistently doing this ourselves that we are qualified and able to address the sins in the lives of our brothers and sisters in the church, which we must do as well.[10]

In dysfunctional organizations, a failure to judge character can lead to abuse because disordered characters can get into positions of power and no one is prepared to judge the character that is producing these behaviors, but instead a great effort is made to manage the sinful behaviors. But let's be clear: you can't manage sin; it will always manage you.

1 Sam 16:7

I don't know how many times I have heard people tell me, "You have no right to judge another man's heart. How can you know what is in his heart? Only God knows a man's heart!" And then an appeal is made to this verse:

> But the Lord said to Samuel, "Do not look at his appearance or at the height of his stature, because I have rejected him; for God does not *see* as man sees, since man looks at the outward appearance, but the Lord looks at the heart."

But the question I then ask is, "Is this a blanket statement of truth, or an objective statement of fact?" That is, is this verse saying, "Only God can judge a man's heart, man is not capable?" Is it a blanket prohibition against judging a person's heart because we have no ability to do so, or is it saying "God judges men's hearts; men are too shallow and only look at the surface gloss?"

I want to suggest it is the latter. It is a comment of rebuke to the family of David, who were more concerned about the outward appearance of his brothers and their seeming suitability for the role of king (capacity and capability) and no consideration was being given for character. And I think this is a subtle swipe at this shallow judgment. David's brothers may have had great capacity and capability, but character? Not so much. Judge character, says God.

Now there is also the famous verse in Jer 17:9, stating:

> The heart is more deceitful than all else and is desperately sick;
> Who can understand it?

---

10. Bargerhuff, *Most Misused Verses in the Bible*, 29.

Taken together with 1 Sam 16:7, it seems to strengthen the argument. "How can I judge another's heart, motive, or character, when we can't judge our own?" But does God not reveal our hearts to us through the faithful exposition of others? If you have held to the belief no man can know another's heart you will find this surprising.

Two verses indicate that one way we understand our own hearts, the gift that God uses to help us see our own heart's wickedness, is another person:

> Do not judge by the outward appearance, but judge with righteous judgment. (John 7:24)

This seems to indicate it is right to look beyond outward appearance, there is a right way to judge, and that it must therefore be possible, and wisdom tells us to do so:

> A plan in the heart of a person is *like* deep water, but a person of understanding draws it out. (Prov 20:5)

It is what counsellors are doing every day in counselling sessions. The way we can know our own hearts, amongst other ways, is by the judgments of wise people who can judge and discern us. Humility would want and welcome this.

SUMMARY

My conclusions from this study of character are as follows:

- God always judges motives and intent. He is not fooled by good behavior.
- Mankind often is fooled by outward behavior. We are shallow judges by nature.
- All of us are self-deceived.
- But all of us can become aware of the nature of our own hearts. This is the work of the gospel and the power of the Spirit.
- One of the ways this occurs is through the wisdom of another who draws us out.
- It is right therefore, to judge motive and character, but this must be done with great caution and humility.

Churches that will not judge character are havens for abusers. A failure to judge character, or to judge it rightly, can lead to injustice. If we assign negative motive incorrectly this is unjust to the one we have judged. If we assign good intent to one with evil intent then we allow this person to be unjust to others. Again, this explains why the leaders of your church must be mature Christians who have resolved their own stuff. (See chapter 6.2, on authenticity.)

Every book on leadership will tell you the same thing: character matters, and we must judge it for the safety of our people. It is too often set as a universal, unalterable truth, that we can't judge others' hearts, we can't know them—only God can. So we take people at face value, and if their behavior gets too off, we'll manage it; if it gets really bad, then maybe we have to act. This shallow understanding of character and judgment is a dysfunction that can lead to abuse.

5.3

Shallow Understanding of Pastoral Care

From somewhere in my mid-thirties I began to preach in churches regularly, mainly my own but often visiting other places. I had a passion for it, although I wouldn't say that I loved it. It was hard work, and by nature I don't like hard work, but as I read and studied Scripture, I would see things and I would question things, and then when I worked them out I had a burning need to explain to others what I had discovered. I was energized by the process. I came alive in the studying and preparation of the sermons. I appeared to have a gift. I could provide insight and meaning to the word of God and apply it. People were moved by it. God's Spirit moved and did great kingdom things in and for people through the ministry of the preached word. It is the evidence of a gift. I take no credit whatsoever.

From time to time, while visiting other churches, people would ask me where I did ministry and where I was pastoring. I would tell them nowhere. Often, they would say. "Well, you should be in ministry." And my standard response was, "God has not called me to ministry." I did this for what I thought was a very good reason.

I had a picture in my head of a pastor. They had a certain air about them. They acted and looked a certain way, and I knew I looked nothing like it. I was sure I would be a square peg in a round hole. If pastors were extroverted, I was introverted. If pastors were patient, I was impatient. If pastors listened, I didn't.

Now of course I wasn't all those things 100 percent of the time, but enough of the time to "know" (how little I really knew!) that God did not want me in ministry. I know some real pastors. Like my preaching, it is a gift. People are moved by the Spirit of God and great kingdom things, miraculous things, are done through their ability to properly care for the souls of those they pastor. I wasn't like those men and women. I have seen some brilliant pastoral care. However, God, in his providential wisdom, called me to ministry despite myself because God needs square introverts who can't talk from time to time, it would seem. But even still, in that role, I was aware of the need for good pastoral carers to join me in the work.[1]

I envy and admire these people, and I am thankful to God for these people. They seemingly have an endless supply of empathy. They are energized by the process of sitting and listening. They can do it again and again, hour after hour. I read their blogs and watch them sit with me and others and think, "Man, I wish I could do that." The church needs preachers, true; it is a vital part of God's work in his kingdom. In fact, it can be argued that the basis for all good pastoral care is solid preaching of the word of God from the pulpit on Sundays. Even so, I daresay the church needs pastoral carers more. (Or more pastoral carers!) I say this for one obvious reason: everybody has heard of the visiting speaker, the travelling preacher, but who has ever heard of the travelling pastoral carer? I'm sure they must exist but they would be a rare bird indeed. We preachers are like a Vitamin B shot—good for a while, one-hit wonders, there and gone. It's easy to do that. But pastoral carers are like your physiotherapist. If you have ever had physiotherapy you will know that it is very up close and personal. They've got their hands all over you. They are down on the floor stretching you, pushing you, working up a sweat with you. And you can't go just once—proper treatment takes many visits. It is a very earthy, get-your-hands-dirty kind of work. It's the work of one soil-bound creature wrestling with another. It is the work of the pastoral carer. The pastoral carer can't just come and visit; they have to live where you live, understand what you understand, taste what you taste.

1. I do think we have confused ourselves a bit about the role of Pastor /pastoral carer. These days in the modern church we have big "P" Pastors who are the people on staff paid to lead the church and small "p" pastoral carers who are lay people who are really good at doing pastoral work but aren't leading the church. This would be people like chaplains and counsellors and mentors and the like. Sometimes a Pastor is also the primary pastoral carer, and sometimes not (i.e, Worship Pastor, big "P" because she is on staff, or at least part of the leadership team). In this book and chapter I am making a distinction between big P and little p pastors because the Bible makes such a distinction. Eph 4:11 indicates Pastor is a spiritual gift, given to the church to lead in a holistic way, a local body of believers. Pastors should be pastoral carers but not all pastoral carers need be Pastors. My concern in this chapter is for the shallow understanding of the nature of pastoral care regardless if one is a Pastor or the pastoral carer.

Eugene H. Peterson, whose work I greatly admire because he was one such pastor, says this:

> Pastoral work has its origin in the act of worship. Community ("common") worship is the biblical setting for pastoral work. Nor is it possible to do pastoral work apart from common worship. Pastoral work has no identity in and of itself. It is derivative work; worship is that from which it is derived.[2]

Pastoral work starts (or ends) on Sunday morning, but continues throughout the rest of the week as what is proclaimed publicly on Sunday is lived out on Monday. The people are sent out to live lives of worship by the preacher, but they are not sent out alone. They are accompanied by the pastoral carer. This is why he/she is more important (in my view) then the preacher. Certainly, the role of pastor /preacher is often filled by just the one person, but a rare and mightily gifted man or woman indeed if they are able to do both exceedingly well.

Now it is important to not think that I am trying to disconnect pastoral work from the pulpit; not at all. In fact, just the opposite. The two are integrally connected. What is said and rested on (the word of God and the tradition of the preaching of the word and truth on Sunday), cannot be divorced from what we do in pastoral work on Monday.

D. Martyn Lloyd-Jones, in *Preaching and Preachers,* speaks of pastoral preaching, dealing with what the Puritans called "cases of conscience,"[3] preaching to the community as if they were dealing with a known problem in a one-on-one conversation with a congregant. They addressed problems of which the preacher was unaware specifically, but knowing the nature of human failings was sure existed in the community. Often in my, as well as his, experience, doing this kind of pastoral preaching had the effect of people coming to me afterwards and saying "This is just what I needed to hear his week!" This kind of pastoral work reduces the workload of the preacher significantly as these people need not make an appointment to see you about something that is troubling them because it has been largely dealt with in the pulpit.

> The preaching had already dealt with the personal problem. Do not misunderstand me, I am not saying that the preacher should never do personal work; far from it. But I do contend

---

2. Peterson, *Five Smooth Stones,* 18.
3. Lloyd-Jones, *Preaching and Preachers,* 37.

that preaching must always come first, and that it must not be replaced by anything else.[4]

Replaced? No. But augmented? Absolutely. Augmented by one-on-one personal pastoral care.

Now one of the things that can occur in the dysfunctional church is a separation of pulpit and pastoring. I ran this serious risk and at times it occurred in my ex-church. Knowing my weakness in the area of pastoral care, I was too often prepared to delegate this responsibility to others. Now this in and of itself is not an issue, but when the issues of the lives of the people are not known to me, the preacher, there can become a disconnect between the life of the community and the life of the preacher. This is not healthy.

When it can become very unhealthy is when there are forms of abuse occurring in the church and the preacher is not airing this issue out on a Sunday morning because it is being kept from him or he is ignorant due to lack of sufficient one-on-one pastoral care. By not being public about this stuff, it effectively acts to sweep it under the carpet, giving the appearance it is not an issue in the community. Abusive behaviors in any form and to any degree are a major pastoral care issue that must be dealt with from the pulpit, as well as personally. Now maybe the preacher isn't saying anything because he doesn't know or is being directed to say nothing, but either way this is a major dysfunction that can enable abuse.

Imagine Mr. Peters is sexually harassing some of the women in the church. Inappropriate sexualized comments and gazes, unwanted touching, this kind of thing. The women have gone to the pastoral team or elders with a complaint. The pastoral team starts dealing with it, but keep the preacher out of the loop. Maybe they say, "It isn't his job" (wrong, it must be), or maybe "He's not good at dealing with difficult people" (doesn't matter, he still needs to know). If interpersonal conflict, manipulation, and abuse are not discussed from the pulpit from time to time in response to what is happening in his community, then the women can start to feel this issue is not a big deal. We fail to pastorally care for them in a vitally important way. We never talk about this stuff, so abuse is thereby enabled.[5]

---

4. Lloyd-Jones, *Preaching and Preachers*, 37.

5. However, a word of caution. It is possible to spiritually abuse people from the pulpit. For instance, if you know Mr. Jones is having an affair and you preach in a none-too-subtle way about people having affairs, it can take the form of passive-aggressive abuse, especially if everybody knows what and who you are talking about. It is right to speak to issues, not people, from the pulpit. Preachers must use discernment

WHAT DOES IT MEAN TO BE A SHEPHERD?

The word "pastor" comes from the Latin word which means "shepherd." It is an outdated word in our modern first-world lives, because gone are the days when we or someone very close to us lived or worked on a farm. The idea of a shepherd is an old picture of an agrarian economy that has started to recede from our modern consciousness.

Nevertheless, it is a very good descriptor for the pastoral role in the local church. Pastors are shepherds[6], and using this metaphor is useful for understanding the role of pastor or pastoral carer.

What do you think of first when you think of pastoral carer? Assuming your experiences are not negative you probably have in your mind a picture of a gentle, kindly, soft-spoken, and deeply empathetic person, who compassionately is able to meet you in your time of need. In the United States, we had a national treasure, Fred Rogers, who had a children's television show for years, *Mr. Rogers' Neighborhood*. He was a Presbyterian minister, and his kindly manner endeared himself to generations of adults and children alike. If you haven't seen him or don't know of him, look him up online, because this is what I first think of when I think of pastoral carer. This is the guy I wasn't and was the picture in my mind that had me hold out of ministry for so long.

Now don't misunderstand what I am about to write next, because Fred Rogers in his gentle kindness was a pastor in the true sense of the word. He was tough when he needed to be and soft when he needed to be and could speak in the face of the worst catastrophes of his time to children to encourage them and their parents. But the appearance of softness and gentleness and kindness hid the steel in him and so it was easy for me to get the impression that pastoral carers are all about softness and gentleness. But if this is all our pastoral carers are, then they are only shallow men or women. Pastoral carers must not be *just* nice people. In fact, if all they are (or primarily all they are) is gentle and nice and sweet and syrupy, then they are more harm than good. This shallow view of pastoring—the kindly, gentle, "get alongside and empathetically journey with you as you struggle" kind of pastor—is only half the need of a good pastoral carer. Nice pastoral carers like this run the risk of drowning their sheep in a lake of syrup. Sometimes pastoral carers need to stop being nice.

---

from the pulpit at all times.

6. Or, better, undershepherds, or stewards of the flock, with their responsibility and authority conferred on them from the Great Shepherd himself, Jesus.

G. K. Chesterton notes: "The virtues have gone mad because they have been isolated from each other and are wandering alone."[7] Compassion and honesty are virtues, but separate them from each other and they become vices and do more harm than good. Just ask the person, for instance, who has been at the receiving end of the honest person who lets you know what they think of you, unfiltered, all the time.

I want to suggest that the Great Shepherd, Jesus, was not always nice. Run through his recorded interactions and you see something more than nice. They include:

- At age twelve talking back to his parents (Luke 2:49–50)
- Calling his friend Simon, the devil (Matt 16:23)
- Rebuking angrily a brood of vipers and whitewashed tombs (Matt 12:34; 23:27–28)
- Overthrowing tables in anger (Matt 21:12–13)
- Being dismissive of his family (Matt 12:46–50)
- Running out of patience with his own disciples: "Have you no faith?" how long have I been with you?" (Mark 4:40; John 14:9)

Now yes there also moments of tenderness and niceness, significantly more so, I would suggest, but Jesus wasn't *exclusively* nice. In fact, if you want to describe the actions of Jesus in one word, and taking all the stories into account, the word I would use is "kind." It makes sense really; kindness is a fruit of the Spirit; niceness is its saccharine substitute.

Kindness as a spiritual gift has associated with it not just niceness, benevolence, and the like, but also the idea of honesty. Take this verse from Ps 141:5, for instance:

> Let a righteous man strike me—it is a kindness; let him rebuke me—it is oil for my head; let my head not refuse it.

Here I think is a vital characteristic that can be missing in the pastoral care in dysfunctional churches—honesty. Jesus was tough when he needed to be and gentle when he needed to be. There was a balance in his approach to dealing with people. A righteous indignation when the actions of others (the Pharisees, for instance) were hurting themselves and others (their souls were in danger), and a gentleness (the woman caught in adultery in John 8). But in both cases, he was being honest.

---

7. Chesterton, *Orthodoxy*, 22.

Pastoral carers have the right and responsibility to be honest. The responsibility comes with the calling. To fail to honestly speak truth into dysfunctional, sinful, abusive or destructive patterns of living and behaving is irresponsible. We have to get away from being afraid to speak the truth in love. C. H. Spurgeon once said: "Leniency to the wicked would turn out to be cruelty to the just."[8] And he is right. It's another way of saying "hurt people, hurt people" He is highlighting the reality that deceived people end up hurting people and we do them or those they hurt no favors by not being honest with them about this. It is in fact cruel.

One of the most overused and yes, abused, words when it comes to pastoral care (in my view) is the word *journey*. "I am going to journey with so and so through this crisis," or "I will journey with them as they deal with this sin," etc. The problem with this idea is this: Who ever heard of a shepherd journeying with his sheep? Journeying, when used in this context, gives the impression of a bunch of sheep wandering in the desert, with no real direction, stumbling from one hole or trap to another. And running around behind and with them is this insipid shepherd who helps them get out of the hole or holds their hand as they cry in the ravine or whatever. Never directing, never giving advice (unless asked for), never admonishing, never exhorting, just journeying and cleaning up the mess as it happens. What a nice, dare I say bad, shepherd!

Shepherds—good ones, anyway—lead (Ps 23:1–2). It is their responsibility. They lead and give advice spoken in love even when it isn't asked for because with the responsibility comes the authority to do so. Shepherds have the right and responsibility to lean into the turmoil and dysfunction that is ruining our lives. Pastors and pastoral carers are called to be ministers of word and prayer. Bring the word of God, both law and gospel, to bear when the actions of an individual run the risk of destroying themselves or others; bring a word of prayer and lament when in seasons of misery and grief.

I have seen too much of the journeying kind of thing, where pastoral carers, in a misguided, shallow attempt to pastorally care for difficult people, engage in interminable conversations about behavior and actions, but never once (like Jesus in the temple) overturn the tables in their lives. Good pastoral care must bring the gospel to bear and turn a mirror to the sin that they harbor that causes them to engage in sinful and hurtful means of coping. I have seen manipulative and abusive ministry leaders allowed

---

8. Spurgeon, "Abundant Pardon," para. 25.

to remain in positions of influence and authority as they are journeyed with, trying to manage their behaviors, rather than being rebuked and being made to stand down. This is the result of a shallow view of pastoral care that sees the role *primarily* as being nice and kind and caring and loving and forgiving. Often the kindest, most loving thing we can do for someone is to allow them to face the consequences of their sin, to face and own their sin and behaviors and the impact it has on others. Otherwise, we just become enablers of sin and dysfunction in our churches. Dr. John Townsend defines enabling this way: "To enable, or rescue, someone is to remove the pain of that person's dysfunction from his experience,"[9] and declares that we should allow people to face the pain and consequence of poor life choices and coping mechanisms they have being using to make sense of the world, methods that fall outside of God's standards:

> God has designed us so that if we live according to his ways, life works pretty well. But if we don't, life begins to fall apart. You don't fight long against gravity, magnetism, or nuclear force. The big realities always win. We should reap what we sow, in the good or bad consequences of our lives.[10]

Life should not be working for difficult people, and we should not be enabling them by shallow views of what it means to love and pastorally care. Rather, we should lovingly be allowing them to face the consequences of the decisions they make in choosing to not do the hard heart work that needs to be done, work that will show them and excavate out of them the things that are at the core of their behavior. If they are in ministry, remove them. If they are members, discipline them. This loves them well. This is biblical kindness. C. S. Lewis reminds us that the love of God is a tough love predicated on his willingness to even die to cure us of our failings:

> Though our feelings come and go, his love for us does not. It is not wearied by our sins, or our indifference; and, therefore, it is quite relentless in its determination that we shall be cured of those sins, at whatever cost to us, at whatever cost to Him.[11]

---

9. Townsend, *Who's Pushing Your Buttons?*, 49.
10. Townsend, *Who's Pushing Your Buttons?*, 23.
11. Lewis, "Mere Christianity," 111.

God is no tougher on us than he is on himself. As Dorothy Sayers said, "God takes his own medicine."[12] As pastoral carers, we do well to remember this.

The kindest thing God ever did for me was cause me to face the reality of the depravity in me. This caused a severe crisis in my life, led to an existential pain, and drove me to the cross. Pastoral carers should do no less. To fail to do this with manipulative or abusive individuals simply enables the abuse to continue. It is kindness that leads us to repentance (Rom 2:4).

Peter L. Steinke, in *How Your Church Family Works*, indicates that this shallow view of pastoral care is anxiety-driven:

> It comes from a sense of helplessness rather than helpfulness. Our glossy good-will, "peace-agree" position, and overprotective involvement with others is an expression of our low tolerance of pain. We cannot stand the tension and conflict that erupts when differences and contrasts appear. Like the ecstasy of romance, anxiety closes the space between people. Ecstasy and anxiety abhor spaces. They liquidate boundaries and limits; they stifle self-definition.[13]

If this sounds familiar, it should. As I explored in chapter 2.2, the need to belong is the fertile soil in which dysfunction and abuse thrive. Energized by their own unseen anxiety, and with little to no capacity to cope with pain in themselves, let alone others, shallow pastoral carers will seek to love the sin out of the sinner, nice them to Jesus, rescue them, carry their burden. It has the appearance of care, but is in fact designed to relieve the anxiety in the carer, not honestly deal with the issue in the one for whom care is given. Sentimentality gets confused with empathy, and the one cared for is never truly cared for at all.

WHAT DOES IT MEAN TO BE A SHEEP?

I have looked at what it means to be a shepherd but now I want to shift focus and turn our eyes to the sheep for a moment and ask "What does it mean to be a sheep? What are sheep for?"

---

12. Sayers, "Greatest Drama Ever Staged," para. 4.
13. Steinke, *How Your Church Family Works*, 63–64.

I am going to push this sheep/shepherd metaphor to its breaking point, but let's see if it can stand the strain. Stick with me here as I ask, "Why do shepherds have sheep?"

In Jesus' day, shepherds had relatively small flocks, 100 or fewer sheep. They were the means of providing a livelihood for the shepherd. The sheep provided wool for personal use, as well as to be bartered and sold for goods and other services. They provided milk for cheese and drinking and (here's where we stretch the metaphor) for meat, for eating. That's right, the shepherd *ate* the sheep. I think we tend to forget or overlook this sobering fact. We like to overly romanticize the role of shepherd, as if he is treating the sheep like they are a pet dog or cat. The sheep were not his pets in the way we moderns think of pets. They were his livelihood, and he, therefore, in the truest sense of the word, exploited them for his benefit.

Ask any modern-day farmer about his relationship with his flock. They care for them, protect them, lead them, and muster them, right up until they send them to market to be slaughtered and eaten. There is real care, and real protection. It would be the very rare, and dare I say soon-to-be-unsuccessful, farmer who did not have a very high ethical standard when it comes to husbanding their animals well. No good farmer wants his animals to suffer. They do this good work of caring for the flock so that they can achieve the purpose of the shepherd: to give their life for the shepherd. That's what sheep are for.

We, who are called to pastoral care, do well to remember this, because as Pastors and pastoral carers, our responsibility is to lead the flock for the benefit of the Great Shepherd. The job of the pastoral carer is to lead the one being cared for into a full measure of devotion, the giving up of one's life, sometimes physically, but always living. As Paul says in Rom 12, a living sacrifice, or in the words of Jesus in Matt 10:39:

> The one who has found his life will lose it, and the one who has lost his life on My account will find it.

Pastors and pastoral carers are called to lead their people on behalf of Jesus into losing their lives for his sake. Which means this *is* the purpose of sheep and the purpose of shepherds. This is why it is such gross abdication of the calling of church Pastors to prey on their flock or allow wolves to prey on the flock.

This is the complaint that God has against the poor shepherds of Israel in Ezek 34:3–4:

> You eat the fat and clothe yourselves with the wool, you slaughter the fat *sheep* without feeding the flock. Those who are sickly you have not strengthened, the diseased you have not healed, the broken you have not bound up, the scattered you have not brought back, nor have you searched for the lost; but with force and with violence you have dominated them.

The under-shepherds exploited the flock for themselves, but failed to protect the flock. Is this not the very definition of abuse? The under-shepherds using the flocks for their own purpose, or failing to protect them from those that do, rather than caring for them for the sake of the real shepherd himself?

Abusers of any sort act like wolves. A sheep that is consumed by a wolf never ends up going to market. It is a loss to the shepherd. In dysfunctional churches, wolves can prey on the flock, leaving a wake of destruction in their path. God holds the wolf, and equally so the shepherd, directly responsible for this tragedy. Imagine a shepherd choosing to journey and be kind and loving and nice with a wolf while it continues to prey and consume the rest of the flock. This happens all too often in dysfunctional churches who call this kind of thing "pastoral care." It makes Jesus furious, and judgment will come. They are his sheep and you had one job—to preserve them for the Great Shepherd. Ezek 34:7–11 highlights God's disgust with the failure of the shepherds of Israel:

> Therefore, you shepherds, hear the word of the Lord: "As I live," declares the Lord God, "certainly, because My flock has become plunder, and My flock has become food for all the animals of the field for lack of a shepherd, and My shepherds did not search for My flock, but rather the shepherds fed themselves and did not feed My flock, therefore, you shepherds, hear the word of the Lord: 'This is what the Lord God says: "Behold, I am against the shepherds, and I will demand My sheep from them and make them stop tending sheep. So the shepherds will not feed themselves anymore, but I will save My sheep from their mouth, so that they will not be food for them.""' For the Lord God says this: "Behold, I Myself will search for My sheep and look after them."

This should be a sobering warning to all who dare call themselves the Pastors and shepherds of God's people.

FOUR DS OF SHEPHERDING

One of the images of a shepherd is his crook. This ancient device is the standard tool we often seen in images of the biblical image of a shepherd. Understanding its purpose will help us get a healthy understanding on pastoral care role. The crook is used to do 4 things: Disciple, Direct, Defend, and Discipline.

I'll look at these briefly in turn.

Disciple

> *The Lord is my shepherd, I shall not want. He makes me lie down in green pastures. (Ps 23:1-2a)*

The first image of the crook I want to explore is it's use by the shepherd to lead the sheep into green pasture. This is a place of rest and delight. For Christians, the greenest pasture is the place where we feed on Christ. He is the believer's green pasture.

A disciple is a learner, or one who follows another for the purposes of learning. A pastoral carer is one who is helping the flock learn about Jesus and learn how to follow Jesus because they are under-shepherds of the Great Shepherd and they are directing them to him. Therefore, we are always and ever called to point the flock to Jesus.

I think we can confuse mentoring with discipleship. In my ministry I fought hard to make a clear distinction between the two. A mentor is an advisor or counsellor, someone who can give you advice and teach you life skills to help you wisely navigate the tricky reefs and shallow waters of life. Mentors are good and necessary, but this is not discipleship, in my view. Mentors can teach and advise across the whole spectrum of all of life's complexities, from finances to education to marriage partners and the like.

Those who disciple, however, are focused solely on the disciplines of what it means to be a learner and follower of Jesus. Now of course these two ideas are not mutually exclusive and there will indeed be some overlap. I would expect that advice about a marriage partner from a mentor would include some of the ideas of the ethics of Christian marriage and the teachings of patience by Jesus. Nevertheless, pastoral carers are primarily concerned with discipling first and mentoring second.

Shallow Understanding of Pastoral Care

Pastoral carers engage in discipling their flock by teaching the disciplines of the Christian life. The old adage

> Give a man a fish and he eats for a day, teach him to fish and he eats forever.

runs true for discipling as well. Pastoral carers are in the business of teaching people how to feed on Christ and his word. They teach the age-old disciplines of

- Prayer
- Mediation on the word of God
- Reading the word of God
- Studying the word of God
- Memorizing the word of God
- Learning to discern good teaching from bad
- Service
- Evangelism
- Missional work
- Giving
- Fasting
- Solitude and silence

In my role in church, I would spend twenty-four weeks with younger men, teaching them these things and helping them learn to be followers of Jesus. I equipped them to be faithful followers of Jesus. They had all the fishing gear and tackle necessary to fish. I left it up to them to actually engage in these disciplines to be better faithful followers of Jesus.

Direct

> *He leads me beside still waters, He leads me in paths of righteousness. (Ps 23:2b–3a)*

A quick tap on the rump and a sheep will know that the shepherd wants him to move along. As I noted previously, pastoral carers are called to lead, not journey. Now there are no shortages of books on church leadership, church models, and the like, and yes, there is an element of that kind of thing in the idea of pastoring. But as I highlighted above, the primary thing that pastors and pastoral carers need to be doing is directing people to a life of full, living sacrifice for their Savior. That means we direct them to Christ. If we want managers then we should hire managers and call them managers, rather than Lead Pastors or Senior Pastors. Let them run and oversee the business of the church, and leave the pastoring to the Pastor and his pastoral carers. Too often Pastors are directing the business of the church first and the souls of the people second. This should never be.

Derek Tidball, in quoting the exegetical work of Martin Bucer on Ezek 34, highlights what Bucer sees as the responsibility of the pastoral ministry. He does this by looking at how the bad shepherd failed, and conversely pointing out what a good shepherd should do. He lists these actions as:

1. to draw to Christ those who are alienated;
2. to lead back those who have been drawn away;
3. to secure amendment of life for those who fall into sin;
4. to strengthen weak and silly Christians; and
5. to preserve Christians who are whole and strong and urge them forward to the good.[14]

This is a good description of what it means to direct. Good pastoral carers direct the sheep in their care, whether it is one or 1,000, to the life of Christ and the Christ of life. And they do this for *his* name's sake. Pastoral carers point others to Christ so that Christ might be made much of and his glories known. This is what it means to lead for *his* name's sake.

Defend

> *You prepare a table before me in the presence of my enemies. (Ps 23:5a)*

To prepare a table in the presence of our enemies is a poetic way of saying we can live at peace because the Shepherd of our souls is watching out

---

14. Tidball, *Skilful Shepherds*, 47.

for us, caring for us, meeting our needs. Even with enemies near, we shall want for nothing. We need not fear, for our God is with us.

The good shepherd, says Jesus, lays his life down for the sheep. The good shepherd sits at the door to the flock. Nothing gets to the sheep without getting past him. The good shepherd defends the flock from unorthodox teachings and unorthodox behaviors, from predators of our souls and predators of our bodies. Like a good goalkeeper in hockey or soccer, nothing gets past.

> Beloved, while I was making every effort to write you about our common salvation, I felt the necessity to write to you appealing that you contend earnestly for the faith that was once for all *time* handed down to the saints. (Jude 1:3)

The church, in her early centuries, wrestled with the idea of what exactly the once-for-all, delivered-to-the-saints faith really entailed. Was Jesus divine or human or both? Is salvation by faith or works or both? What is the relationship of the Old Testament to the New Testament and Jesus? As these and many other questions were raised, theologians attempted answers. Over the early centuries, those ideas that had no merit or failed the test of agreeing with Scripture were tossed aside and considered heresies. It was vital work to which the early church saw herself called. This is what G. K. Chesterton called the thrilling romance of orthodoxy.[15] The councils of Nicaea and Chalcedon (amongst others), guided by the Holy Spirit, gave the stamp of approval to the early church for the doctrines of the orthodox faith.

Today's pastors, shepherds, preachers, and teachers are the custodians of these early centuries of work. It is their duty to ensure that these important truths are never forgotten. We hold these treasures, say Paul, in earthen vessels (2 Cor 4:7). Let not the weakness of the vessel diminish the glory of the contents. The treasure is great indeed, but shepherds are not only to protect against false teaching, but false behaviors as well, which stem from false teaching. And the false teaching need not be just the major themes or creeds of the gospel. Any teaching which causes a schism, or factionalizes a church, is to be guarded against.

A look at an interesting little verse in Titus 3:10–11 will be helpful here:

---

15. Chesterton, *Orthodoxy*, 93–94.

> Reject a divisive person after a first and second warning, knowing that such a person has deviated from what is right and is sinning, being self-condemned.

Note the word "divisive" is a translation of the Greek word *hairetikos*, from which we get the word "heretic." The old King James Version even translates it this way. Now why this is interesting is because the etymology of the word "heretic" in the English has led to a meaning of a person who differs in opinion from established religious dogma; that is, unorthodox belief systems. For instance, Pelagianism[16] is considered a heresy in the church today.

So why aren't modern translators translating the Greek word this way? Because at the time of writing the Bible, the word didn't mean that. A heretic wasn't a false teacher, *per se,* but one who followed a false teacher and lived a life, therefore, that was out of step with community norms. We might call this heteropraxy:

> The true notion of the word is that of one who is a promoter of a sect or party. The man who makes divisions in a church, instead of aiming to promote unity, is the one who is intended. Such a man may form sects and parties on some points of doctrine on which be differs from others, or on some custom, religious rite, or special practice; he may make some unimportant matter a ground of distinction from his brethren, and may refuse to have fellowship with them, and endeavor to get up a new organization. Such a man, according to the Scripture usage, is a heretic, and not merely one who holds a different doctrine from that which is regarded as orthodoxy.[17]

False belief systems or divisive distinctions that lead to disunity and can cause division in the flock are to be addressed quickly, and the "heretics" removed if there is no repentance.

According to the pastoral advice of Paul to another pastor, admonish once or twice, then remove. Disruptive, factionalizing behavior can only be allowed to go on *ad infinitum* if the pastoral carers are not prepared to defend the flock. This is a dysfunction that can lead to or enable abuse. Pastoral carers are called to remove from the flock those whose

---

16. A fifth-century teaching by Pelagius that dismissed the impact of original sin and declared that goodness still existed in mankind sufficient to enable one to choose good or evil. This effectively taught that a person could help themselves in achieving salvation, without the intervening grace or work of God.

17. Barnes, *Notes on the Whole Bible,* loc. 238841 of 325133.

unrepentant behavior, due to the unorthodoxy or heteropraxy, causes division within the church.

And lastly and most importantly, shepherds are called to defend the flock against those who would be predators amongst them. The church is a ready playground for wolves. With access to children, families, women, and the aged, the church is full of vulnerable people. Couple this with the close intermingling of the lives of these vulnerable ones with people in positions of authority and power and you have a recipe for predation. Any shepherd that is not doing everything humanly possible to keep its vulnerable lambs safe from predators risks the very wrath of God.

Discipline

> *Your rod and your staff they comfort me. (Ps 23:4c)*

The last D of a good shepherd is disciplining. It is a specific, and the ultimate, form of defending the flock. Church discipline is one of the most contentious ideas regarding the role of Pastor or pastoral carer. But as I have already explored, to swing the pendulum the other way towards niceness is just as shallow a view of the role as would be if we only had harshness and discipline.

We tend to see discipline as uncaring and unloving, and hence we want to avoid it. Failure to discipline when necessary is one evidence of a peacekeeping, conflict-avoidant church. I'll have more to say about that later, but it is a dysfunction that can enable and allow for abuse. Pastors must discipline.

The rod or staff of the shepherd was used to discipline the sheep, a sharp whack to the rump or flanks would instantly reveal the displeasure of the shepherd. It helped keep the sheep in line out of trouble and on the right path. This is done for the sheep's own good; this is indeed merciful.

And in extreme cases the sheep are to be removed from the fold when their beliefs or behavior are a serious threat to themselves or others, lest they flock become contaminated by a false teaching or a way of behaving which this teaching evokes. As Paul said, "A little leaven leavens the whole lump of *dough*" (Gal 5:9).

As a failure to discipline well is a major dysfunction in churches that can enable and allow abuse, I will explore this further in the next chapter.

SUMMARY

In this chapter I have explored the idea that a shallow view of pastoral care is a dysfunction that can enable abuse.

- Good pastoral care starts in the pulpit, with preachers who are immersed in and amongst the lives of the sheep to whom they speak. There can be no separation of pulpit and pastor.
- Pastoral carers are called to be kind. This means being compassionate and honest, gentle and firm, in equal measure.
- Good shepherds are under-shepherds called to lead their flock. This means guiding them to the full measure of the devotion of a sheep, which is to lay its life down for the chief shepherd.
- Good shepherds, Disciple, Direct, Defend, and Discipline in balanced proportions.

5.4

Shallow Theology of Discipline

> *Now if your brother sins, go and show him his fault in private; if he listens to you, you have gained your brother. But if he does not listen to you, take one or two more with you, so that on the testimony of two or three witnesses every matter may be confirmed. And if he refuses to listen to them, tell it to the church; and if he refuses to listen even to the church, he is to be to you as a gentile and a tax collector. Truly I say to you, whatever you bind on earth shall have been bound in heaven; and whatever you loose on earth shall have been loosed in heaven. Again I say to you, that if two of you agree on earth about anything that they may ask, it shall be done for them by My Father who is in heaven. For where two or three have gathered together in My name, I am there in their midst. (Matt 18:15–20)*

I THINK ONE OF the most well-worn sections of my Bible is Matt 18. During the last few years of my ministry, I pored over and prayed about this section of the Bible more so than any other. It probably goes to show what was going on in our community at that stage of my ministry. Often in church the leadership is confronted with the reality that they will have to engage in some form of church discipline. What also seems apparent is churches have no clear idea what that should look like. Leadership groups are not particularly interested in going there. This dysfunction, a shallow view of church discipline, is closely linked to the shallow view of pastoral care and it enables abuse.

As I showed last chapter, shepherds of the flock must be prepared to discipline for the sake of the integrity of the church and for the safety of the souls of those in their care. If we believe pastoral care is *solely or primarily* about being a nice, kind, loving, caring, and journeying-with kind of person, then the last thing we will want to do is excommunicate those in our flock who are causing harm, and so we never consider it. And of course it is indeed the last thing you want to do. It is the nuclear option, but it *is* an option, and should be always on the table in a healthy environment in which the shepherds of the flock are seeking to both honor their Lord and protect the sheep.

How you go about understanding Matt 18:15–20 will determine your ideas on church discipline. Now granted, Matt 18 is not the sole location the church can go to consider the idea of discipline within the local church; in fact far from it. But if you major on this section, as many churches do, and approach it the right (wrong!) way, then you will have a very shallow view of discipline indeed. And so, although this chapter is ostensibly about church discipline, in reality it is an expose of Matt 18 and its context within an abusive environment.

Is Matt 18 primarily about reconciling interpersonal conflict, or is it primarily about church discipline? There must be a balanced approach to ensure both loving care and willingness to reconcile conflicting parties on the one hand, and dealing honestly and harshly with unrepentant sin in the community on the other. Too low a view of church discipline allows for the wolves amongst us to keep feeding; too harsh and we drive wounded sheep from our presence. Godly wisdom and balance are needed. In dysfunctional organizations, fear of getting discipline wrong, or perhaps a misunderstanding of its theology, means this vital tool of shepherding may be either kept in the tool shed or used inappropriately. Church discipline is either not practiced or wielded too quickly and/or harshly. We err on the side of niceness or harshness. Either way, sheep get eaten. It is a dysfunction that can lead to abuse.

In order to understand what this passage is dealing with, we first have to get our heads around a tricky little translation problem.

Matt 18:15 in the ESV starts with these words: "If your brother sins *against you* . . ."

But note these other translations:

NASB: "Now if your brother sins . . ."
NET: "If your brother sins . . ."
NIV 1984: "If your brother sins *against you* . . ."
NIV 2011: "If your brother or sister sins . . ."

Now one of the things to notice is that when translators of the Bible struggle to come up with a uniform translation, something is up. Between 1984 and 2011, the translation committees of the NIV went from including the words *against you* to removing them. It usually means that the original manuscripts are not clear. Some manuscripts have these two words, some don't.

Matt 18:15 reads in the NA28 (the standard Greek critical text of the New Testament): "If your brother sins [against you] go and show him his fault in private. If he listens, you have won your brother."

What the bit in the brackets is indicating is this is a textual variant that is not present in some of the manuscripts translators are using to translate the Bible. Now usually textual variants in the Bible have little effect, but this one is significant. Is the offense a general offense that is observable and we are seeking to correct a brother? Or is the offense one directly against your person?

I am inclined to the short reading for two reasons. Firstly, the earliest manuscripts have the shorter reading. Earlier is closer to the initial document and so we must lean in favor of this. And secondly, I like the strength of the argument put forward by the NET Bible® translation committee. They highlight that, firstly, when intentionally changing text, scribes added words, they didn't subtract. Secondly, the scribes were not taking dictation, where they might mishear a word and record it in error. Unintentional changes in this way are unlikely as the manuscripts were copied by sight not sound.

The point being made is that scribes, when intentionally changing text added words, they didn't subtract. Unintentional changes are unlikely as the manuscripts were copied by sight not sound. What the NA28 is showing is that *against you* is a variant reading, not present in the oldest manuscripts and mostly likely added later.[1] The NASB translators agree with this thinking. The reason for doing this is speculative, and clearly there is no agreement. Good Bible scholars far more credentialed than I will ever be, disagree as to which translation is best. They have to make a decision as best they can, hence the variations in translations.[2] But I also

---

1. The NA27 referenced by the NET translation committee also includes this variation.

2. Metzger, *Textual Commentary on the Greek New Testament*. Classifies this as type "C," which means it's a toss-up. Arguments for the longer variant have as much merit as the shorter, meaning textual criticism cannot be the sole determiner of what was in the original.

think that the context of this phrase prefers the shorter variant, which is a catch-all that deals with all forms of sin including abuse, whereas the longer reading may not. Let's explore this now by thinking about cases of abuse.

HOW TO (NOT) USE MATT 18—
THE CASE OF THE NARCISSISTIC BULLY

The question I want to consider is, if the translation is "sins *against you*" or "offends *you*," what kind of thing would this constitute? Think of the following offenses or sins, to list but a few:

- Slander
- Insult
- Adultery
- Theft
- Gossip
- Rape
- Physical assault

Is a longer reading of Matt 18:15 concerning itself with all of these situations? Certainly, some make sense. I might slander you or gossip about you and you take offense, and so, following the Matt 18 process, you come and see me and we deal with it. But think about rape? Is Jesus suggesting that a woman who is raped should see her rapist alone and engage in a Matt 18 process of reconciliation? In their recently released book, *A Church Called Tov*, McKnight and Barringer recognize that using this section in Matt 18 in cases of abuse is "morally inexcusable and psychologically violent."[3] I completely agree.

If we understand anything about Jesus and his concern for the weak, oppressed, broken-hearted, etc, then I don't think it is too far a stretch of imagination that he would be aware of the dynamics of abuse and not require an abused woman to meet alone with her abuser. Surely Jesus would know these words of Psalm 82:3–4:

---

3. McKnight and Barringer, *Church Callled TOV*, 49.

Shallow Theology of Discipline

> Vindicate the weak and fatherless; Do justice to the afflicted and destitute. Rescue the weak and needy; Save *them* from the hand of the wicked.

Jesus cares for the abused. Given this, it is obvious there are common-sense limitations to our application of a longer variant translation of Matt 18:15 which make it unworkable. If the longer variant is right, then we have to argue for exceptions (like abuse) that are based on common sense, compassion, etc., and this can often be hard to argue as it appears to be antibiblical, liberal, or wanting to push an agenda. If we take the shorter variant as the words of Christ then we have a far broader understanding of offense that would include abuse. The passage then becomes *not about personal offense, but sin in general*. We don't have to perform compassionate gymnastics with the text.

The shorter variant has the force of the words of Paul in Gal 6:1-2. I believe Paul is likely looking back at the words of Jesus in Matt 18 when he writes:

> Brothers *and sisters*, even if a person is caught in any wrongdoing, you who are spiritual are to restore such a person in a spirit of gentleness; *each one* looking to yourself, so that you are not tempted as well. Bear one another's burdens, and thereby fulfill the law of Christ.

When viewed in light of this passage, Jesus, when speaking in Matt 18, can be seen to be telling the church to deal with sin in others in a gentle, compassionate, but firm way. This is what Paul means by "fulfill the law of Christ." This would be a compassionate and loving thing to do, to call a brother aside and confront him with his sin and its impact.

With cases of abuse, if we take the longer variant, we are suggesting abused people meet one on one with an abuser. Given the trauma of abuse this is unlikely to ever happen in reality. To see what I mean by this, let's consider this passage in cases of narcissistic and bullying kinds of abuse (as an example) and see how unworkable it is if the longer variant is correct.

Look at the word Jesus uses in Matt 18:15. The translators use words like "show him his fault," or "tell him his fault." But the word used is *elegcho*, which is a much stronger word then appears in the English. Thayer's Greek lexicon defines the word:

> to convict, refute, confute, generally with a suggestion of shame of the person convicted by conviction, to bring to the light, to

expose, to find fault with, correct by word, to reprehend severely, chide, admonish, reprove, to call to account, show one his fault, demand an explanation.[4]

Imagine a relatively timid elderly woman is confronted by a bully in church. She is offended, and frankly frightened by this aggressive behavior. Do you honestly think she is going to privately go confront this person with the kind of strong confrontation the word here suggests? Or what if the person who offends her is an elder or pastor of the church? Are we going to demand she meet them alone? She simply can't or won't. To demand she go into a room alone with a bully or one who holds authority and power over her is abusive in its own right.

Herein lies the difficulty with the longer version of the text in cases of abuse. It simply is unreasonable and uncaring to expect people to face their abusers one on one. However, a strict adherence to this idea of conflict resolution by a leadership team can lead to further abuse. The offended party gets effectively victim-shamed for not following a "biblical method" of resolving offense and interpersonal conflict.

Now, should the offended party somehow manage to get up the courage to face this kind of bullying abuser, they are likely to leave feeling unheard and shamed. This is a common outcome when dealing with narcissistic abuse. It comes with the territory. Matt 18 says if the first rebuke fails, then bring one or two others, but by this stage I suspect most people don't want any more to do with bullying behavior and so let it go. You can't shame (as *elegcho* requires) a narcissistic bully, by the very definition of the idea. They will end up making you think you were at fault. They are good at it. Should you try to be this hard as the Greek speaks with a narcissistic type bully, they will end up playing the victim. And let's be honest, people haven't got the gumption to do this with a bully.

And even if you do follow through, the idea that "you will win your brother back" never happens, because narcissistic bullies who offend you are never interested in being reconciled, just being right, and in control. It is a narcissistic tendency to avoid accountability for the very actions for which they are responsible.

Now, feeling unheard by the bully, and unsupported by the leadership team, people end up leaving a wide berth around this person and no reconciliation happens. The bully knows that a conscientious church is going to require a Matt 18 process, so now the offended party, gossiping

---

4. Thayer, *Thayer's Greek-English Lexicon of the New Testament*, 202.

and grumbling in the background, is confronted by the elders, who say "Matthew 18. Go be reconciled." The offended party ends up being in the wrong; the bully is smugly acting self-righteous. The elders have become unwitting pawns in this game. By putting pressure on the offended party to follow Matt 18 is spiritually abusive, in my view, in circumstances where there is a power imbalance (the offender is an elder or in a position of authority) or in cases of abuse (including psychological, sexual, spiritual, etc.), which, as I have shown in chapter 1.2, is a misuse of power.

This leaves the narcissistic bully free to continue in their abusive behavior because the elders adhere to a strict Matt 18 mindset for resolving any and all offenses. The bully is able to present themselves as self-righteous, declaring "I was prepared to reconcile," and the rest of the flock just accept they are going to be abused because nothing really is going to be done about it.

Of course, seeing that conflict is not being resolved because of the abusive nature of the bully, and the unwillingness of the offended to go alone, the elders may choose to offer to sit in and help resolve the conflict. The reality is this is not conflict at all. This is abuse and Matt 18 has nothing to say to this. The leader's willingness to mediate a solution is simply an admission that this longer variant is not workable in cases of abuse, because Jesus didn't give the option of mediating a solution in Mathew 18.

OFFENSE

Another reason to prefer the shorter variant is because the Greek phrase translated sins *against you,* if it is right, would be one of the few places in the New Testament where sin is translated as being against *you,* the person. Sin is ultimately against God, and normally when this word appears it means to sin against God's holy standard. The Greek word *hamartanō,* the word for "sin," means "to miss the mark or to miss or wander from the path of uprightness and honor, to do or go wrong." It is always against God. For instance, even though King David sexually abused Bathsheba and had her husband killed, he still recognized ultimately the sin was against God in his great psalm of repentance:

> Against You, You only, I have sinned and done what is evil in Your sight. (Ps 51:4)

A shorter rendition maintains the biblical understanding of sin being against God; the longer rendition makes sin against you.

It becomes evident from simply a common-sense perspective (in cases of abuse it is not workable or advisable) and biblical perspective that Matt 18 is not primarily about interpersonal conflict and reconciliation (the longer variant), but rather dealing with all forms of observable sin in the community (shorter variation) and dealing with it effectively.

It is troubling to me that entire conflict-resolution policies of churches are based on a section of Scripture that has this important textual variation about it. Relying on the longer variation and then making it your prime means of conflict resolution can lead to abuse being enabled, as I have shown.

The words of Edwin Friedman ring true here:

> Actually religious institutions are the worst offenders at encouraging immaturity and irresponsibility. In church after church, some member is passively-aggressively holding the whole system hostage, and no one wants to fire him or force her to leave because it wouldn't be 'the Christian thing to do.' It has nothing to do with Christianity.[5]

He's right. It has to do with poor pastoral care, the poor judging of character, and unwillingness to engage in biblically mandated discipline. These things are driven by fear and anxiety.

A WALK THROUGH MATT 18

I want to pull Matt 18:15–20 apart a little bit. What I am hoping to show is that Matt 18:15–20 is not about interpersonal conflict resolution, but rather about how the church should rightly deal with sin in individuals within the local church context. As I move through this passage this should become evident. Let's start with this question:

Who Is My Brother?

I am aware that asking that question can sound very much like asking the "Who is my neighbor?" question of the famous good Samaritan parable. If I ask "Who is my brother?" am I just looking to justify myself and to find a way to not love the unlovable? Am I looking for loopholes?

---

5. Friedman, as quoted in Steinke, *How Your Church Family Works*, 64.

Perhaps. I am aware that this could be an unresolved emotion in me, but I think not.

This passage is about *your* brother, not "a" brother. The word is "your," the genitive case, a possessive pronoun. This is *your* brother, which speaks of a relationship which goes beyond merely "a" brother. I notice that the NLT translates this "any believer" but I think that is too broad an option in that translation. The word *adelphous*, translated "brother," can be a "Christian" or fellow believer, or fellow countryman, and is used in this way frequently in Scripture, but the modifier "your" makes me believe that the right meaning for the word is: "A fellow believer united by the bonds of affection."[6]

As in Matt 23:8 ("But as for you, do not be called Rabbi; for *only* One is your Teacher, and you are all brothers *and sisters*."), where Jesus is speaking directly to the small band of men called disciples, it is used in the same way in John 21:23.

There is more than just common belief in Jesus in mind here, but a more familial "united by the bonds of affection." Now in one sense, as we have seen in chapter 4, we all have a need to belong, and in so doing I have a bond of affection for all Christians, but in another more important sense, I am limited as to the numbers for whom I have real bonds of affection. I visited a church of 5,000 people once. We were all there (as far as I knew) because of our common affection for Christ, and hence the "bonds of affection." But in another more personal sense, I had no relationship with these people at all. They were "brothers" in the sense that they self-declared to be in Christ, but otherwise they were complete strangers.

Jesus, here in Matt 18, was talking to his disciples, men who had a common life shared together, further strengthening the idea of a bond of affection, which was the product of sharing their lives together over time. This is amplified by the idea in verse 16 in that there is a community, a church, a close group of people who know this person and you, people that can be called in as witness to the case.

Let's take an absurd example. Imagine that I am a first-time visitor at the church of 5,000 and someone seriously offends me by making crude sexual innuendoes to my wife. If we consider the longer variant of Matt 18 to be right, I would, to be true to my beliefs, need to go through an entire three-step Matt 18 process. It will never happen, of course, if for no other reason than because it is totally impractical. However, if

---

6. Thayer, *Thayer's Greek-English Lexicon of the New Testament*, 11, definition 4.

the shorter variant is right, and this behavior is observed by a "brother," that is, someone local in the church who knows this fellow, they can pull him aside and start a three-step process with him within the context of his local community. This is sensible and workable. This man wasn't my brother, but the brother of his church family members, and it is their responsibility to engage and discipline their own. This is one reason God has given us the local church.

Offense

Verse 17 indicates that the ultimate response is excommunication. What kinds of offenses warrant this solution? Surely Jesus has in mind serious sins; otherwise, the whole process here is overkill. Yes, all sin is serious and is against God, but some sins have the potential to hurt and discredit the church in such profound ways that excommunication is the right and only solution to nonrepentance. Things like abuse for instance; or, as in my example above, crude sexual remarks to women which go undealt with, and which badly reflect not only the heart of the person making them, but a church which would turn a blind eye to such things.

The sins in mind here would be things like stealing, coveting, character assassination, or physical, sexual, verbal, or any other kinds of assault or abuse. I want to suggest that the sin here is of such seriousness that a failure to repent of it calls into question the bona fides of the declaration of faith of the one we call brother, take Judas as an example.

Gain Your Brother

The Greek word in verse 15 translated "gain" (also meaning "acquire") has an interesting use in the New Testament. First Peter 3:1 uses the word to show how a wife can can "win" or "gain" her husband; likewise in 1 Cor 9:19–22 where Paul uses the word to mean "gaining" or "winning" people to Christ. It is most frequently used with the sense of leading someone to salvation. In context with verse 17 here, what Jesus is saying is that the offense is of such sufficient seriousness in the first place that a failure to repent of it would suggest that the person was never a kingdom citizen at all. Kingdom people repent of serious sin. Nonkingdom people do not (1 John 1:8–10). If they repent, you win them. If they don't, they remain lost.

Here we see the motive of speaking to the offense: to win the sinner to salvation, or to affirm their salvation. Jude 22–23 puts it this way:

> And have mercy on some, who are doubting; save others, snatching them out of the fire; and on some have mercy with fear, hating even the garment polluted by the flesh.

Witnesses

Verse 16 is vital. "Take one or two others along with you, that every charge may be established by the evidence of two or three witnesses." Can I suggest that these two or three witnesses... witnessed the sin? They saw what happened, or they have seen the fallout and can confirm the seriousness of the situation. They objectively can affirm this happened and it is objectively sin. This is a reference to the OT (i.e., Deut 19:15), where in order for a *serious* accusation to stand, it can't be my word against yours. There have to be witnesses. Matt 18:16 is saying that a person has committed a serious offense, or is in a state of serious sin, and others have seen it and can affirm the accusation. A person goes in mercy and grace and confronts another on their own, but if they will not repent, then these witness to the offense are called in. We tend to soften or miss this a bit by suggesting that the two witnesses are there to watch the way you two handle the conflict, or to witness you accusing the other person and seeing if they repent or not. I don't think this notion had any biblical or cultural merit in Jesus' day. This is about a small group of people in the community calling you to account, an intervention if you will, in order to win you back to Christ.

Which brings to light the question: What happens if there are no witnesses and it is serious? Like rape, for instance? The section in Deuteronomy 19 gives the pattern to follow. Send the case to independent investigators to figure it out. That is the purpose of the law and police.

Tell It to the Church

This is a public denunciation of the behavior, the affirmation by the witnesses and the confirmation that this individual is not accepting or choosing to accept the wrongness of their actions, and not engaging in repentance.

Notice this is public. No secret, closed-door meeting, no star chambers. Open, honest accountability by all involved. Here in the court of public discussion, both parties lay out their case and the church decides. Here is where the godly wisdom of the elders is necessary. These meetings could easily turn into a witch hunt and character assassination; hence why two witnesses are so important. And if the offender is still unrepentant?

Verse 17 means literally to remove yourself from him, or remove him/her from the community. For instance, Paul, in 2 Thess 3:6, says remove yourself from the unruly person, or 1 Cor 5:5, deliver such an offender to Satan for the destruction of the flesh. The purposes of these actions are the holiness of the community, unity, peace, and ultimately, the restoration of the individual to Christ.

What does Jesus mean when he says treat a person as a gentile and a tax collector? "Gentiles" is a term for "nations," and was a catch-all word in the time of Christ for all non-Jews. It was a term of scorn equal in opprobrium to "tax-collector."[7]

To be a gentile in the minds of the Jewish people was to be other. The Jewish people, the children of Abraham, had the oracles, the promised land. They were the chosen ones of God. The gentiles had none of these things and were none of these things. The gentiles, or the peoples of the nations, were heathens, idol worshippers, unwashed, and unclean. Quoting the Talmudic tractate Abodah Zarah, Alfred Ederhsheim[8] details the contempt the Jews had for the gentile people, describing a "bitter hatred." He declares "The best among the Gentiles, kill, the best among the serpents, crush its head." Gentiles were lower than a snake's belly!

Tax collectors, in the minds of the Jews, were even worse. The Roman authorities liked to use locals where they could to collect the taxes because it would be harder for a local to be deceived about the income and wealth of those from whom they collected. To be a Jewish tax collector was seen as traitorous. One of God's chosen children in cahoots with the occupying Roman army was, in their minds, simply unforgivable. Jesus equates tax collecting (Matt 5:46) with a class of people known as sinners (Luke 6:32–34). Tax collectors were not only traitors in the minds of the Jewish people, but unclean simply as a result of the fact they interacted with them so much and handled their money. Jesus was

---

7. Blair, "Gentiles," 414.
8. Edersheim, *Life and Times of Jesus the Messiah*, 90–92.

speaking to the cultural milieu of his day. His words were weighty, and his disciples knew it.

When Jesus tells the disciples to treat an unrepentant brother like a gentile or tax collector, he is telling them to treat them as if they are not elect. Treat them as if they do not belong to the family of God. Treat them as if they are no longer, or were never, a brother. To put it in common church jargon, treat them as if they aren't saved.

Which means love him, care for him, journey with him, yes, but not only this. To simply be nice is to fail them and our Savior, and fail to protect the church. Jesus means to discipline them, and church discipline has consequences:

> Church discipline is the act of removing an individual from membership in the church and participation in the Lord's Table. It is not an act of forbidding an individual from attending the church's public gatherings. It is the church's public statement that it can longer affirm the person's profession of faith by calling him or her a Christian.[9]

Although I largely agree with this, it falls short in cases of abuse. In these, removing the offender from the church's public gatherings shows compassion for the one offended, especially if the abuse happened to someone in the church. For instance, it makes no sense, and is pastorally insensitive to the abused, to allow a sexual abuser who is unrepentant to continue to attend the public gatherings of the church in which the abuse occurred.

This is how D. A. Carson explains it:

> First, the offense may be so serious that the only responsible decision that the church can make is to thrust the offender out of the church and view him or her as an unconverted person (Matt 18:17). In other words, the offense is excommunicable because of its seriousness. In the NT as a whole, there are three categories of sins that reach this level of seriousness: major doctrinal error (e.g., 1 Tim 1:20), major moral failure (e.g., 1 Cor 5), and persistent and schismatic divisiveness (e.g., Titus 3:10). These constitute the negative flipside of the three positive "tests" of 1 John: the truth test, the obedience test, and the love test. In any case, though we do not know what it is, the offense in Matt 18 is excommunicable because of its seriousness.[10]

---

9. Leeman, *Church Discipline*, 27.
10. Carson, "On Abusing Matthew 18," 2.

Too often churches and other organizations err on the side of Jesus "niceness" with respect to this passage. Here is the balance; extending grace and dignity to the offender by speaking to them behind closed doors, demonstrating love and grace in a public meeting and offering mercy and the goodness of the gospel. The offender is given every chance to repent and be forgiven. Their removal from the community is an act of mercy, for both the community in that it protects them and for the offender. In losing community, the offender sees the depths of what their sin is really costing. It is a kindness, leading hopefully, in time, to repentance.

Verse 17 is about excommunication and church discipline, and we allow dysfunction and abuse to continue in our communities if we don't see it this way.

This view is further reinforced by the last three verses of this section, which are often ignored by those who hold views of this section as primarily about interpersonal conflict resolution. Jesus is affirming the right of the leadership of the church to make assessments as to the nature of a person's state of salvation. This is a grave responsibility.

If someone has been witnessed engaging in one or more egregious acts, and remains stubbornly unrepentant, then it is right for the leadership to affirm that this person (like Judas) was never a Christian in the first place. If the church makes this assessment, then this is true. If we bind this on earth, if we agree on this on earth, then it is agreed upon in heaven. This is about giving church leadership authority to make these decisions, all in the name of protecting the flock and maintaining the good name of the church. This is a serious business. No wonder churches don't do this well, or at all; the responsibility is great, but the consequence of not doing it is far worse.

SUMMARY

What I have tried to do in this chapter is explore the usage of Matt 18:15–20 as a tool for reconciliation and discipline within the context of abuse. What I have concluded is that:

- a shorter variant of verse 15 sin, rather than sin *against you*, better deals with the full spectrum of sin and abuse from both a common-sense perspective and biblical perspective.

- this passage is about discipline within the context of the local church, and not about interpersonal conflict.

- this passage is primarily about gently and graciously bringing one in a state of sin back from the brink.
- ex-communication is the nuclear option that must be exercised in cases of unrepentant sin in order to maintain the safety of the flock and the integrity of the church.
- using this passage as a pattern for interpersonal conflict can enable and entrench abusive behaviors in the church.

Churches that fail to exercise discipline leave the church open to abuse. This failure to discipline is a dysfunction of poor shepherds whom Christ will one day hold accountable for abandoning their God-given responsibilities. Souls are in danger. The church must be prepared to bind and release in wisdom, gentleness, humility, and faith to the glory of God.

6

The Herbicide
(What Will Kill It?)

Repent, for the kingdom of God is at hand
—Jesus (Matt 3:2)

It would be neglectful in the extreme if I were to look at the concepts of dysfunction and abuse within the church and not give some consideration to the reality of the problem of sin.

Calvinists are known for their systematic theology which spells out the aptly named TULIP, the "T" standing for total depravity. What is less well known is that the principally competing protestant theology, Arminianism, also holds to this same theological point of view. That is, original sin and its effect, the total depravity of mankind. Whatever main theological Protestant school you adhere to, sin and its effects on mankind are agreed upon as the root of all mankind's ills.

This doctrine determines that the sin of Adam is placed on the account of all mankind (Rom 5:12). Although the specifics of the sin we may commit are different, we are still identified with Adam and are therefore partakers of his guilt and the just condemnation of sin this entails. In the words of Arminius:

> The whole of this sin is not peculiar to our first parents, but is common to the entire race and all their posterity, who, at the

time when his sin was committed, were in their loins, and who have since descended from them by natural propagation.[1]

Scripture declares the impact of this original sin on mankind's depravity by clearly stating:

- Mankind fell from a state of glory to a state of sin (Rom 3:23)
- This sin placed man under God's condemnation (Rom 6:23)
- Mankind cannot, in and of himself, please God or have fellowship with God (Eph 2:1–3)
- Only the gracious work of God the Holy Spirit can draw a sinner to God (John 6:44)

To be totally depraved means:

- it is a matter of the entire person-mind, body, will
- all acts of altruism have an element of improper motive—good acts are never entirely selfless
- sinners are unable to extricate themselves from their sinful condition—an act of God's grace is necessary.[2]

Calvinists and Arminians both agree on these ideas. However, although the idea of original sin and the total depravity of man might be tenets in our stated beliefs as Protestant Christians of whichever persuasion, we can live out our lives as practical Pelagians.

Pelagius was a British monk that held to the idea that: "The soul created by God specially for every person is not tainted by any supposed corruption or guilt."[3]

The outworking of this theology is that people could, by their own innate goodness and efforts, make themselves right with God. It allows for the belief that by exercising free will, a person, encumbered by original sin, could find their way to God. This flies in the face of clear Scripture and was officially renounced as a heresy by the church at the Council of Ephesus in AD 431.

Now although this is a seemingly esoteric wandering through ancient Christian theology, I go there to show that although we can declare

---

1. Arminius, *Works of James Arminius*, 2:156.
2. Erickson, *Christian Theology*, 645–47.
3. Erickson, *Christian Theology*, 649.

"No good in us," we can still act as if there is good in us. We can fail to fully understand the impact and depth of sin on our souls. We can act as if the war against sin ends when we come to a faith in Christ, when in fact that is when the war against sin really begins.

It is only through the gracious work of God in opening my eyes to the depth of the depravity of the sin in my soul (a kindness; see Rom 2:4) that the battle against sin can really begin. The life of a Christian is a battle against the ever-present indwelling of sin and its nature and the death it is producing in us (Rom 7:24).

What the gracious work of God is doing in us is revealing not only the depth of our sin as it pervades all of our motives and actions, but also the very name of the sin itself. It is one thing to say "I am a sinner, saved by grace," it is another to actually give the sin a name: pride, anger, lust, envy, gossip, gluttony, idolatry, lying, apathy, thieving, abusing, mistreating, mistrusting, misusing. I'll wait while you fill in the list.

The point is that sin has a name and we do well to not just make blanket statements like "I am a sinner." This has the effect of minimizing the actual behavior and the sin nature behind it. Statements like "I am a liar" paint a clear picture of both the reality of sin and its outworking in our life.

We can live and act like Pelagius, behaving as if we can live good, moral lives without needing the ever-present grace of God in our lives. But,

> Here's the question: how wholesome, faith-driven, and Christ-centered is the conversation that you have with yourself every day? Do you remind yourself of your need? Do you point yourself once again to the beauty and practicality of God's grace? Do you tell yourself to run toward him in those moments when you feel like running from him?[4]

The solution to the problem of dysfunction of abuse begins and ends with the daily application and preaching of the gospel into the very hearts of us fallen-yet-saved creatures. The gospel is not just for the unsaved, but even more so for those of us who are saved. We must remind ourselves of the exact nature of the sin and death that are working themselves out in us and constantly repent of these things. We must remind ourselves that there but for the grace of God go I, as we see sin doing its killing work in others. We must forever remind ourselves of the mercies of God and bless his name in public for the might of his saving grace towards us.

---

4. Tripp, "You Talk To Yourself," para. 6.

6.1

The Gospel

IT SEEMS, THEREFORE, LIKE a natural thing to declare that the way to kill the bitter fruit of dysfunction, and its potential associated abuse in our churches, is by means of the gospel. But it is a weird thing as well. Natural, in the sense at least for evangelical churches or those from that tradition (of which the church I belonged to was one), because evangelical churches are all about the gospel. It is her *raison d'etre,* and one of the things of which she is most proud. Our church, for instance, "prided" itself in close adherence to the gospel. No works-based righteousness would ever pass our lips. We proclaimed the 5 Solas. Heck, I even preached on them in October 2017 to commemorate the 500th anniversary of Luther's 95 theses. Grace, grace, and more grace—we were all about grace.

The gospel was the thing those others weren't adhering to. You know, *them,* with their robes and incense and stained-glass windows. Those others, all liturgical and formulaic and religious. No priests with us though, just the priesthood of all believers. Not phony priests interfering with little children. No, not us, no way, we lived in the freedom of the fullness of the gospel.

And not just any gospel, the *true* gospel, not that glitzy televangelist health-and-wealth thing that promised much, but delivered little. Yeah, those people are the ones with all the abuse and dysfunctional problems because they watered down the gospel and got away from truth. "For them," I mused, "it's all about power and money and religion—any number of other things. All those others got away from the gospel and now all this dysfunction and abuse in those churches is God's judgment on them."

So, of course it's natural. Good churches are gospel-abiding, gospel-preaching churches, and so the means of killing the bitter fruit of dysfunction and abuse and preventing such things in the first place has to be the gospel, because abuse can't happen in churches that are all about salvation and Jesus and the gospel. Good evangelical churches, standing firm on the word of God, adhering to the apostolic doctrines. "Standing on the promises, not sitting on the premises," as we used to joke.

Which is exactly why it is so weird, because if the #Churchtoo movement is telling us anything, even the most gospel-soaked communities can be havens of dysfunction and abuse. If they are all about the gospel, how is it then that abuse is happening in gospel-proclaiming evangelical churches? Adherence to, preaching of, and proclaiming aloud the gospel, it seems, is no hedge against sin and abuse in the church. And this is just the point: we can proclaim it, preach it, declare it, print it, love it, and yet not always live it. And as I survey the churches across the globe whose ex-members report abuse, this is all too common a theme: the gospel is not being lived.

In dysfunctional and abusive churches, the gospel seems to have been reduced into something like a sales pitch for the business that we are in, designed to ensure that people hear about Jesus and are won to Jesus. The gospel is all about salvation from sin, being made right with God, getting entry into heaven, declaring Jesus is Lord. And if, by proclamation of the justifying saving work of Christ, we win people to our church, all the better. It affirms to us that we are doing the right thing.

But the gospel is so much more than this. I fear that gospel-proclaiming churches have a hole in their understanding of the wholeness and fullness of the gospel.

THE HOLE IN THE WHOLE GOSPEL

> And we know that God causes all things to work together for good to those who love God, to those who are called according to *his* purpose. For those whom He foreknew, He also predestined *to become* conformed to the image of his Son, so that He would be the firstborn among many brothers *and sisters*; and these whom He predestined, He also called; and these whom He called, He also justified; and these whom He justified, He also glorified. (Rom 8:28–30)

There are three broad ideas that this important passage from Paul highlights, which are also evident elsewhere in his writings and in other locations in the Bible, and that is that salvation has a tripartite sense to it, each of which is a deeply rich idea in itself:

- Justification: That is, being made right with God
- Sanctification: Being set apart, made holy, being transformed into the image of the Son
- Glorification: The resurrection of the body, and the Christian eschatological hope.

When we talk about the saving work of Christ, therefore, when we proclaim the gospel, we are talking about all three things. Salvation is not just something that occurs for the Christian in the past, but is a present, continuous kind of thing that God is doing in us and for us by the power of his Spirit until he finishes the work in the new age. This is what Paul is contending in 1 Cor 1:18:

> For the word of the cross is foolishness to those who are perishing, but to us who are being saved it is the power of God.

Notice the language; "those of us who are *being* saved," not those of us who *were* saved. Those outside of Christ are in the present state of perishing; those in Christ are presently, currently, continually being saved.

I believe part of the issue as to how and why gospel-preaching communities can still find themselves dysfunctionally enabling abuse is that the idea of salvation as sanctification is either little understood or ignored.

Well understood is the kind of gospel that, when preached and believed, gets us right with God, the sort that stamps our entry ticket into heaven, as it were. People will declare, "I asked Jesus into my heart and now I am saved," and what is popularly understood by that is, Jesus washed away their sins by his blood, they are now forgiven, and will one day make it to heaven. This is a layman's understanding of salvation and glorification (Rom 8:30). But the same saving grace that justifies and glorifies is the same saving grace that is actively at work in the Christian through the Spirit to sanctify. And sanctification is the place that I think is where we find the hole in the wholeness of the gospel.

Theologians spend swimming pools of ink trying to describe things like the relationship between:

- Justification and sanctification
- Law and gospel
- The work of the Spirit and our duty

But what is not in question, and what Paul is declaring in Romans 8, is that the Trinity is at work in the fullness of our salvation:

- The saving work is initiated by God
- Jesus does the redeeming work
- The Holy Spirit is working within us

The desire to obey God and be like Christ is all a work of grace. As Paul puts it in Phil 2:13,

> for it is God who is at work in you, both to desire and to work for *his* good pleasure.

If a person desires Christlikeness, this is the work of God the Holy Spirit in the life of the believer. No natural man would ever choose to be like Christ. No unsaved person would ever voluntarily bend the knee to the lordship of Jesus. This is the sense and impact of John's words in 1 John 4:13-15:

> By this we know that we remain in Him and He in us, because He has given to us of his Spirit. We have seen and testify that the Father has sent the Son *to be* the Savior of the world.

But God, having placed this desire in us, also empowers us through his Spirit to do these things to which he calls us. This is entirely a work of grace, by faith:

> Therefore, as you have received Christ Jesus the Lord, *so* walk in Him, having been firmly rooted and *now* being built up in Him and established in your faith, just as you were instructed, *and* overflowing with gratitude. (Col 2:6-7)

We received Christ by faith (justification), we are called to walk with Christ by faith (sanctification), and God, who has begun this work in us by faith, will complete it until the end when we finally see Christ face to face (glorification).[1]

---

1. I am aware of views that declare that some can lose their salvation; I do not hold to this view. I believe those who endure to the end will be saved (Matt 24:13) and that those who are saved will endure.

We are being (present tense) transformed into the image of the Son, which presupposes, therefore, that whatever we are becoming, it is certainly not from a base of inherent goodness. Original sin's stain has done (and is doing!) its work in us, and God, through the process of sanctification, is rinsing this out. Perhaps this is why dysfunctional churches don't get this part of the gospel right. Perhaps they have too low of a view of sin, its pervasiveness, and its ability to creep up on us and slay us at any time. The process of being transformed and spiritually formed occurs within a community that recognizes that simply being justified has not dealt with the sin problem within us.

> The fertile field for formation is a community genuinely aware of the depth of their sin and the reality of their spiritual thirst. True formation requires that the community deeply understands that they cannot cure the sickness of their soul through willpower alone.[2]

As has frequently been said, sin's *power* is gone, but it is still ever-*present*. And we must deal with its presence until we are *perfected*.

Now here is where I think dysfunctional churches get it wrong. As I described earlier in chapter 1.1, healthy churches, and the individuals within them, are sensitive to the stimuli of both word and Spirit. Dysfunctional churches, conversely, are not. A healthy community is a thirsty community, seeking the living water to be their living and life-changing force. And it is by means of both word and Spirit that God primarily saves us. That is, by sanctifying his people. If God is in the business of transforming us as individuals and as gospel communities into images of his Son, then we need to be constantly attuned to the sanctifying and convicting work of the Holy Spirit within our midst as he speaks to us through word and prayer. This is partly what it means to be a gospel-informed, gospel-soaked community—we don't just preach that Christ justifies, we live in a way that demonstrates how Christ sanctifies, constantly growing to become like the Christ who is doing this work in us.

But this raises important questions: Are biblical propositional truths the only truths that can be brought to bear on a sinful people? Is this the only way God speaks to his people? Is this the only sanctifying power available? The biblical truths, these special revelations and graces, are the primary means no doubt, but are there not also common graces that can be used to inform the people of God? If the gospel is the good news that

---

2. Wilhoit, *Spiritual Formation*, 63.

God is creating for himself a new people then he will stop at nothing to allow this to happen. According to his sovereign plans he will reveal truths as he sees fit to grow and change his people.

There is wisdom of the ages that may not be biblical. That is, you can't find a chapter and verse about it. But there are objective truths that exist that can be used to inform and thereby be Spirit used to transform a people. These extrabiblical truths may not be sufficient for justification, but can and are used by God for sanctification. In his commentary on Titus, Calvin wrote, "All truth is from God; and consequently, if wicked men have said anything that is true and just, we ought not to reject it; for it has come from God."[3] Here is a common grace: God using, from time to time, any mouthpiece to present what is true. It is not the messenger of truth that matters, but its source.

So even if some social scientist, starting from a viewpoint of evolutionary humanism, is able to describe the way we as a society organize ourselves, or how the human psyche works, we as biblical Christians can acknowledge the real source of this truth as God, even if this is not the starting point of the one who declares it. The social sciences, psychology, social psychology, and other disciplines, can have much to say and are helpful in informing churches and church communities, as we have seen in previous chapters. These truths can be a sanctifying force for a receptive people. To reject these things because they are not biblical is to reject one of the sanctifying graces of God for his church, and, therefore, cause us to end up with a hole in the whole of God's saving and sanctifying work.

It is easy to have blind spots on our periphery; we can fail to recognize that God's sanctify and saving work for his people includes these other things. This is a form of tunnel vision, wherein the community is focused firstly, centrally, and—most importantly—*only* on the biblical truths of the Bible as the means of God sanctifying his people. But there are truths (wisdom, if you will) at the periphery of their vision to which these dysfunctional communities are blind. Yes, God uses his word to sanctify his people, but he also uses the fullness of all truth, as well as experiences, wisdom of others, and sufferings to help form his people. Failing to recognize the fullness of the sanctifying means of God and denying its power in their midst is one way church communities can have a hole in the wholeness of the gospel which can allow for dysfunction and abuse.

---

3. Calvin, *Commentaries on the Epistles*, 300–1, commenting on Titus 1:12.

For example, I was once told I had spent too much time listening to psychologists and counsellors and not enough time meditating on Scripture. This reflects a fear and bias against anything nonbiblical which helped to maintain the dysfunction in the place, because as a church we were deliberately telling people to not listen to any form of truth of which we were suspicious.[4]

THE GOSPEL AS HONOR

When I read the gospels, I read about Jesus and the kingdom of God. And if there is one thing that is blindingly obvious to any first reading of the gospels, it is that Jesus—and the kingdom he represents—is so very anti-power and control, and so very in favor of the poor and disempowered. The gospel is the *gospel of the kingdom* (Matt 24:14), not just *the gospel*, and so as gospel people we should be proclaiming what it means to be kingdom people, and clearly living that out. Something has gone wrong with our living out of the gospel if we are disempowering the poor and weak. Or ignoring them. Or worse, using them. If we allow the weak and most vulnerable amongst us to be used and abused, or when we hear about it and choose to actively cover it up, then we have missed the point of the gospel by a mile.

Right from the beginning of his ministry, Jesus made this clear:

> The Spirit of the Lord is upon Me,
> Because He anointed Me to bring good news to the poor.
> He has sent Me to proclaim release to captives,
> And recovery of sight to the blind,
> To set free those who are oppressed. (Luke 4:18)

I don't care how many buildings you build, sermons you preach, baptisms you perform, or declarations of "Jesus is Lord" you make. I don't care how many ministries you run or how many missionaries you support. If you allow, enable, or engage in abusive actions in your church, you have missed the heart of the gospel. You have missed the heart of Jesus.

There are too many unhealed, wounded, and brokenhearted people in dysfunctional churches, people who are being held captive, blind and bruised and not set at liberty, not because of undealt with sin in their

---

4. Discernment is always necessary to know what to keep and what to jettison. This is the value of listening to disparate Christian voices and being part of a living church community.

own lives, or because of a failure to know Jesus,[5] but because of what the shepherds in those churches are doing to them and allowing to happen to them. They are captives in their own flock. We have dishonored them and this is a great and grievous sin.

It is too easy to want to spiritualize the words of Jesus in Luke 4:18. Yes, there is a spiritual metaphor intended, but Jesus is also speaking directly to the physical malady that the fall has wrought on mankind. Jesus has walked into a religious community that was actively spiritually abusing its people. Jesus is speaking into that. Jesus is seeking to restore *shalom*. The gospel of the kingdom is not only about declaring, "The king has come," but also demonstrating in real practical ways what submission of all things to this king actually looks like. Kingdom people are called to demonstrate the restoration of all things to their prefall state, even if they do so imperfectly before the new age to come.

Take the words of Jesus in Luke 14:7–14. This passage starts with these words:

> Now He *began* telling a parable to the invited guests when He noticed how they had been picking out the places of honor *at the table*, saying to them . . .

What I want to note here is that this story, the seeking places of honor at a wedding feast, does not at first glance seem like a parable. There are no farming or agrarian society metaphors, no mustard seeds, no hidden treasures. In fact, if Luke had not highlighted the fact that this was a parable you might miss it because it is such a normal-sounding, everyday kind of story about people being invited to a wedding. But because Luke tells us it is a parable, he is indicating it is pointing to something far more important than just the basic story being told. This is about kingdom life and what living in the kingdom looks like. What Jesus wants us to see is that unlike our earthly kingdoms, where people are ambitious and greedy for honor over and among other people, kingdom people are humble and willing to step back so others might be honored.

Honor and shame were big deals in the culture in which Jesus found himself. Honor was a deeply held cultural value in his day, which was understood as

---

5. There is no shortage of people held captive to their own sin as well.

the positive value of a person in his or her own eyes plus the positive appreciation of that person in the eyes of his or her social group.[6]

In honor-based societies, how I am viewed is as important as how I view myself, and this complex interplay is at work in the hearers of these parables:

> The multiple criteria for honor—wealth, ancestry, age, education, legal status, physique, character, and virtuous action—made the quest for honor ubiquitous across the social scale, while the very diversity of these marks of value ensured that strength in one dimension could be challenged by criticism of weakness in another. And challenge was indeed the very essence of this culture. Honor was derived from comparison, from placing oneself (or being placed by others) higher on some hierarchal scale, in which one person's superiority means that another is comparatively demeaned.[7]

Jesus is proclaiming the overturning of this social system of honor and shame. He indicates in this parable that you are likely to be shamed (v. 9) when someone of greater honor shows up and puts you in your place. Here we see the counterpositions of shame and honor, shame as the opposite of honor. Jesus' point is clear: in the kingdom, those who seek to honor themselves will be shamed and humbled, and the humble and seemingly shameful amongst us will be honored. And not just in this life, but more importantly in the life to come. Jesus' words in verse 11:

> For everyone who exalts himself will be humbled, and the one who humbles himself will be exalted.

are an eschatological warning, and not just some temporal concern for the present. This is the intent of the teaching: in the coming kingdom, those who sought honor in this life will be shamed, and those that were shamed in this life will be honored.

Now shame is a marvelously wonderful and complex emotion, but effectively it is opposed to guilt in that guilt is something I have done wrong. Guilt says, "I did this wrong"; shame says, "I am wrong." Guilt is about actions; shame is about personhood. Shame has many names: unclean,

---

6. Malina and Neyrey, "Honor and Shame in Luke-Acts," 25.
7. Barclay, *Paul and the Gift*, 433.

defiled, disgraced, worthless, loathed, vile, scorned, shunned, disgusting. Guilt says "That behavior is disgusting"; shame says "I am disgusting!"

What Jesus is doing here is saying that if you seek to promote yourself, you run the risk of being exposed. Being exposed is shameful. You run the risk of being stripped bare; people will see you for what you really are. The thing you fear the most, the loss of honor, is the thing you risk the most by seeking honor for yourself, and in particular clambering over others to do so.

Jesus amplifies this teaching with a more typical parable just a few verses later. In Luke 14:15–24, Jesus tells of a great banquet to which many were invited but none attended. The invitees were too busy with the mundane things of life to be bothered by such niceties as accepting the invitation. I liken this to being invited to a high tea with the Queen of England, and telling her you do laundry on that day and so you can't make it. The insult is breathtaking, and with this parable Jesus' listeners would have felt the breadth of that insult. The behavior is shameful as it seeks to shame the one who invited in the first place. It seeks to declare "you are not worthy of our attention." So, in justifiable anger, the man invites "the poor and crippled and blind and lame" (v. 21).

Now the point of this parable is primarily about the nation of Israel and her rejection of the call by God, and so God, therefore, rejects her, opening up the doors wide to any and all that will come. The any and all are the lowly and shamed. As a parallel to the first parable, those who are in the low places (v. 10) is equivalent to the "poor and crippled and blind and lame" (v. 21). For those in this unblessed, shameful condition, it was considered the fault of them or their parents and the just punishment of God (e.g., John 9:1). In Jesus' day, to be in that low class of people was to be cursed and shamed, dirty, outcast, vile, other.

The point Jesus is making in both of these parables is clear: to be invited to sit with the king is to be given the greatest honor. Shame has been scorned and turned on its head.

The most common occurrence of the word "honor" in the Old Testament are translations of some form of *kabowd*, while in the New Testament the word *atimia* is most commonly referred to as "honor." These terms are generally used with reference to the honor granted fellow human beings. The root of *kabowd* means "heavy" or "weighty." When used with respect to people it means, therefore, that when we honor someone, we give weight to them or elevate them and grant them respect.

In the context of this kingdom parable, what Jesus is saying is those things that are considered shameful, the low, the vile, the disgusting, those things we would call unblessed, become elevated, honored, and respected by the fact that God invites them through Christ to feast at his table. In a spiritual sense, all of mankind is poor and lame and shameful as a result of original sin and the total depravity it has caused, but God does us the honor of inviting us to sit at his table, through Jesus Christ. This is what we are called to remember at every eucharist meal.

If, therefore, the gospel is about honoring the otherwise dishonorable amongst us, then abusing, using, mistreating, or harming the flock of God within our churches is anti-gospel and anti-Christ. If we are enabling abuse and abusers, or seeking to turn a blind eye to it or them, or sweeping it under the carpet by attempting to manage our image and the fallout, rather than standing up for the victim, then we are also anti-gospel and anti-Christ. Adherence to, and understanding of, the gospel as being the restoration of honor is one means of killing the bitter fruit of dysfunction and abuse that can occur within our churches.

Gospel of the kingdom people are called to elevate the weakest amongst us, not protect those who seek to honor themselves by stepping over the downtrodden. We heap shame upon those who suffered the shame of abuse by not dealing with it openly and running it out of our churches. We need to hear the cry of the abused amongst us. God help us to honor them and elevate them to places of honor, and openly shame those who have abused them.

THE GOSPEL AS HOPE

In truly dysfunctional and abusive organizations, hope can be lost. Just listen to the grief, pain, and sense of injustice coming from the lips of countless thousands of survivors of every kind of abuse from churches and it breaks your heart. How could "Christians" treat fellow brothers and sisters in Christ like this? Yet they do, sadly too often and every day. These survivors often have lost hope. Hope in the church, hope in justice, hope even in God. How many Christians have walked out of dysfunctional and abusive churches never to return to a church or even to their faith? Rightly does Jesus say:

> but whoever causes one of these little ones who believe in me
> to stumble, it would be better for him to have a great millstone

fastened around his neck and to be drowned in the depth of the sea. (Matt 18:6)

A righteous indignation should swell in the breast of believers for what is being done in churches to Christians in the name of Jesus.

Hope is embedded in the gospel: without the gospel there is no hope, and without hope there is no gospel. Donald Capps describes hoping as projecting our minds, and hence ourselves, positively into the future.

> If hoping involves the perception that what is wanted will happen, it follows that our projected hopes will be envisionings of what is realizable. Hopes are not projections of what we believe to be impossibilities, as the projection of impossibilities would not make for hope but hopelessness and would, therefore, be grounds for despair. When we hope, we anticipate the realization of what is projected.[8]

Capps goes on to list three things that can destroy hope:

- Despair: The perception that what is wanted will not happen.
- Apathy: The state of desirelessness (acedia) and a strong element of not caring what is going on around us.
- Shame: Our most deeply and immediately felt reaction to the failure of hopes to materialize.[9]

Underlying all these ideas is the concept of trust, a rock-steady belief that the things for which we dared to hope are undergirded by a trustworthiness in the one who can deliver them. For Christians, the trustworthiness of God or those God appoints undergirds our hopefulness.

Hope is closely linked to trust. We place our hope in those things we feel are trustworthy. However, churches and people in churches are not always worthy of our trust. Misplaced trust means misplaced hope. When the church breaks our trust, we can lose hope. But this was a false hope to begin with. We begin to heal of this when we place our trust in the One who is worthy of our trust. And then hope springs anew.

For example, biblical hope is the certainty of the resurrection, the assurance of new life:

---

8. Capps, *Agents of Hope*, 71.
9. Capps, *Agents of Hope*, 98–136.

The Gospel

> And He who sits on the throne said, "Behold, I am making all things new." And He said, "Write, for these words are faithful and true." (Rev 21:5)

Note that Jesus is not saying that he is making new things, but all old things are being made new; real life being restored, the prefall condition returning to all mankind. Hope is the wonderful work of grace. Hope is the work of Christ. Hope is the heartbeat of the gospel. God is trustworthy because of the certain fact of the resurrection, the certainty that he will restore *shalom*.

How, then, is it possible for a church that proclaims to be a gospel people to actually be so if its actions or neglect cause its members to lose hope? What kind of gospel are the church members experiencing? Are the following things really the result of the gospel?

- Members hoped for acceptance and belonging, but by being abused or neglected it is demonstrated that they have not been accepted.
- Members who, due to the repeated actions of the shepherds, become numb to the abuse and dysfunction around them.
- Members who, when abused, or if they choose to speak up about the abuse, are shamed.
- Members who feel the shame of belonging to something shameful, a community that failed to live up to the promise of the gospel.

These experiences by church members in dysfunctional and abusive churches are the antithesis of a hopeful environment. We project (to use Capps's phrase) that it should be realizable that the church be a safe place. Too often this is not realized. We project that abuse will be dealt with in an open and transparent way. As gospel communities it is right for us to want to hope for these things, and when they do not materialize, we lose hope. To cause people to lose hope is a grievous sin.

SUMMARY

I have explored the idea that it is only by the full application of the gospel that churches can rid themselves of the dysfunction and abuse which plague them.

In dysfunctional churches, too often bitter fruit exists because of the failure of the church to be whole-gospel people. We have avoided the application of the fullness of truth; all of God's truth which is meant to be a sanctifying force in our lives. With tunnel vision, we too often reject anything that is considered unbiblical.

We have failed to see that the gospel is the means by which God honors a dishonorable people. To fail to honor the weak amongst us, and instead honor the dishonorable, defined as those that seek to honor themselves, is to miss the heart of the gospel.

And lastly, the means by which we allow the gospel to kill the bitter fruit of dysfunction and abuse is to allow the gospel to restore hope to the wounded and hurting, the grieving and suffering. Hope that those amongst us who have been hurt will come to realize caring community, protection from wolves, and the honoring of the shamed self.

Unhealthy churches have lost sight of the gospel, despite their protestations to the contrary. The gospel is a herbicide that when properly applied will kill the bitter fruit of dysfunction and abuse. However, any good weed killer will have several broad-spectrum components to better ensure its ability to kill. We will look in the next chapter at another such important component of this herbicide: authenticity.

6.2

Authenticity

Vulnerability sounds like truth and feels like courage. Truth and courage aren't always comfortable, but they're never weakness"
—Brené Brown[1]

Be present as the watcher of your mind—of your thoughts and emotions as well as your reactions in various situations. Be at least as interested in your reactions as in the situation or person that causes you to react. Don't judge or analyze what you observe. Watch the thought, feel the emotion, observe the reaction.
—Eckhart Tolle[2]

AUTHENTICITY IS THE FLAVOR of the day. Everyone is talking about being authentic, living their authentic life, being their authentic selves. And to declare that authenticity is a vital means of killing abuse and dysfunction in our church runs the risk of getting this idea confused with modern culture's understanding of what it means to be authentic.

Authenticity can be hard to define. We know when we meet an authentic person, but putting our finger on exactly what we mean by that can be far more difficult.

1. Brown, *Daring Greatly*, 37.
2. Tolle, *Power of Now*, 55.

Charles Taylor, the Canadian philosopher, has done a culturally significant job of helping to define what we as moderns typically mean by being authentic:

> There is a certain way of being human that is my way. I am called upon to live my life in this way, and not in imitation of anyone else's life. But this notion gives a new importance to being true to myself. If I am not, I miss the point of my life; I miss what being human is for me.[3]

For Taylor, authenticity is a moral concept, in that we as people have a moral responsibility to live our life to the fullest. To be authentic means to answer the question, "What is the good life?" And the answer is, "The good life is to be all I can be." We are called in this modern idea of authenticity to determine our identity without the cultural constrictions of religion (for example) that bound our ancestors. Freed from those bonds, disenchanted in Taylor's words, we are now able to discover who we really are and what we really can be, and are free to authentically live that out.

These ideas can be seen playing themselves out in much of today's sexual politics. If I believe I am a man trapped in a woman's body then to not live as man would be inauthentic. Since I have a moral imperative in this secular culture to be authentic, then to be prevented from living out my identify as a man would be immoral, as would any ethic that would prevent me from living as such. Hence this explains why religion is in the crosshairs of much of today's secular society.

This is not the kind of authenticity I am thinking about when I speak about being authentic. I am defining authentic people as being both *honest* and *vulnerable*, free to be what God is calling us to be as we rest in our identity in Christ. Unlike Taylor's assertion that I need not imitate another, as Christians our highest privilege, the means to the authentic self, is to be imitators of Christ himself. It is his identity that informs our own. Authentic people live in the honesty and vulnerability of what it means to struggle into the identity we have in Christ.

THE HONEST SELF IS SIN-AWARE

One way to think about being honest is to think of its opposite. Surprisingly, this does not mean not being a liar, at least not in the way you

---

3. Taylor, *Multiculturalism*, 30.

may think, but rather, to be honest, or one's honest self, means to not be a hypocrite.

Hypocrisy is an idea we get. It is one of the first accusations we lob at our enemies. We use words or phrases like "phony," "false," "putting on airs," "putting on an act," or "affectations." Hypocrites, as the derivation of the word suggests, are mask-wearers, people playing a part like stage actors.

There are two kinds of hypocrites. One is the sort that Jesus was always at war with. This is the *double-standard* kind of hypocrite, the "Do as I say, not as I do" person. One rule for me and one rule for everyone else. This kind of hypocrisy is what most nonreligious people tend to think of when they think of church or church people. And let's be honest, not without some justification. To see church leaders flaunting their wealth and "earning" it by making promises to people who can least afford it, and in the name of Jesus, is indeed a most vile form of hypocrisy.

This kind of hypocrisy also shows up in dysfunctional and abusive churches. As I showed in the previous chapter, the gospel we proclaim may be about the poor and shamed, but when abuse is highlighted in these organizations the wagons get circled around the abuser rather than the abused. This is both shameful and hypocritical in the extreme.

But a second kind of hypocrisy is the *two-faced* form of hypocrisy, which is enormously prevalent in most of us, whether we are religious or not. This is the behavior where we present ourselves as one thing in public, but inside and privately we are another thing altogether. This is the hypocrisy of the pastor who proclaims Christ on Sunday but acts out his secret pornography addiction on Monday. Or the Sunday school leader who tells the class Jesus loves the little children, but then sexually assaults them. Or the deacon at church who is beating his wife. Or the good doctor at church who has a secret drinking problem. Or the single young woman who teaches Sunday school at church, but has had an abortion, because telling the truth about sex out of marriage in her church was a seemingly more awful proposition then terminating the pregnancy.

And what makes this dishonest is that these people are putting on a mask. They want you to see them as good Jesus people, but they are dishonest with others, and often with themselves, particularly as to the depth of their issues or the grasp it has on them. They are in denial as to the reality of sin's grip, and this face of denial is the face they let others see. This is not to say they are not grieved or anxious about the behaviors they keep behind the mask (unless they are sociopaths or psychopaths), it just that they are not ready or willing to be honest about the struggle.

To be an authentic person is to be an honest person in that the true self is made known to others. But more importantly, the true self is actually known to self, because without truly knowing ourselves we cannot have others see us as we really are. This is a vital concept. It is not possible for people to see the real you if you are not aware of who the real you actually is.

This is why understanding total depravity and original sin is so important. Calvin, in his monumental *Institutes*, puts it this way:

> For there exists in man something like a world of misery, and ever since we were stripped of the divine attire our naked shame discloses an immense series of disgraceful properties, every man, being stung by the consciousness of his own unhappiness, in this way necessarily obtains at least some knowledge of God.[4]

Man must know himself, his *true* self, and cannot do so without a knowledge of God:

> On the other hand, it is evident that man never attains to a true self-knowledge until he have previously contemplated the face of God, and come down after such contemplation to look into himself.[5]

And in the honest examination of himself he will see himself in the light of God's countenance as falling well short of the glory of God (Rom 3:23). We play a fool's game when we play at mask-wearing, as if others can't know what we know. That is, the cesspool within.

We are *simul justus et peccator*, both saint and sinner, and true honesty starts here. Saved by grace, we are a people who now in the light of the word and Spirit (as we have seen) are being transformed into the very image of Christ himself. This is partly why God has given the world the church. That we may encourage and support one another as we walk this pilgrim's journey:

> But God has put this word into the mouth of men in order that it may be communicated to other men. When one person is struck by the word, he speaks it to others. God has willed that we should seek and find his living word in the witness of a brother, in the mouth of man. Therefore, the Christian needs another Christian who speaks God's word to him. He needs him again and again

---

4. Calvin, *Institutes* 1.1.1.4.
5. Calvin, *Institutes* 1.1.2.5.

when he becomes uncertain and discouraged, for by himself he cannot help himself without belying the truth. He needs his brother man as a bearer and proclaimer of the divine word of salvation. He needs his brother solely because of Jesus Christ. The Christ in his own heart is weaker than the Christ in the word of his brother; his own heart is uncertain, his brother's is sure.[6]

To be authentic people means to be honest with ourselves, God, and others about the real struggles we face in the working out of our faith. This is why James encourages us to confess our sins to each other (5:16). It is one of the graces God gives us. However, in dysfunctional churches which can enable abuse, this kind of self-confessing honesty can be discouraged, either through a failure of others to pattern honest confessing behaviors, or by simply being dismissed or disregarded by others when you try to confess. People soon learn what is acceptable or not. And in more insidious ways open confession can be used by manipulative and abusive individuals to control and coerce. Pastors may get people to confess their sexual sins for instance and then use this information in a kind of blackmailing way to control people, all the while engaging in sexually deviant behaviors himself.

THE HONEST SELF: SELF-AWARE

An authentic community is not only one where people are honest with one another about their struggles with sin, but one where individuals within it are self-aware or becoming so.

Many of the problems we face are the result of our own thought patterns, actions, and ways of reacting to situations, patterns that we may not be conscious of but which are most likely obvious to everyone else. I might complain that nobody likes me, but fail to recognize that my bullying behavior or lack of empathy might actually be the reason I have no friends.

Howard Gardner would call self-awareness *intrapersonal intelligence*, seen as the ability to have a view of oneself that correlates with reality. In his words it is:

> ... the capacity to form an accurate veridical model of oneself and to be able to use that model to operate effectively.[7]

6. Bonhoeffer, *Life Together*, 9.
7. Gardner, *Multiple Intelligences*, 9.

Gardner was famous for postulating that there are many types of intelligences that exist beyond just what the standard IQ would measure. Things like musical intelligence or social intelligence. Taking this one step further, Daniel Goleman[8] added emotional intelligence. Gary Collins, in his counselling text, describes people with a high EQ (Emotional Quotient) as people that exhibit a range of skills amongst which are:

- Self-awareness: The ability to recognize and understand your moods and emotions, and to know how these influence others
- Self-control: The ability to control impulses and think before acting
- Sensitivity to the emotional makeup of others, along with the skill in treating people according to their abilities and emotional makeup.[9]

Self-aware people have a high EQ, which is vital because it is low EQ, the inability to detect how you come across or empathize with or understand the emotions in others, that keeps dysfunctional communities alive. Poorly self-differentiated individuals are low-EQ people. Emotionally healthy individuals not only do not engage in the manipulative behaviors we have seen previously, but are able to detect them when they are being used and willingly can call them out. They are emotionally aware. They feel things and the feelings inform them rightly of both what is going on for them and in them, and, equally importantly, what is going on in others.

Self-aware people are able to detect what they are feeling in any given situation—be it anxiety, fear, joy, ecstasy, etc.—give a name to it, and connect it to the physical world at the moment they experience it.

For me, self-awareness has taken over fifty years. I can remember being in a conversation with a particularly manipulative individual at church. This was long before I had a language for, and an understanding of, manipulative behaviors. Following the conversation, I spent five minutes in agitation, pacing around the main hall. Someone saw me and asked me why I was so upset, and the answer was I actually had no idea.

It was only several years later, when I realized this individual had used false guilt as a means of covert aggression, that I realized that the agitation I felt those years earlier came from a lack of self-awareness in me. I had a lack of understanding as to why I was susceptible to this form of manipulation (I had my own unresolved stuff), as well as a lack

---

8. Goleman, *Emotional Intelligence*.
9. Collins, *Christian Counseling*, 261.

of awareness of the anxiety it was producing in me and a lack of understanding as to what this individual was actually doing in that conversation. As a result, I was manipulated and used. This is why self-awareness is so vital and a means of killing abuse and dysfunction in a church. I would like to think that today the outcome of that conversation with me would be totally different. Self-awareness, being honest with ourselves, is vital if we want to stop dysfunction and abuse in its tracks.

VULNERABILITY

Vulnerability is "the willingness to show up and let ourselves be seen," so says Brené Brown. At the time of this writing, Brené Brown's TED talk on vulnerability has had over 11 million hits.[10] This short talk has had an amazing impact. It demonstrates that people at the core of their being really want to be vulnerable, really want to be seen, and really want to show up. "Vulnerable" comes from the Latin word meaning "wound" or "able to be wounded." Nobody naturally volunteers to be wounded; hence fear keeps vulnerability at bay.

Now some people are naturally vulnerable, children for instance, and, in patriarchal societies, women. Sadly, young women walking home alone at night are vulnerable. But the vulnerability that is at the heart of authenticity is a deliberate choice rather than an innate characteristic. Here is where vulnerability and our status and identity as children of the living God intersect. Vulnerability is the way to love.

Vulnerability takes courage. It is a willingness to be exposed to harm. It means taking a risk, but not being risk-taking. Risk-takers get an adrenaline rush from always being on the knife's edge of life and death. But taking risks in the authentic, vulnerable sense is exposing yourself to meaningful risk. And what is meaningful risk? Love for one. I love how C. S. Lewis puts it:

> To love at all is to be vulnerable. Love anything and your heart will be wrung and possibly broken. If you want to make sure of keeping it intact you must give it to no one, not even an animal. Wrap it carefully round with hobbies and little luxuries; avoid all entanglements. Lock it up safe in the casket or coffin of your selfishness. But in that casket, safe, dark, motionless, airless, it

---

10. Brown, "Power of Vulnerability."

will change. It will not be broken; it will become unbreakable, impenetrable, irredeemable. To love is to be vulnerable.[11]

Love and loving others are mankind's highest good, as in love we best reflect the nature of God, who is himself love. To become vulnerable and open to being wounded for the cause of love is indeed a meaningful risk worth taking. But not just romantic love in some kind of *The Bachelor* attempt to manipulate gullible women into declaring their love to a man they barely met kind of thing. Yep, that is vulnerable all right. There is real vulnerability in romantic love, but mankind's highest good comes in vulnerability to the biblical love in the sense of *agape*.

This selfless, sacrificial, "for the good of the other" kind of love is risky because, as we have seen, sin runs deep, not only in the one loving, but also in the one being loved. No expressions of *agape* are entirely devoid of self-motive, as total depravity does its work in us, and all too often this selfless giving of ourselves is not replicated. Jesus knows this all too well.

What happens when two self-unaware, nonvulnerable people meet? Their interaction is surface at best. There is no real connection and this is in fact the environment where most manipulation occurs. If I am manipulative for whatever reason, I am most likely not-self-aware.[12] If you also are not self-aware, then this is the ideal breeding ground for manipulation and abuse. Neither person is really present. Nobody showed up, just the false selves that can enable abuse.

When one self-aware, vulnerable person meets the opposite, this is also the place where no connection is really made. The healthier of the two individuals may seek to help, connect with, and understand the other, but will soon tire of being used or being seen to be used and will speak the truth into this relationship. This should be the nature of counsellor-client relationships, where healthy, self-aware (hopefully!) counsellors are seeking to highlight to their clients those hidden places within themselves that are at the root of why they are speaking to a counsellor in the first place. The client will accept this and start to grow, and real connection can occur, or they will balk and walk away and miss the opportunity for growth. I have seen this as a pastor when I highlighted the sin and dysfunction in the heart of another, and their reaction was to accuse me of being unloving and then effectively run away.

11. Lewis, *Four Loves*, 121.
12. At least not in that moment.

Only when both parties have self-awareness and are vulnerable can real connection, and hence real *agape*, occur in a relationship. It is only through vulnerable *agape* that we are able to truly engage and connect with the others in our lives. Opening oneself up to this kind of love is a risk worth taking, because only in this way can real relationships form. When the real me shows up (I am authentic) and the real you shows up (you are authentic) then meaningful relationships are made.

Vulnerable relationships are one in which honesty abounds, real connecting takes place, apologies can be proffered without fear, and forgiveness offered without strings attached. There is, of course, a limit to the number of these relationships we can have, but when churches are full of these open, accountable, honest, vulnerable relationships, then you have a church that is full of authentic people. Manipulation and lies, deceit and abuse cannot thrive. There is nowhere for them to hide. The herbicide does its job. The bitter fruit is killed.

SUMMARY

Dysfunctional churches which can allow abuse are inauthentic communities. They play the roles of good Jesus people, but inside are a seething mess of hidden secrets, neuroses, fears, and anxieties. Unable to detect these things in themselves, or finding the church to be an unsafe place to reveal these things, sin and abuse can abound.

Authentic people are honest people. They are honest with the sin and the struggles they face in this life. They don't hide these things from each other, but rely on each other to strengthen and comfort one another. They don't play the game of happy Christian out of fear of what people may think if they aren't happy, happy, happy all the time. They recognize and understand the fallen world in which they find themselves, and the impact of sin and death in them and how it affects them. They can live in the twin worlds of praise and lament with equal peace because they rest in their identity as saved children of God. Authentic Christian people are safe in the arms of a God who can handle their complaints and reside in their praises, and who they know sovereignly reigns over all.

Authentic people are honest with themselves in that they are self-aware, able to see and feel and react in emotionally healthy ways to the circumstances in which they find themselves. They aren't afraid of their emotions; they don't seek to stuff them down nor do they try to splatter them all over the place. They are emotionally healthy and in control, and if not, due to any number of legitimate mental health issues, are honestly and openly dealing with these things.

Authentic people are willing and desire for people to be honest with them. "As iron sharpens iron," the wise man says (Prov 27:17). Authentic people know that one of the ways that God grows us and sanctifies us is through the honest words of a faithful friend, harsh though they may seem at times (Prov 27:5–6). Authentic people, therefore, are humble people, as they willingly accept they have blind spots that only faithful others can reveal.

And lastly, authentic people are vulnerable people. They are willing to take the risk and be courageous in opening themselves up to others so that real connections, real *agape* love, real community can be formed, and real Christlikeness formed.

The bitter fruit of dysfunction and abuse cannot grow in such environments. May God lead us to repent of our inauthentic selves.

7

The Resistant Species
(What If It Won't Die?)

THE RESISTANT SPECIES

I OFTEN JOKE THAT my favorite gardening tool is glyphosate, a cheap, easy-to-apply, broad-spectrum weed killer. Once a year I dutifully walk around the house with my small spray bottle and attack the weeds that so aggressively take over in winter. And then I wait. The product is effective, although it takes about a week to see that the weeds are going to die, and about two weeks before they go. But there is one weed growing around the house that is resistant to the spray. Probably due to its overuse in agricultural areas, this weed species has built up a resistance to this product. It just doesn't matter how much you put on, it has no effect.

Sadly, some churches are so entrenched in their dysfunction that they are immune to truth and transparency. The gospel is never fully lived and there will never be real authenticity. The dysfunction won't die. It has been said that, "The same sun that softens the wax hardens the clay." The same gospel that breaks a person can harden them. The calls to vulnerability fall on deaf ears. The dysfunctional fruit will not die.

Ultimately, the problem at the heart of dysfunctional and abusive churches is the leadership. If abuse is occurring or enabled, or if the organization is dysfunctional, this is a direct result of a dysfunctional leadership that has enabled it. If you are not part of the leadership team of your church and you find abuse and dysfunction occurring in your community, there is little you can actually do. You can try to bring awareness, but if my experience is anything to go by, the more you call them out the more abused *you* will become. Be prepared for the storm that is coming your way.

CRIMINAL BEHAVIOR

Some forms of abuse (i.e. rape or child sexual abuse, abuse of an elderly person or disabled person) are clearly legal issues. A legal line has been crossed and so it is seemingly obvious that if this kind of behavior occurs the police should be called in. Churches are not suited to, and neither are they professionals in, legal matters. I say the seemingly obvious here because unfortunately in dysfunctional organizations often these allegations of illegal behavior are not brought to the legal authorities. Dysfunctional organizations will demand that the investigation of allegations of rape and abuse remain in-house. If the accusation is against one of the members of the leadership team then the conflict of interest is obvious. By taking these accusations directly to the legal authorities, a church demonstrates to the accuser that they have and will continue to take their allegations seriously and are prepared to let professionals trained in these things to handle it well.

Church Cares[1] is a wonderful resource for local churches which helps to inform churches dealing with all forms of abuse on handling these situations well.

For those of you in churches where allegations of rape and abuse have been made, and the alleged perpetrator is in a leadership role, I emphasize that you should demand that the leader be stood down and removed from the role. "Innocent until proven guilty" is a great legal principle, but when dealing with pastoral issues of the human heart, where souls are at risk, we must be extra cautious. This is the thrust of Deut 19:15–21. It is highly unlikely that a person would make up an allegation of abuse just to get a leader in a church to be dismissed, and if the allegation is of a criminal sort, proper criminal investigations will soon figure this out.

Pastors, elders, and other ministry heads who have been accused of criminal activity should remain stood down until a complete independent and *transparent* investigation has been completed by properly trained law enforcement agencies. If a false accusation has been made then you have

---

1. https://churchcares.com.

a new set of problems; a church discipline issue with respect to the one who falsely accused the other, and a new legal issue associated with the one who made such a false claim.

There is also the case of workplace bullying, and you may find pastors abusing paid staff, or as in my experience, staff being bullied by unpaid staff and having a workplace that was manipulative and abusive. This may violate the workplace laws of the jurisdiction in which your church exists. Rom 13 makes it clear that God has put the authorities in place, not so we might fear them, but so they may exercise their God-given power in the maintenance of good order.

When behaviors in the local church are abusive and violate the laws of the land, it is the right and responsibility of the local church to see these laws enforced. They are both immoral and illegal. The church can deal with the immorality of it, but leave the legality of it to the authorities.

If your leadership is not prepared to handle cases of abuse in a healthy manner as outlined by Church Cares, or by GRACE[2], as another example, then you should recognize that your church is not a safe place. You should then start to reconsider your attendance there.

NONCRIMINAL BEHAVIOR

The problem for many cases of abuse in the church is that it is of a nonlegal variety. There is nothing in the statute books about spiritual abuse or narcissistic manipulation. And although a pastor or someone with spiritual authority in the church (a ministry leader, for instance) who has sex with an adult member of his church has crossed an ethical boundary and it is rightly an abuse, it is not in and of itself a legal matter; it is a moral matter and how it is handled will tell you much about the health of the leadership of your church.[3]

Of course, the other problem for the average attendee of a church is that dysfunctional churches keep this kind of abuse hidden behind closed doors. Whisper campaigns abound, but since nobody actually knows anything, often nothing gets done. Dysfunction continues and abuse can thrive. The accused will be protected and the accuser further victimized.

---

2. https://netgrace.org.

3. In some states is it a violation of the law for person in positions of trust, which includes clergy, to engage in sexually exploitive relations with a member of their congregation, even if consenting adults. You should check the relevant laws in your jurisdiction.

This is why I have written this book. To show the average person what dysfunctional churches can look like. This should attune you to the fact that it is possible for abuse to be happening and the need for you to be vigilant for the safety of yourself and others. Entrenched dysfunction will not deal with abuse well, but will seek to hide it, minimize it, and sweep it under the carpet. Unhealthy organizations have no language for, or understanding of abuse, and giving them resources or speaking out about these things, although great in theory, is unlikely to have the positive effect you would wish for. Those who speak up will likely be scapegoated.

This does not mean you should not speak up, but it is just a warning that you should not expect a positive outcome. In dysfunctional organizations, those that speak up about the dysfunction and abuse will become the problem. The system will need to silence you, or failing that, drive you out.

Now a word of caution here. You may see much of the dysfunction I have laid out—unquestioned authority, unity at all cost, poor theology of forgiveness and the like—but just because these things exist does not mean abuse is *necessarily* happening within the walls of the church. Only that it is much more likely. Abusers can smell this kind of thing a mile away. They will show up, I promise you. If no abuse is happening within the church you have a better chance of stopping the dysfunctions than after abuse begins to occur. But once abusers get control of churches and their ministries, only a crisis will drive it out, and even then that is not a guarantee.

Churches that have had their dysfunction exposed will enter into a crisis, and can do one of two things: seek the truth by open and transparent means, or seek to maintain their image by giving the appearance of truth-seeking.

SEEK TO MAINTAIN THEIR IMAGE

This looks like any one or more of the following, all of which are designed to keep the leadership team unaccountable and in control:

- Stonewalling any investigation—Simply refusing to take the allegations seriously.
- Highlight how hard this is for the church—Note: no mention of the pain of the abused or the impact on the whistle-blower. This is designed to get sympathy and is a form of playing the victim.

- Minimize the accusations (i.e., "It wasn't abuse, it was inappropriate behavior," "It was an affair, not sexual abuse of a parishioner, etc.," "She isn't abusive, she is just difficult.").
- Scapegoating the whistle-blower—Those that highlight dysfunction and sin in sick organizations are seen as great transgressors that must be driven out of the community. The whistle-blower is denigrated, character-assassinated, and sought to be forgotten as quickly as possible.
- Investigating in-house—Keeping independent investigators away.
- Using pseudo-independent investigators—The church industrial complex is a vast network of good ol' boys. Those in church leadership have a vast network of people who know them and they know any one of which can be called in as an "independent" investigator. The problem is that the leadership group who are allowing dysfunction in the first place have appointed this person. It gives the appearance of taking allegations seriously, but it will be a white wash. It is like a criminal getting to pick their own judge at a trial.
- Refusing church-wide open discussions—Only one-on-one, closed-door meetings occur. This gives the appearance that the church is taking the situation seriously, but it is really a divide-and-conquer technique, designed to maintain control. If everyone got in a room together the real scope of the issue might come out.
- Distract attention—Engaging in sudden bursts of energy, new programs, new buildings, new baptisms, new pastors, new websites and logos, all designed to indicate that the allegations cannot be true, or we would not be able to do these great things for God. If God is blessing us (so goes the thinking), then we can't be in sin. The allegations are false and the whistle-blower is/was the problem.
- Peacekeeping, rather than peacemaking, that looks like:
  - bad apologies—"I am sorry that you felt like that," but with no acknowledgement of the wrong done and the real pain caused.
  - pursuing forgiveness, demanding forgiveness, and denigrating a failure by the abused to forgive, which becomes the focus, rather than truth, justice-seeking, and dealing openly with the reason things need to be forgiven in the first place.

This list could go on for pages, but what you will notice is that all of these behaviors are manipulative—they are all designed to maintain the image the community has of itself and its leaders, and is the exact opposite of open, transparent truth and justice-seeking. If allegations of abuse and dysfunction have been made in your church and the leadership is not actively, openly, and honestly seeking truth then you have hard decisions to make. So, what do you do if you or someone you know in your church has been abused, and your leadership team chooses to handle it poorly?

ary # 7.1

Justice

PRAY, SPEAK UP, AND be prepared to leave. I have said it before and I say it again, dysfunctional organizations that are enabling abuse are not safe places, for you or anyone who attends. I don't care how many great ministries are being done, or how many friends you may have there.

Speaking up in the face of these things takes the courage of a prophet, and as Bible history shows, it rarely goes well for the prophet. However, once you see and understand abuse and its features, and once you notice it in your church, there is no going back. You either have to deliberately turn a blind eye to it, and become part of the culture and the problem, or call it out.

Deciding to stay to help make the changes is noble, but often misplaced. If abuse and dysfunction have been highlighted to your leadership and they are busy managing their image and not taking the steps necessary to root it out, then your decision to stay behind to "help make changes" is actually just enabling behavior. If you are staying, then your motive must be to seek justice and truth. And put a time frame on it, put pressure on your leaders to achieve this, and if they fall short, leave.

I was a member of my ex-church for twenty-five years. We exhibited dysfunctional behaviors for most of it, I just never saw it. It was subtle, isolated, low-level. I was an unknowing participant in it. I enabled it, and perpetrated it, and in the end was a victim of it. Once I saw it, I tried to stop it, and, being unable to do so, I had no choice but to walk away from everything. My job, my church, my friends and social network, any future career prospects. I have lost relationships with people whose children we raised together, people with whom I had meals. Couples I married. All lost. It is heartbreaking. The grief is real and I will never be truly over it, but I have come to live with it. But I am not innocent here. As part of the leadership team, I was culpable for the abuse that was occurring, even long before I ever saw it or had a language around it. Losing these things, although life-altering and deeply painful, is the necessary and right judgment of God on me. Justice on behalf of those that our dysfunctional church hurt over the decades is being served, at least in part by me, regardless of what the other culpable leaders may or may not do.

If you or someone you know is coming out of an abusive environment, failing to see justice done is probably the hardest thing. No acknowledgment has been made, no apologies offered, no forgiveness sought. To be scapegoated and cast away by a community you have done life with, and for daring to speak out, is heart-rending. And the cry goes out from the depths of the heart: "Where is the justice in all this?"

In Luke 12, Jesus tells a parable of a man who leaves people behind to manage his farm, and the managers, thinking the master is a long way from ever coming back, engage in abusive treatment of the other servants (v. 45). Jesus, in this parable, describes three types of managers:

- Those that will be slaughtered—they actively abuse
- Those that will be beaten heavily—they actively disregard, turn a blind eye
- Those that will be beaten lightly—they passively disregard, are unaware

The point is that God will hold his leaders accountable. This is a sobering parable for those in positions of leadership within the church. God *will* hold his leaders accountable. Those that actively abuse, will be treated as if they are not Christians:

> (he) will cut him in two, and assign him a place with the unbelievers. (Luke 12:46)

Let the impact of this sink in. Abusive behavior is diagnostic behavior. Those that engage in it are exhibiting behaviors that demonstrate they are unsaved, not elect, destined for hell. We need to be as blunt as this because Jesus is.

Those leaders that actively disregard this behavior, turn a blind eye, as it were, will also be judged. Their salvation may not be at risk, but they should expect to face the wrath of Christ, either sometime in this life or

Justice

the life to come. Those that dare to declare Jesus as Lord would be wise to heed. By highlighting abuse and dysfunction in your local church, even if the leadership ignores it, heaps judgment on them. Justice has begun, although it may not ever be completed in your lifetime. They are no longer ignorant. Like the Pharisees in Jesus' day, they may choose to kill the messenger but the blood of their own judgment is on their heads. He who has ears to hear, let him listen.

Then there are those like me, ignorant due to my own lack of authenticity, who are in positions of leadership in the church, but ignorant of the abuse occurring around them:

> but the one who did not know *it*, and committed acts deserving of a beating, will receive *only* a few blows. (Luke 12:48)

Ignorance is no excuse. God rightly judges.

There are no shortages of advocates in the world who work tirelessly to help bring justice to the oppressed and abused. They seek to turn a light onto the darkness. They are a grace God gives to the church and oppressed, but despite their passion and energy, their work may go unrewarded for decades. The dysfunction in some churches, and the overarching bodies, can take a long time to kill.

The difficulty for many who come out of abusive churches is that they will never see justice done, at least not in this lifetime, and this can be very hard to take. God declares himself to be a God of justice, but often so many never see it. The cry of the poor and oppressed goes out "How long!" They must trust him.

> But there is nothing covered up that will not be revealed, and hidden that will not be known. Accordingly, whatever you have said in the dark will be heard in the light, and what you have whispered in the inner rooms will be proclaimed on the housetops. (Luke 12:2–3)

> Vengeance is Mine, and retribution;
> In *due* time their foot will slip.
> For the day of their disaster is near,
> And the impending things are hurrying to them. (Deut 32:35)

The longer God patiently waits to bring justice to the oppressed, the more severe the judgment will be on those on whom judgment is due. The waiting can be hard for those who seek justice. It is easy to want to take justice into your own hands. Vengeance, however, is God's business.

7.2

Lament

My God, my God, why have You forsaken me?
Far from my help are the words of my groaning.
My God, I cry out by day, but You do not answer;
And by night, but I have no rest.

(Ps 22:1–2)

March 24th is a day tattooed on my brain. When high emotion is attached to an event, we can remember it with great clarity. On that day, as my old church was celebrating the opening of its new extension, thirty-five people who had left in the previous eighteen months gathered for a service of lament. One group of people praising God for a new building, thirty-five people grieving at the true cost of that building—themselves. The lament was not because a new building had been built, but rather a meeting of grieving people to remember what was lost, and most importantly, the way in which they had lost it. They, as a community, were undercared for, underheard, undervalued, scapegoated, or just plain ignored. Truth was not sought on their behalf and justice not done. These are deep wounds indeed.

This service of lament was an important marker in this small, disaffected community. It marked an end, a burial, if you will, of past hopes and dreams, and the beginning of a new future. They spoke of the things they loved about the place, the good that was done, and wrote these things down on pieces of paper to keep for themselves as a reminder that not all was terrible. In fact, most was not.

But they also wrote down the things they lost, and the pains they suffered, the relationships severed, and then at the end collected their losses together in a pile and set fire to them. They prayed that their grief and prayers would be a sweet aroma, lifting up like smoke to the presence of God himself. They prayed for justice and reconciliation, and then left. This little community will never meet again like this. It had come to an end.

Lament is the proper and godly cry of an authentic people who have been the victims of abuse and want justice for themselves and others. Lament cries out "Why?" It is right that we start there, but we must not remain there.

This service of lament helped us to grieve well. Unresolved grief can leave us stuck emotionally and psychologically. It can drive us and control us. Naming our pain and speaking of it honestly with ourselves and God is one of the ways we move forward. Jesus gets it. He is a man acquainted with sorrow and grief. He gets betrayal. As the Great High Priest, he intercedes on our behalf:

> Therefore He is also able to save forever those who come to God through Him, since He always lives to make intercession for them. (Heb 7:25)

Grief is the right reaction to what was lost, but there is also the anxiety and shame that can be experienced for having attached yourself to something that proved to not be what you had hoped. Lament helps us to give voice to these things. The certain law of life is this: To live is to lose. Naked we enter this world, and naked we will leave it. It does not make the losses any less painful, but it does give them perspective. A wise friend said to me once that eventually we must move in our grief of abuse from the "why," as in "Why did God allow this?," to the how and what, as in "How will you be gloried in this?" and "What will you do for your saint now?" These are healing questions for us. This is the hard, adult work that must be undertaken. As we get to this place, we become aware that God is moving us out of the wilderness into the place where we can start to rest in his sovereign goodness and promises of justice.

Lament reorients us. It reminds us that we are not in control, that the world and its sin and its impacts on us are great. The gospel always begins with lament; hope finds its birthplace there. Hope springs out of the fertile ground of lament, watered by our tears, and grows in the light of the sunshine of God who turns his countenance on us and declares "Soon." Too often we want to short circuit the journey from grief to praise, but we must rest in lament until it does its work in us. Our faith is strengthened and our confidence in God assured in lament. It is his means of graciously helping us deal with our grief.

A PRAYER OF LAMENT[1]

> Why, Lord, must evil seem to get its way? We confess that our sin is deeply shameful; but the wicked are openly scornful—they mock your name and laugh at our dismay. We know your providential love holds true: nothing can curse us endlessly with sorrow. Transform, dear Lord, this damage into good; show us your glory, hidden by this evil.
>
> Why, Lord, must any child of yours be hurt? Do all our pain and sorrow somehow please you? You are a God so jealous for our praises—hear this lament as a prayer that fills the earth.
>
> We plead: Repair the brokenness we share. Chastise no more, lest it destroy your creatures. Hear this lament as intercessory prayer, and speak your powerful word to make us hopeful. Amen.

---

1. *Worship Source Book*, 113–14.

Epilogue
The Sweet Fruit

O watch and wait with patience,
And question all you will
His arms of love and mercy,
Are round about thee still—
O Heart bereaved and lonely, Fanny Crosby

The Lord God planted a garden toward the east, in Eden; and there He placed the man whom He had formed. Out of the ground the Lord God caused every tree to grow that is pleasing to the sight and good for food; the tree of life was also in the midst of the garden, and the tree of the knowledge of good and evil.

(GEN 2:8–9)

And he showed me a river of the water of life, clear as crystal, coming from the throne of God and of the Lamb, in the middle of its street. On either side of the river was the tree of life, bearing twelve kinds of fruit, yielding its fruit every month; and the leaves of the tree were for the healing of the nations.

(REV 22:1–2)

SIN HAS A THOUSAND families, one of which is abuse. And the bitter fruit of abuse comes in many genera: sexual, spiritual, physical, psychological, emotional, and within those genera there is no shortage of horrible species: betrayal, dismissal, neglect, abandonment, pain, and loss. A veritable cornucopia of sin.

Legions of people have walked out of churches, cults, and sects having tasted the bitterness of spiritually and sexually abusive leaderships. It has poisoned their lips, embittered their stomachs, and left its lasting mark for a lifetime.

God only knows the thousands of woman and children sexually assaulted and abused by men in the church, so-called "men of God" who preyed on these vulnerable lambs for their own pleasures, only to have the rest of the church cover it up, sweep it away, and then blame the victim. The bitterness of this is wicked. Abuse, in all its forms and in any measure, is evil and we must state it as such.

But this is just the point: *God knows*. Now for those still reeling from the impact of their dysfunctional churches, accepting the fact that God knows can be almost as triggering as the reminder of the events that caused the grief in the first place. If God knows, then why?

I have no intention of trying to give trite, clichéd answers as to why, because I don't know. I'm not God. I have no answer to why. Victor Frankl, a psychiatrist and a survivor of the Holocaust, declared that finding meaning and purpose to our lives gives us hope and resilience.[1] But too often God is not answering why, no matter how much we ask. Instead, to find meaning, we must ask the questions God is answering, questions like "Who?" and "When?"

Those who have tasted the bitter fruit of abuse cry "How long, Lord, when will we see justice and who will bring it for us?" The answer is found at the beginning and the end of the Bible.

The Bible starts and ends with a garden. And both have trees, but note the marked difference: one tree is missing at the end.

In the first garden exists a tree declared to be the tree of the knowledge of good and evil. And there is nothing particularly wrong with the tree. It is a good tree, placed by a good gardener in a good garden, and for good reason. Adam and Eve are given clear instruction: "Don't eat of it," but as we know all too well, they do.

To eat of the tree is to announce a declaration of independence from God. To eat of it is to determine what is good and evil. In Adam, humankind has come to decide for themselves what makes for *shalom* and what doesn't. People weren't going to let God make those decisions any longer. We rebel against the right of God to determine *shalom*, and as a result we destroy it. The tempter's voice in Gen 3:5–6—"you will be

---

1. Frankl, *Man's Search For Meaning*.

like God"—confirms this view. To eat of the forbidden fruit is to usurp God from his rightful position of Holy Declarer of good and evil. We are not supposed to be like God, determining for ourselves and others what makes for *shalom*. This is God's business.

To eat of this fruit introduces shame. The man and woman are instantly aware of their nakedness (Gen 3:7). In eating of the fruit, mankind is exposed in all their warts and bumpy knobbiness. Everything to hide and no feasible way to hide it. Fig leaves indeed!

This fruit, this breaking of *shalom*, is a bitter fruit, it exposes us all and we all must eat our share of it. As a child, I remember reading a book about a woman who would help parents with their naughty children. One such story was a young girl who would refuse to eat her vegetables. This woman tells her parents, "leave her with me for one week." On the first day the girl is given only chocolate things to eat; cakes and ice cream and milkshakes. Needless to say, the child is delighted. The next day it is vanilla and so on for a week. Every day the child is filled to sickness with sweets of every kind. By the end of the week the girl is craving healthy food.

I view God and his dealings with mankind in the same way: by the time we get to the book of Revelation, mankind has had his fill of this bitter fruit. He has declared for himself the nature of *shalom* for the last time. We chose to eat this fruit and God has given mankind his head.[2] Like a glutton, he has gorged himself until he can eat no more.

And then the Gardner steps back into the garden. No tree of the knowledge of good and evil now need exist. It can no longer tempt mankind, as we will have lost our taste for such nonsense; now only the tree of life. And behold the leaves—not fig leaves to cover our shame, but leaves that heal. The healing of nations, the restoration of *shalom*, no more war between people, the human family one. This is the future which awaits us; no one ever using anyone ever again.

I want to remind you of Luke 12 again. There are three kinds of leaders in church

- those who abuse,
- those who turn a blind eye,
- those who never knew but should have

---

2. An equine idiom referencing dropping the reins of one's horse. It means to allow one to have their own way without restraint.

And not a one of them has committed the unpardonable sin. Jesus died for these people too. And as we have seen, only the first will face eternal judgment should they fail to repent. The other two? As hard as it may be to spit these words out of your mouth, even if there is no repentance in this life, no forgiveness, no confession, no restitution, in a word, no justice ... now ... they will ... if in Christ ... still ... be ... saved. Now that doesn't mean there is no justice, far from it. The words of Paul are instructive here:

> For we must all appear before the judgment seat of Christ, so that each one may receive compensation for his deeds *done* through the body, in accordance with what he has done, whether good or bad. (2 Cor 5:10)

Those who abuse or those who ignore abuse or those who should have known and did nothing will stand before Christ one day and give an account. At risk of being accused of sin-levelling[3], so, too, will you and I, and well in fact we all will. Nobody is getting away with anything. It is easy to get all self-righteous about the things, heinous as they may be, that have been done to us, and demand God judge, but if we are honest with ourselves, there are sins that we are unrepentant of as well. Now maybe they haven't had the same impact on others that abusive behaviors can have. Maybe we haven't assaulted the souls of those in our care, and discarded them as so much refuse. I am not minimizing this at all. But ultimately, we offend a Holy God. Has he no right to demand justice from all of us and for all of us, for the contemptuous acts of sin done against his holy name? And for those in Christ, the final judgment will be done, justice will be delivered, and then the healing can begin. Those outside of Christ will be lost for eternity, but those in Christ will be healed.

The friends and family you lost, the people who betrayed you, abandoned you, used you, and ignored you, in Christ, by his unfathomable grace, will be restored to you. *Shalom* will be returned, the bitter fruit a distant memory of a nightmare gone by. Yes, those who turned blind eyes out of anxiety or fear or naiveté or whatever form of sin will finally have their eyes opened. Jesus will do this. Jesus. They will see, they will know, they will understand and they will weep.

And then God will wipe every tear from their eyes. Tears of sorrow and tears of shame.

And they will be returned to you, and you to them, because of Jesus—the sweetest fruit of all.

---

3. Declaring that one sin is just as bad as another, i.e., lying and rape.

Bibliography

Arendt, Hannah. "Authority in the Twentieth Century." *The Review of Politics* 18.4 (April 7, 1956) 403–17.
Arminius, James. *The Works of James Arminius*, vol. 2. 3 vols. London Edition. Grand Rapids: Baker, 1986.
Arthurs, Jeffery D. *Preaching as Reminding*. Downers Grove, IL: IVP Academic, 2017.
Baker, Hunter. *The End of Secularism*. Wheaton, IL: Crossway, 2009.
Ball, R. Glenn, and Darrell Puls. *Let Us Prey: The Plague of Narcissist Pastors and What We Can Do about It*. Eugene, OR: Cascade, 2017.
Barclay, John. *Paul and the Gift*. Grand Rapids: Eerdmans, 2017.
Bargerhuff, Eric J. *Most Misused Verses in the Bible: Surprising Ways God's Word Is Misunderstood*. Bloomington, MN: Bethany House, 2012. Kindle.
Barnard, Robert Seldon, Jr. "An Examination of Dysfunctional Behaviour in Christian, Evangelical, Mission Organizations and Strategies for Managing the Consequences of Dysfunctional Behaviour." PhD diss., Oxford Centre for Mission Studies, 2004.
Barnes, Albert. *Notes on the Whole Bible*. Omaha NE: Patristic, 2019. Kindle.
Baumeister, Roy F., and Mark R. Leary. "The Need to Belong: Desire for Interpersonal Attachments as a Fundamental Human Motivation." *Psychological Bulletin* 117.3 (1995) 497–529.
Berger, Peter L. *The Sacred Canopy: Elements of a Sociological Theory of Religion*. Reprint Ed. New York: Anchor, 1990.
Bergin, G. Fred, ed. *Autobiography of George Muller, or a Million and a Half Answers to Prayer*. Denton, TX: Westminster Literature Resource, 2003.
Birch, Adelyn. *30 Covert Emotional Manipulation Tactics*. n.l.: Self-published, 2015. Kindle.
Blair, P. A. "Gentiles." In *New Bible Dictionary*, edited by J. D. Douglas, 414. Second edition. Leicester, UK: InterVarsity, 1982.
Bloomer, George. *Authority Abusers*. New Kensington, PA: Whitaker House, 1995.
Bond, Casey. "How MLMs and Cults Use the Same Mind Control Techniques." *Huffpost*, August 13, 2019. https://www.huffpost.com/entry/multilevel-marketing-companies-mlms-cults-similarities_l_5d49f8c2e4b09e72973df3d3#.
Bonhoeffer, Dietrich. *Life Together*. London: SCM, 2012. Kindle.
Boyd, Gregory A. *Benefit of the Doubt*. Grand Rapids: Baker, 2013.
Bradshaw, John. *Bradshaw on: The Family*. Revised Ed. Deerfield Beach, FL: Health Communications, 1996.

Brewer, Marilynn B. "The Social Self: On Being the Same and Different at the Same Time." *Personality and Social Psychology Bulletin* 17.5 (1991) 475–82.

Brewer, Marilynn B, and Wendi Gardner. "Who Is This 'We?' Levels of Collective Identity and Self Representations." *Journal of Personality and Social Psychology* 71.1 (1996) 83–93.

Brown, Brené. *Daring Greatly: How the Courage to Be Vulnerable Transforms the Way We Live, Love, Parent, and Lead*. New York: Penguin Life, 2013.

———. "The Power of Vulnerability." Houston: TEdx Houston, 2010. https://www.ted.com/talks/brene_brown_the_power_of_vulnerability?language=en.

Brueggemann, Walter. *The Prophetic Imagination*. Second edition. Minneapolis: Fortress, 2001.

Calvin, John. *Commentaries on the Epistles to Timothy, Titus and Philemon*. Grand Rapids: Eerdmans, 1948.

———. *Institutes of the Christian Religion*. Peabody, MA: Hendrickson, 2008.

Capps, Donald. *Agents of Hope: A Pastoral Psychology*. Eugene, OR: Wipf and Stock, 1995.

———. *The Depleted Self*. Minneapolis: Augsberg Fortress, 1993. Kindle.

Carson, D. A. "On Abusing Matthew 18." *Themelios* 36.1 (2011) 1–3.

Challies, Tim. "Character Is King." https://www.challies.com/articles/character-is-king/.

Chesterton, G. K. *Orthodoxy*. London: Project Gutenberg, 2004.

Collins, Gary R. *Christian Counseling: A Comprehensive Guide*. Third edition. Nashville: Thomas Nelson, 2007.

DeGroat, Chuck. *When Narcissism Comes to Church: Healing Your Community from Emotional and Spiritual Abuse*. Downers Grove, IL: IVP, 2020.

Denhollander, Rachael. "Read Rachael Denhollander's Full Victim Impact Statement about Larry Nassar." *CNN*, January 30, 2018. https://edition.cnn.com/2018/01/24/us/rachael-denhollander-full-statement/index.html.

Dever, Mark, and David Platt. *Nine Marks of a Healthy Church*. 3rd ed. Wheaton, IL: Crossway, 2013.

Dillehay, Tilly. "How the Rod Can Point Children to God." https://www.thegospelcoalition.org/article/rod-point-children-god/.

Downen, Robert, et al. "Abuse of Faith: Investigation Reveals 700 Victims of Southern Baptist Sexual Abuse over 20 Years." *The Houston Chronicle*, February 10, 2019. https://www.houstonchronicle.com/news/investigations/article/Southern-Baptist-sexual-abuse-spreads-as-leaders-13588038.php.

Earls, Aaron. "Churchgoers Split on Existence of More Sexual Abuse by Pastors." *Lifeway Research*, May 21, 2019. https://lifewayresearch.com/2019/05/21/churchgoers-split-on-existence-of-more-sexual-abuse-by-pastors/.

Eberstadt, Mary. *It's Dangerous to Believe: Religious Freedom and Its Enemies*. New York: HarperCollins, 2016. Kindle.

Edersheim, Alfred. *The Life and Times of Jesus the Messiah*. Grand Rapids: Eerdmans, 1980.

Erickson, Millard J. *Christian Theology*. 2nd ed. Grand Rapids: Baker Academic, 1998.

Fogarty, Thomas. "The Family Emotional System." *Family Therapy* 2.1 (1975) 79–97.

Frankl, Victor E. *Man's Search for Meaning*. New York: Pocket, 1992.

Freyd, Jennifer J. "Violations of Power, Adaptive Blindness and Betrayal Trauma Theory." *Feminism & Psychology* 7 (1997) 22–32.

Bibliography

Friedman, Edwin H. *A Failure of Nerve: Leadership in the Age of the Quick Fix.* 10th Anniv. ed. New York: Church, 2017.
Gardner, Howard E. *Multiple Intelligences: New Horizons in Theory and Practice.* New York: Basic, 2008.
Gibbs, Eddie. *Leadership Next.* London: InterVarsity, 2005.
Goleman, Daniel. *Emotional Intelligence: Why It Can Matter More Than IQ.* London: Bloomsbury, 1995.
Grudem, Wayne. *Sytematic Theology.* Nottingham, UK: IVP, 2011.
Hamilton, Craig. *Wisdom for Leadership.* Sydney: Matthias Media, 2015.
Handwerker, W. Penn. *The Origin of Cultures: How Individual Choices Make Cultures Change.* Walnut Creek, CA: Left Coast, 2009.
Harsey, Sarah J., et al. "Perpetrator Responses to Victim Confrontation: DARVO and Victim Self-Blame." *Journal of Aggression, Maltreatment & Trauma* 26.6 (July 3, 2017) 644–63. https://doi.org/10.1080/10926771.2017.1320777.
Johnson, David, and Jeff VanVonderen. *The Subtle Power of Spiritual Abuse.* Bloomington, MN: Bethany House, 1991. Kindle.
John XXIII, Pope. *The Pope's Caress.* Sherbrooke, QC: Mediaspaul, 2000.
Jordan, Judith V. "The Meaning of Mutuality." *Work In Progress* 23 (1986) 1–11.
Kerr, Michael, and Murray Bowen. *Family Evaluation: An Approach Based on Bowen Theory.* New York: Norton, 1988.
Langberg, Diane. *Redeeming Power: Understanding Authority and Abuse in the Church.* Grand Rapids: Brazos, 2020.
Leeman, Jonathan. *Church Discipline: How the Church Protects the Name of Jesus.* Wheaton, IL: Crossway, 2012.
———. *Political Church: The Local Assembly as Embassy of Christ's Rule.* London: Apollos, 2016.
Lewis, C. S. *The Four Loves.* Orlando: Harcourt, 1960.
———. "Mere Christianity." In *The Complete C. S. Lewis: Signature Classics*, 1–177. New York: HarperCollins, 2002.
———. *The Weight of Glory.* Kindle. London: William Collins, 2013.
Lloyd-Jones, D. Martyn. *Preaching and Preachers.* Grand Rapids: Zondervan, 1971.
Malina, Bruce J., and Jerome H. Neyrey. "Honor and Shame in Luke-Acts: Pivotal Cultural Values of the Mediterranean World." In *The Social World of Luke-Acts: Models for Interpretation*, edited by Jerome H. Neyrey, 25–65. Peabody MA: Hendrickson, 2008.
May, Rollo. *Power and Innocence: A Search for the Sources of Violence.* New York: Norton, 1972.
McKnight, Scott, and Laura Barringer. *A Church Callled TOV.* Carol Stream, IL: Tyndale Momentum, 2020.
McManaman, Douglas. "Narcissism and the Dynamics of Evil." *Catholic Education Resource Center*, 2008. https://www.catholiceducation.org/en/culture/catholic-contributions/narcissism-and-the-dynamics-of-evil.html.
Metzger, Bruce M. *A Textual Commentary on the Greek New Testament.* 2nd ed. Stuttgart: German Bible Society, 1994.
Miller, Alice. *For Your Own Good.* New York: Farrar Straus Giroux, 2002.
Mounstephen, Philip. *Bishop of Truro's Independent Review for the Foreign Secretary of FCO Support for Persecuted Christians: Final Report and Recommendations.* London: Crown, 2019.

Mullen, Wade. *Something's Not Right: Decoding the Hidden Tactics of Abuse.* Carol Stream, IL: Tyndale Momentum, 2020.
Murray, John. "Love and Its Correlatives." *Banner of Truth*, 2020. https://banneroftruth.org/uk/resources/articles/2020/love-and-its-correlatives/.
Nouwen, Henri J. M. *In the Name of Jesus: Reflections on Christian Leadership.* Study Guide Edition. Chestnut Ridge, NY: Crossroad, 2002.
Novšak, Rachel, et al. "Therapeutic Implications of Religious-Related Emotional Abuse." *Journal of Aggression, Maltreatment & Trauma* 21.1 (January 1, 2012) 31–44. https://doi.org/10.1080/10926771.2011.627914.
Oakley, Lisa, and Justin Humphreys. *Escaping the Maze of Spiritual Abuse.* London: SPCK, 2019.
Pattison, Stephen. *Shame: Theory, Therapy, Theology.* Cambridge: Cambridge University Press, 2000.
Peterson, Eugene. *The Pastor: A Memoir.* New York: HarperCollins, 2011.
Peterson, Eugene H. *Five Smooth Stones for Pastoral Work.* Grand Rapids: Eerdmans, 1992.
Phelps, Libby. *Girl on a Wire: Walking the Line between Faith and Freedom in the Westboro Baptist Church.* New York: Skyhorse, 2017. Kindle.
Piper, John. *God's Passion for His Glory.* Wheaton, IL: Crossway, 1998.
Reagan, Ronald. "Address at Commencement Exercises at Eureka College, Eureka, Illinois." *Ronald Reagan Presidential Library & Museum*, 1982. https://www.reaganlibrary.gov/archives/speech/address-commencement-exercises-eureka-college-eureka-illinois.
Richardson, Ronald W. *Family Ties That Bind.* 4th ed. Bellingham, WA: Self-Counsel, 2011.
Roberts, Barbara. "Crying Out for Justice." https://cryingoutforjustice.blog/tag/barbara-roberts/.
Rohr, Richard. *Everything Belongs: The Gift of Contemplative Prayer.* New York: Crossroad, 2015. Kindle.
Rose, Jessica. *Psychology for Pastoral Contexts.* London: SCM, 2013.
Rubin, Julius H. *Religious Melancholy and Protestant Experience.* New York: Oxford University Press, 1994.
Ryle, J. C. *Expository Thoughts on John, Volume 3.* 3 vols. Carlisle, PA: The Banner of Truth Trust, 1873.
Sande, Ken. *The Peace Maker.* Third edition. Grand Rapids: Baker, 2004.
Satir, Virginia. *The New Peoplemaking.* Mountain View, CA: Science and Behavior, 1988.
Sayers, D. L. "The Greatest Drama Ever Staged." *WACMM*, 1963. http://www.wacmm.org/Sayers.html.
Schein, Edgar H. *Organizational Culture and Leadership.* 3rd ed. San Francisco: Jossey-Bass, 2004.
"Sexual Misconduct and Churchgoers: National Survey of Protestant Churchgoers." http://lifewayresearch.com/wp-content/uploads/2019/06/Sexual-Misconduct-and-Churchgoers-Report-6.14.2019.pdf.
"Shorter Catechism of the Assembly of Divines: The 1647 Westminster Confession and Subordinate Documents." 1648. https://www.apuritansmind.com/westminster-standards/shorter-catechism/.

Bibliography

Simon, George K. *In Sheep's Clothing: Understanding and Dealing with Manipulative People*. Marion, MI: Parkhurst Brothers, 2010. Kindle.

Smedes, Lewis B. *Forgive and Forget*. Revised. New York: HarperCollins, 2007.

Spurgeon, Charles Haddon. "Abundant Pardon." https://www.ccel.org/ccel/spurgeon/sermons20.xlvi.html.

Steinke, Peter L. *How Your Church Family Works*. Lanham, MD: Rowman & Littlefield, 2014.

Straton, WIlliam Bruce. *The Formation of Christian Character: A Contribution to Christian Ethics*. Edinburgh: T. & T. Clark Limited, 1908.

Strong, James. *Strong's Exhaustive Concordance*. Nashville: Broadman, 1981.

Taylor, Charles. *Multiculturalism and "The Politics of Recognition."* Princeton: Princeton University Press, 1992.

Thayer, Joseph H. *Thayer's Greek-English Lexicon of the New Testament*. 4th edition. Grand Rapids: Baker, 1977.

Tidball, Derek. *Skilful Shepherds: Explorations in Pastoral Theology*. Nottingham, UK: Apollos, 1997.

Tolle, Eckhart. *The Power of Now: A Guide to Spiritual Enlightenment*. Novato, CA: New World Library, 2004.

Townsend, John. *Who's Pushing Your Buttons?: Handling the Difficult People in Your Life*. Nashville: Thomas Nelson, 2004. Kindle.

Tripp, Paul. "You Talk To Yourself." https://www.paultripp.com/wednesdays-word/posts/you-talk-to-yourself.

Volf, Miroslav. *Free of Charge: Giving and Forgiving in a Culture Stripped of Grace*. Grand Rapids: Zondervan, 2005.

Watson, Thomas. *A Body of Divinity*. Grand Rapids: Baker, 1979.

Wilhoit, James C. *Spiritual Formation as if the Church Mattered: Growing in Christ through Community*. Grand Rapids: Baker Academic, 2008.

Wolff, Robert Paul. *In Defense of Anarchism*. New York: Harper & Row, 1976.

The Worship Source Book. Second edition. Grand Rapids: Faith Alive, 2013.

www.ingramcontent.com/pod-product-compliance
Lightning Source LLC
Chambersburg PA
CBHW062007220426
43662CB00010B/1259